Handbook for Critical Reading

Handbook for Critical Reading

Don Meagher
Miami–Dade Community College

HARCOURT BRACE COLLEGE PUBLISHERS

Fort Worth   Philadelphia   San Diego   New York   Orlando   Austin   San Antonio
Toronto   Montreal   London   Sydney   Tokyo

Publisher	Christopher P. Klein
Senior Acquisitions Editor	Carol Wada
Developmental Editor	Camille Adkins
Product Manager	Ilsa Wolfe-West
Senior Project Editor	Charles J. Dierker
Production Manager	Lois West
Art Director	Sue Hart

ISBN: 0-15-503057-4

Library of Congress Catalog Card Number: 96-75655

Address for Editorial Correspondence:
Harcourt Brace College Publishers, 301 Commerce Street, Suite 3700, Fort Worth, TX 76102.

Address for Orders:
Harcourt Brace & Company, 6277 Sea Harbor Drive, Orlando, FL 32887-6777. 1-800-782-4479, or 1-800-433-0001 (in Florida).

Harcourt Brace College Publishers may provide complimentary instructional aids and supplements or supplement packages to those adopters qualified under our adoption policy. Please contact your sales representative for more information. If as an adopter or potential user you receive supplements you do not need, please return them to your sales representative or send them to:

Attn: Returns Department
Troy Warehouse
465 South Lincoln Drive
Troy, MO 63379

Printed in the United States of America

6 7 8 9 0 1 2 3 4 5 039 10 9 8 7 6 5 4 3 2 1

for
Mary Esther, my mother
and
in memory of Francis, my father

Preface

The purpose of this book is to familiarize you with all of the aspects of analytical and critical reading and to provide you with the reading strategies necessary to succeed in college. To do so, you will read both explanations of reading strategies and examples of written passages that illustrate each aspect of reading that is discussed. This book is meant to be a reference work that you can refer to in order to increase your understanding of what you read.

Understanding what you read not only makes the act of reading much easier, but it also makes reading much more pleasurable, and it makes you better able to evaluate and critique an author's style and content. The goal of the first four chapters of this book is to increase your capacity for both personal and critical involvement in reading. To address reading comprehension, Chapters 1–4 will focus on some of the basic strategies for understanding what you read, including strategies for reading textbooks, defining unfamiliar words, determining main ideas and major supporting details in paragraphs and longer passages, and recognizing how ideas are related to one another and organized into pieces of writing.

In understanding an author's main idea and organizational scheme, both the context and the way ideas are organized in relation to one another are important. Nevertheless, understanding what you read often involves more than what the author actually says. Sometimes it is necessary to go beyond the context—even beyond the words on the page—to understand what an author means, suggests, or tries to accomplish. In such cases, you must draw upon your background knowledge, personal experience, logic, and imagination to interpret an author's words or to infer what an author may only suggest. In Chapters 5 and 6, you will focus on these inferential and interpretive skills as they involve figuring out an author's implied meanings, intention, and attitude, as well as understanding the meanings of carefully chosen words and figurative expressions. Chapter 7 will then apply many of these inferential and interpretive skills in the reading of imaginative literature, including literary nonfiction, fiction, and poetry.

The word "argument" probably brings to mind a quarrel between people involved in a disagreement. One may even imagine two people yelling at each other and hurling insults back and forth. And the word "persuasion" might suggest a calmer, more refined attempt to convince. However, when referring to types of writing, these terms have somewhat different meanings. In Chapters 8–10, the terms *argument* and *persuasion* will be used to refer to two types of writing whose purpose is generally to persuade. The terms argument and *argumentation* refer to attempts to present a convincing case for a certain opinion on a controversial topic primarily through the use of reasoning and structured support. Persuasion, like argumentation, also involves an attempt to convince, but it relies more on emotional appeals to an audience's needs and desires than it does on logical reasoning. In Chapters 8–10, you will examine things to look for in order to recognize persuasive writing, examine ways that writers use persuasion to convince through less than reasonable means, and consider the parts of an argument and how to evaluate arguments in terms of their inner logic.

My hope is that this book will be a useful resource for students in reading and English courses, as well as in any course or academic situation requiring the comprehension, analysis, and evaluation of complex reading material. If this book is indeed useful, it has become so through the contributions of several people who I would like to thank for their help. First, I would like to thank Camille Adkins and Carol Wada of Harcourt Brace—Camille for her encouraging and intelligent support and Carol for being where I could find her and for trusting me in the first place. I would like to thank for following people who read drafts of this book and offered valuable suggestions for its improvement: Margaret Ehlen, Ivy Tech State College; Laurel Watt, Inver Hills Community College; Cathy Leist, University of Louisville; Gale Parker, San Jacinto College; David London, Miami–Dade Community College; James Nystrom, Dixie College; Donna Clack, Schoolcraft College; and Eileen Schwartz, Purdue University–Calumet.

Table of Contents

CHAPTER 1

Reading Textbooks

In your college courses, your instructors undoubtedly ask you to read many things, including both fiction (imaginative literature) and nonfiction (writing based on actual events, experiences, or thoughts) from both primary sources (original writings) and textbooks (books organized for the study of a subject). However, most of what you are asked to read is nonfiction, and much of this is in the form of textbooks, especially for introductory or survey courses.

For this reason, your success in college depends in part on how effectively you approach textbook reading assignments. Textbooks summarize and synthesize the vast amounts of information in a subject area or academic discipline. Authors write them to introduce students to subject matter that would otherwise require reading many different books and articles by many different authors to gain the same information.

Unlike most other reading material, college textbooks have been structured to aid students' understanding. Being able to take advantage of these structural aids will make your reading of textbooks both easier and more time-effective. This chapter will first briefly consider the format or structure of textbooks, including an examination of graphic illustrations commonly used in textbooks, and will then discuss some strategies for reading textbooks effectively, including ways to get the most out of text material and to read for different purposes.

Chapter Outline

Recognizing Textbook Features

1a Textbook Format
    Preface
    Table of Contents
    Appendices
    Glossary
    Index

1b Chapter Format
    Introductions
    Lists of Key Terms
    Marginal Notes
    Inserts
    Review Questions
    Chapter Summaries
    Suggested Readings

1c Graphic Illustrations
    Maps
    Diagrams
    Flow Charts
    Pie Graphs
    Line Graphs
    Bar Graphs
    Tables

Using Textbook Reading Strategies

1d Previewing Strategies
    Surveying
    Questioning

1e Active Reading Strategies
    Marking
    Annotating
    Notetaking
    Reciting

1f Reviewing Strategies
    Reviewing
    Outlining and Mapping
    Paraphrasing and
      Summarizing

1g Reading for Different Purposes
    Varying Rate
    Skimming
    Scanning
    Reading to Retain
    Information
      Taking Objective Exams
      Taking Essay Exams

Recognizing Textbook Features

In order to increase your understanding of what you read in textbooks, it helps to know how they are structured. What follows are descriptions and examples of the most common features you can expect to find in college textbooks.

1a   Textbook Format

Most textbooks contain several parts in addition to the actual chapters, each of which is there to help you use the book and to get the most out of its contents.

Preface   The preface of a textbook is an opening statement, usually no more than a few pages long, in which the authors explain their reasons for writing the text, their qualifications for writing the book, the readers they intend it for, the structure of the text, the emphasis of the book, and any special features contained in it. Reading the preface will give you a good sense of what to expect in the book.

Table of Contents   The table of contents generally appears right before or right after the preface and is a list of the chapters and other sections of the book in the same order in which they actually appear. A glance at the table of contents can help you see how ideas are related to one another in the text and how the author's choice of material reflects the emphasis of the book as a whole and of each chapter individually.

Appendices   Following all the chapters, which contain the main body of information in the textbook, you will sometimes find an appendix or several appendices near the end of the book. An appendix contains additional information to supplement the main text that does not fit conveniently into any one chapter. The appendices will probably be referred to throughout the text, so it is a good idea for you to know where they are located and what they contain.

Glossary   Also in the back of many textbooks you will find a glossary that provides definitions for technical words or specialized vocabulary used in the book. You will probably find a glossary easier and quicker to use than a dictionary because of its convenient location and because the definitions are often especially written to apply to the words as they are used in the subject field covered by the text.

Index   Usually located at the very end, an index is an alphabetical list of all the main topics and important information contained in the entire book, with page numbers to refer to the exact location of the information. In addition to allowing you to quickly and easily locate any information contained in the book, an index can also be used as a way to quiz yourself in preparation for a test on the information listed for a specific topic, or on the entire contents of the book in preparation for a final exam.

1b Chapter Format

Just as a textbook has a format planned to make it easy for students to use, so are the individual chapters designed with several convenient learning features to make them easy to read and learn from.

Introductions   Textbook chapters often begin with some introductory material to provide a preview of the contents of the chapter. This is done to provide you with a framework of information before you begin to read, which will make the material easier to comprehend and remember. You will often find this introductory material in the form of a list of objectives to help you focus your reading, a chapter outline that indicates the headings and subheadings to come, or an overview paragraph that introduces the topic, discusses the importance of the information in the chapter, or relates the chapter contents to other chapters in the book.

Lists of Key Terms   Sometimes you will also find a list of key terms at either the beginning or the end of a chapter. Such lists provide definitions of some of the important words that appear for the first time in the chapter and that need to be understood in order to fully comprehend the material.

Marginal Notes   Some textbooks include wide margins containing notes that comment on the text, questions for you to think about while reading, examples or illustrations of key concepts, or definitions of important terms. These marginal notes can be useful both for understanding the material as you read it and for reviewing it afterwards.

Inserts   You will sometimes find textbooks that include material inserted at the end of a chapter or in places within the chapter, often in boxes or in other ways that set it apart from the main text. These inserts provide information of some special interest and often include short essays, articles, commentaries, applications, or examples that are meant to clarify more general ideas from the chapter. It is a good idea to read an insert after reading the main text near it, so you can get the general point first and then see a more specific discussion.

Review Questions   At the end of a chapter, you will often find review questions, which are meant to test your comprehension of what you have just read. These questions ask you to recall and explain the main points from the chapter. For this reason, review questions are ideal for reinforcing what you have learned and for studying for a test.

Chapter Summaries   Many textbooks include summaries at the end of each chapter that briefly restate the main points. Reading a summary before reading a chapter can help you to understand the material while you read, and reading it afterwards can help you to tie the ideas together and review what you have learned.

Suggested Readings   Many textbooks include a list of readings at the end of each chapter that you can refer to for additional information on the topic of the chapter. These may provide useful starting points for research papers on topics covered in the chapter.

1c   Graphic Illustrations

Besides the written text itself, graphic illustrations represent the next most significant form in which textbook authors present information. Often complicated ideas, interrelationships, or processes can be expressed much easier and more clearly with pictures or other illustrations than in writing alone. For this reason, it is very important for you to pay careful attention to illustrations and to understand what they represent, especially when the author refers to them in the text.

When looking at a graphic illustration, always read any accompanying explanatory information, including a title (suggesting what it is about), a key or legend (interpreting any symbols used), or a caption (explaining or summarizing the contents of the graphic). Also, try to summarize to yourself the meaning of the graphic and the main points it illustrates. In addition to photographs and realistic drawings or paintings, there are several types of graphic illustrations commonly used in textbooks to represent complex ideas that you should be familiar with.

Maps   Maps are graphic representations of specific geographical areas and sometimes include legends or keys to help you interpret any symbols, numbers, or shading used.

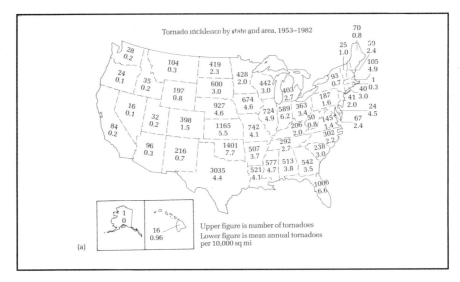

Robert Gabler, Robert J. Sager, and Daniel L. Wise, *Essentials of Physical Geography,* p. 181.

This map shows the number of tornadoes occurring between 1953–1982 and the average (mean) number occurring per ten thousand square miles each year. You can also tell that more tornadoes have occurred in the Midwest and South, with fewer in the Middle Atlantic, Northeast, and West.

Diagrams   Diagrams are outline drawings of objects and often include labeled parts.

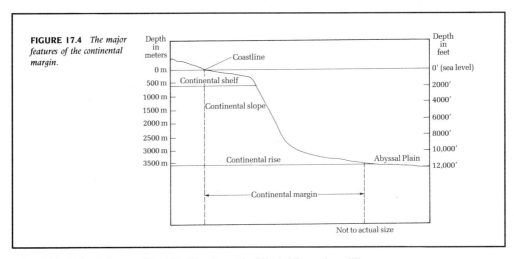

Robert Gabler, Robert J. Sager, and Daniel L. Wise, *Essentials of Physical Geography,* p. 374.

The caption for this diagram of the ocean floor states that it depicts the "major features of the continental margin." The numbers listed vertically on the outside borders indicate the depth of the ocean for each part of the continental margin. It is clear from the diagram that from the coastline, the continental margin first slopes down gradually (continental shelf), then drops sharply (continental slope), then finally levels off (abyssal plain) at about twelve thousand feet.

Flow Charts   Flow charts use boxes or other shapes and lines or arrows to show a step-by-step procedure or process.

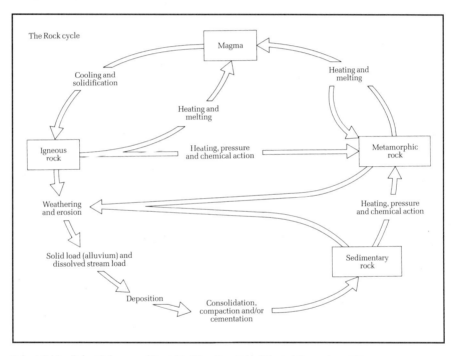

Robert Gabler, Robert J. Sager, and Daniel L. Wise, *Essentials of Physical Geography,* p. 515.

This flow chart of the rock cycle illustrates the process by which molten rock (magma) hardens into igneous rock, becomes sedimentary rock through a weathering process, changes into metamorphic rock by heat and pressure, and finally reverts to magma if it melts. The arrows indicate how the transformations occur. The arrows in the middle of the flow chart show that not all rocks go through all of the stages, but sometimes steps are bypassed or reoccur.

Pie Graphs   Pie graphs are circles divided into wedge-shaped sections, each representing a percentage of the whole.

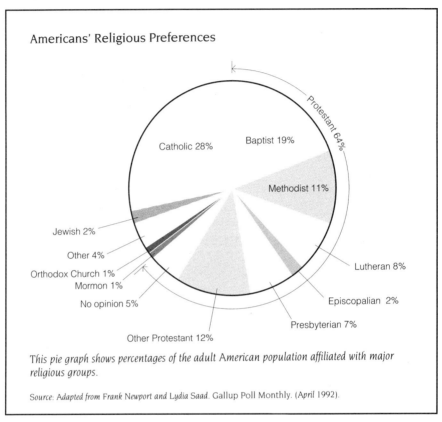

Americans' Religious Preferences

This pie graph shows percentages of the adult American population affiliated with major religious groups.

Source: *Adapted from Frank Newport and Lydia Saad. Gallup Poll Monthly. (April 1992).*

Christopher Bates Doob, *Sociology: An Introduction*, p. 253.

As both the title and a caption state, this pie graph shows Americans' religious preferences. From the percentages of the whole population indicated by the size of each section and by the percentages listed for each religious affiliation, it seems clear that the majority of Americans, about 89 percent, consider themselves to be Christians of one denomination or another, and that Catholics form the largest single denomination.

Line Graphs   Line graphs use straight or curved lines to represent changes over time or to compare changes for two or more measures.

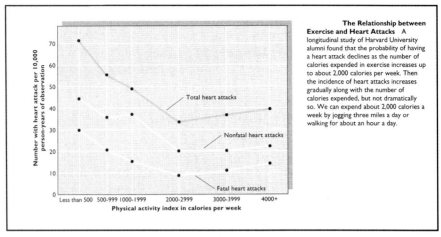

The Relationship between Exercise and Heart Attacks A longitudinal study of Harvard University alumni found that the probability of having a heart attack declines as the number of calories expended in exercise increases up to about 2,000 calories per week. Then the incidence of heart attacks increases gradually along with the number of calories expended, but not dramatically so. We can expend about 2,000 calories a week by jogging three miles a day or walking for about an hour a day.

Spencer A. Rathus and Jeffrey S. Nevid, *Adjustment and Growth: The Challenges of Life,* p. 193.

The caption to the right explains how the data shown in the line graph were collected and what they mean. The numbers going up the left side indicate the number of heart attacks, and the numbers along the bottom show amounts of physical activity. It seems clear from both the lines on the graph and from the caption that both insufficient and excessive exercise can contribute to heart attacks.

Bar Graphs   Bar graphs incorporate a series of horizontal or vertical bars, each representing an amount.

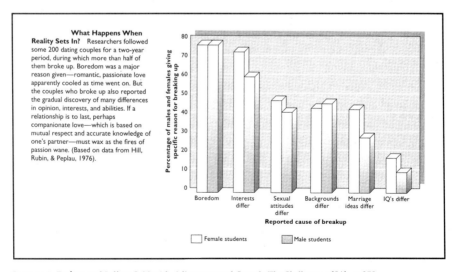

What Happens When Reality Sets In? Researchers followed some 200 dating couples for a two-year period, during which more than half of them broke up. Boredom was a major reason given—romantic, passionate love apparently cooled as time went on. But the couples who broke up also reported the gradual discovery of many differences in opinion, interests, and abilities. If a relationship is to last, perhaps companionate love—which is based on mutual respect and accurate knowledge of one's partner—must wax as the fires of passion wane. (Based on data from Hill, Rubin, & Peplau, 1976).

Spencer A. Rathus and Jeffrey S. Nevid, *Adjustment and Growth: The Challenges of Life,* p. 358.

This bar graph shows what the caption to the left explains: A survey of student couples has indicated the reasons they broke up. The caption interprets the data by stating that a relationship may survive the decrease in "the fires of passion" if there is an increase in the "mutual respect and accurate knowledge of one's partner." In addition, the differences in the responses of female and male students as shown by the differently shaded bars suggest their different reasons for ending relationships.

Tables   Tables are lists of facts or statistics in columns and rows, usually in two different directions, with labels for each.

Table 9.2   Some Important Statistical Facts in the Lives of Whites, Blacks, and Hispanic-Americans

Issue	Total population	White	Black	Hispanic
Median family income	$35,353	$36,915	$21,423	$23,431
Percent of persons below poverty line	13.7%	10.7%	31.9%	28.1%
Education[1]				
Four years of high school or more	78.4%	79.9%	66.7%	51.3%
Four years of college or more	21.4%	22.2%	11.5%	9.7%
Owner-occupied units	64%	67.3%	42.4%	39%

	TOTAL POPULATION	WHITE		NONWHITE	
		Male	Female	Male	Female
Life expectancy (in years)[2]	75.4	72.6	79.3	68.4	76.3

[1] All education figures are for people 25 years and older.
[2] The life expectancy figures compare whites to nonwhites.

Source: U.S. Bureau of the Census. Statistical Abstract of the United States: 1992, No. 41, No. 44, and No. 103.

Whites fare better than blacks and Hispanic-Americans on all these measures. Hispanic-Americans average higher income than blacks while blacks tend to be better educated.

Christopher Bates Doob, *Sociology: An Introduction*, p. 344.

This table shows what the title states: "Some Important Statistical Facts in the Lives of Whites, Blacks, and Hispanic-Americans." In this case, a caption underneath the table conveniently summarizes the significance of the data shown in the table, which clearly shows the differences in economic and educational achievement among white, black, and Hispanic Americans.

Using Textbook Reading Strategies

While the textbook features briefly described above are all quite common, not every text includes them all. When they are present, you should of course take full advantage of them. However, there are a number of useful strategies that you can use regardless of how many learning aids a text may include. One of the most common of these strategies is known as *SQ3R*, which stands for Survey, Question, Read, Recite, and Review. This and other similar methods all involve strategies in three basic stages: previewing, active reading, and reviewing.

In the rest of this chapter, you will first read descriptions of the previewing, active reading, and reviewing reading strategies, including illustrations of how these strategies can be used on two sample pages from an introductory biology textbook. You will then read about how to apply these strategies when reading for different purposes.

1d   Previewing Strategies

Before actually reading the chapter, two strategies can help you understand what you will read. These previewing strategies include surveying the material and formulating some questions that you want to answer from your reading.

Surveying   The first step in effective reading involves taking a few minutes to preview the entire chapter to get an overview of the contents. This can be done by *skimming,* or quickly looking through the chapter and selectively reading the parts that suggest the main points and key concepts.

When surveying a chapter, look for the following features that can give you a good overview of the contents: the *title* expresses in a few words the topic of the chapter; the *introduction* or *conclusion* may include lists of objectives or actual summary statements; the *first and last few paragraphs* may also contain summaries of the main ideas in the chapter; *headings and subheadings* represent the main points of each section of the chapter; *margin notes or questions* may summarize or suggest many of the important points; words in **boldface** or *italic* type or that are set off in a different color may indicate important terms; and *pictures, graphs, charts,* or *inserted material* often illustrate or summarize important points.

Surveying is very useful in gaining a general idea of what the chapter is about, in helping you remember what you may already know about the topic, and in forming a conceptual framework within which to fit the information you will read.

Questioning   Another effective previewing strategy is to formulate questions that you will attempt to answer in your reading of the chapter. An easy way to do this is to turn all the headings and subheadings into questions that you will try to find the answers to in the section introduced by each one. This questioning strategy will help you to focus on the essential information contained in the different sections of the chapter.

1e   Active Reading Strategies

Once you have introduced yourself to the chapter by surveying and questioning, you are ready to begin reading the entire chapter. However, rather than merely reading straight through, you will gain much more by reading *actively* with a few strategies that will increase your understanding and retention of the material, as well as make it easier to come back and study the chapter later on. An important *active reading* strategy is to try to find answers to the questions that you formulated out of the chapter headings and subheadings during previewing.

Marking   When reading the chapter, an effective way to indicate the main points is to mark them with a colored highlighter or to underline or circle them with a pen. However, marking is only effective when what you highlight or underline actually represents the main points rather than less important details or examples. This of course requires you to be able to distinguish between main ideas and supporting details, a skill that will be discussed in Chapter 3. For this reason, you may find that highlighting or underlining is most effective during a second reading of the material after you have given some thought to what you have read.

The physical act of marking helps you focus on the material, which both aids in your comprehension and helps you remember what you have just read. If you have highlighted, underlined, or circled the main points as you read through the chapter, you will have made studying the material so much easier by indicating for yourself all the most important things to focus on when you come back to review.

Annotating   As effective as marking is for recognizing the main points during your initial reading and for later study, annotating is perhaps even more effective. Annotating involves writing notes in your own words in the margins of the textbook. Annotating also includes the use of personal symbols or codes that indicate the significant points or words in the text.

Annotating is especially effective because it requires you to restate the author's significant points in your own words. As with marking, you may find that annotating is most effective when it is done during a second reading, after you have decided what you feel are the most important points to mark in the text or to comment on in margin notes.

Your margin notes should be very brief and should summarize key points and indicate the location of key ideas. In addition to summary comments in the margins, some common symbols that you might use include the following:

T (thesis)

MI (main idea)

S (summary)

Ex (example)

Def (definition)

1, 2, 3 (major points)

? (unclear points)

* (important points)

When used along with marking, annotating is probably the most effective method of reading for information.

Notice how both annotating and marking strategies are used on the following sample pages from a biology textbook.

Notice on the following sample textbook pages how the reader has both marked and annotated. The heading is turned into a question, key points are underlined, important terms are circled, and margin notes and symbols (a star and arrows) suggest main points, definitions, and examples.

What is

1-D Evolution and Natural Selection ?

Main point of Biology

A living organism is the product of interactions between its genetic information and its environment. This interaction is the basis for the most important concept in biology, that organisms evolve by means of natural selection—point 8 in our preceding list.

def The theory of evolution states that today's organisms have arisen by descent and modification from more ancient forms of life. For instance, most biologists believe that human beings evolved from now-extinct animals which looked something like apes, and that this happened through accumulation of changes from generation to generation. In more modern terms, we can say that evolution is the process by which the members of a population of organisms come to differ from their ancestors.

Like many other great ideas in science, the theory of evolution by means of natural selection presents a simple explanation that makes sense of a great many observations of the natural world. Soon after Charles Darwin proposed this theory, his champion, Thomas Huxley, remarked, "How extremely stupid not to have thought of that!"

The theory is based on three familiar observations:

Based on 3 things

1. Organisms are variable. Even the most closely related individuals differ in some respects.
2. Some of the differences among organisms are inherited. Inherited differences between individuals result from differences in the genetic material that they inherited from their parents. Because parents and offspring have very similar genetic material, they tend to resemble each other more closely than they resemble organisms to which they are less closely related.
3. More organisms are produced than live to grow up and reproduce. Fish and birds may produce hundreds of eggs, oak trees thousands of acorns, but only a few of these survive to reproduce in their turn.

def Some of the inherited variations among organisms are bound to affect the chances that an individual will live to reproduce. Individuals with some genetic variations produce more offspring (which inherit this genetic material) than do others. This is called natural selection and it produces evolution, a change in the proportions of different genes from one generation of a population to the next. *another def*

Ex To take an example of natural selection producing evolution, the length and thickness of an animal's hair is largely determined by its genes. A very cold winter may kill many individuals with short, sparse hair. Individuals with longer, thicker fur are more likely to survive the winter and reproduce in the following spring (Figure 1-11). Because more animals with thicker fur breed and pass on the genetic material that dictates the growth of thick hair, a larger proportion of individuals in the next generation of the population will have genes for thick fur. The genetic makeup of the population has changed somewhat from one generation to the next, and that is evolution. The agent of natural selection in this case *agent of nat. selection* is low temperature, which acts as a selective pressure against those individuals with short, sparse hair.

Result The result of natural selection is that populations undergo adaptation, a *def* process of accumulating changes appropriate to their environments, over the course of many generations. The selective pressures acting on a population "select" those genetic characteristics that are adapted, or well suited, to the environment. For instance, through selection, populations living in cold areas evolve so as to become better adapted to withstand the cold.

In this discussion of evolution, we use "environment" as a catchall word meaning much more than merely whether an organism lives in a forest rather

Karen Arms and Pamela S. Camp, *Biology: A Journey into Life,* p. 12

In the first of these sample textbook pages, the reader has drawn lines between the three sections: a definition of evolution, a discussion of the basis of the theory of evolution, and some results of evolution. Also, notice on both pages that he has marked definitions ("Def") and examples ("Ex") for both the text and the photographs that accompany it.

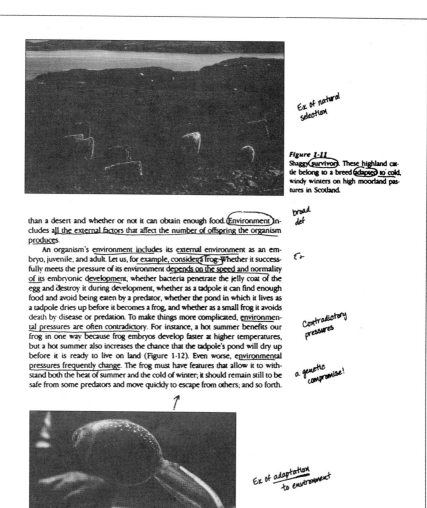

Ex of natural selection

Figure 1-11
Shaggy survivors. These highland cattle belong to a breed adapted to cold, windy winters on high moorland pastures in Scotland.

broad def

than a desert and whether or not it can obtain enough food. Environment Includes all the external factors that affect the number of offspring the organism produces.

Ex

An organism's environment includes its external environment as an embryo, juvenile, and adult. Let us, for example, consider a frog. Whether it successfully meets the pressure of its environment depends on the speed and normality of its embryonic development, whether bacteria penetrate the jelly coat of the egg and destroy it during development, whether as a tadpole it can find enough food and avoid being eaten by a predator, whether the pond in which it lives as a tadpole dries up before it becomes a frog, and whether as a small frog it avoids death by disease or predation. To make things more complicated, environmental pressures are often contradictory. For instance, a hot summer benefits our frog in one way because frog embryos develop faster at higher temperatures, but a hot summer also increases the chance that the tadpole's pond will dry up before it is ready to live on land (Figure 1-12). Even worse, environmental pressures frequently change. The frog must have features that allow it to withstand both the heat of summer and the cold of winter; it should remain still to be safe from some predators and move quickly to escape from others; and so forth.

Contradictory pressures

a genetic compromise!

Ex of adaptation to environment

Figure 1-12
A tadpole, which will develop into an adult frog. (Biophoto Associates)

Karen Arms and Pamela S. Camp, *Biology: A Journey into Life,* p. 13

Notetaking　In addition to marking and annotating, notetaking on paper is also an effective active reading strategy. Notetaking generally takes longer than annotating because you are moving back and forth from paper to the text, but some students prefer it to the other methods and find that it helps them to stay involved with the material. One common method of notetaking is to jot down notes in outline form, using indentations, letters, and numbers to indicate main ideas and major details.

Another common method is called the Cornell Method and involves dividing a page of notebook paper into two sections, a two-inch section on the left and a six-inch section on the right with a line drawn between them. Then after you finish reading a section in the textbook, you jot down brief one or two sentence summaries in your own words in the six-inch section, skipping a line between each summary. Finally, you reread your summaries, underline key words or short phrases, and copy these words into the two-inch column immediately to the left of the summary statement. This method will provide you with extremely convenient study notes. The words to the left can be used to remind you of the key ideas that you will have summarized on the right. The following illustrates the use of the Cornell Method for the two sample textbook pages on pages 14 and 15:

Evolution	<u>Evolution</u> is the process by which organisms change over many generations.
Natural selection and selective pressure	Evolution is based on <u>natural selection</u> and <u>selective pressure</u>. The environment and inherited differences in individuals, affect which ones survive.
Adaptation	<u>Adaptation</u> is the result of natural selection and represents the ways groups change to fit into environments.

Reciting　An effective strategy for discovering the main points in your reading that can assist you in marking, annotating, and notetaking is to recite or repeat to yourself the essence of what you have just finished reading. After reading a section in a textbook chapter, or after a few minutes of sustained reading, close the book and say to yourself what you remember just having read. Then go back over what you have read and mark the most significant points that you have remembered and make your annotations or notes accordingly. This technique can help you identify the main points and reinforce what you have understood.

Reciting is also an effective way to study your notes later on. By reading aloud what you have written in your notes, you can reinforce what you have learned. And by reciting from memory what you have just read, you can reinforce your learning even more.

1f   Reviewing Strategies

As effective as these reading strategies may be in getting the most out of the material, you will surely need to go back over a chapter at a later time to study for a test or to complete some writing assignment related to it. If your marking, annotating, and notetaking have been thorough and clear, this last stage in your textbook study system will be much easier than it would otherwise be.

Reviewing   Reviewing a chapter involves going back over all that you have done in the previewing and reading stages in order to reinforce and study what you have learned. To review a chapter, first read back over everything you have marked and read all of your annotations and any marginal notes included by the authors in the text. Then read over any notes you have taken on separate paper. If any review questions are provided at the end of the chapter, be sure that you can answer them all. A final way to review is to look back over the chapter, questioning yourself by imagining the headings and subheadings as questions and by quizzing yourself on all the bold print or italicized words in the text.

Outlining and Mapping   Whether the chapter notes you have kept from your reading are in the form of annotations in the margins or notes on separate paper, one of the most useful and effective ways of organizing these notes to reinforce your learning is to organize them into an outline or concept map. An *outline* is an organized list of the author's main ideas and important supporting points that shows the relationships and relative importance of ideas by using indentation, lettering, and numbering. A *concept map* portrays the same information but in a diagram rather than a list. You may find that you prefer one of these methods more than the other in some situations. You would do well to try them both and see which you prefer.

Outlining   To be effective, an outline should not include every point from a chapter, but should, as with marking, annotating, and notetaking, include only the most important points that you feel you will need to learn and remember. To outline a chapter, you should first write a sentence that sums up in your own words the overall main point of the chapter. Then follow this summary statement with single words or short phrases, also in your own words, that represent the author's main points. List these points in the order in which they occur in the chapter, using letters, numbers, and indentations to show how they are related to one another. Notice how this has been done in the following example of an outline based on the information in the two textbook pages on pages 14 and 15.

Thesis: Evolution is a major theory in the science of biology.
- A.   Evolution
  - 1.   Inherited changes
  - 2.   Charles Darwin
- B.   Basis of evolution
  - 1.   Three things
    - a.   organisms differ
    - b.   differences inherited
    - c.   few reproduce
  - 2.   Factors in inherited variations
    - a.   natural selection
    - b.   selective pressure
- C.   Adaptation
  - 1.   Successful characteristics
  - 2.   Role of environment

Mapping   Like an outline, a concept map also shows how the main points relate to one another. However, a concept map is a diagram of the ideas and does not necessarily portray them in the order they were mentioned, but does show them only in relation to one another. When you are mapping, begin by drawing a circle or box in the middle or at the top of a piece of paper, and write in the overall main point. Then indicate the main points and the important supporting ideas from the chapter by using boxes, circles, and lines to connect them in ways that make sense to you. Notice how this is done in the following map, which contains the same information as the outline above but in a more graphic way:

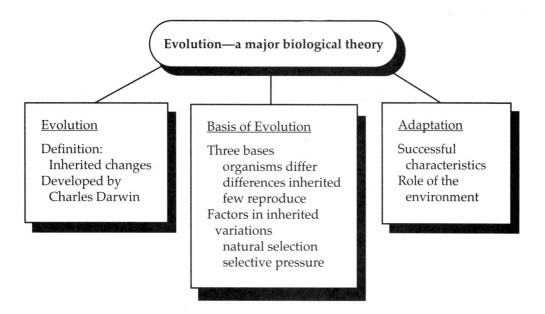

Paraphrasing and Summarizing   Outlining and mapping both involve expressing the author's key points in your own words. This is called *paraphrasing*. The listing of the author's main points and key supporting ideas in an outline or a concept map is also similar to the process of *summarizing*, which involves a restatement in sentence and paragraph form of the author's main points. Paraphrasing and summarizing are perhaps the best tests of how well you have understood what you have read. For this reason, they represent very effective strategies for reviewing what you have read, as well as important skills in taking notes and in writing essay exams and research papers.

Paraphrasing   To paraphrase something means to use your own words to restate the author's essential meaning. When you paraphrase, you are expressing the same meaning as the author has but, except for perhaps a few key terms that can't be restated, you are using your own words to do so. For example, in the passage from the biology textbook above, the authors introduce the theory of evolution by explaining it as follows: "The theory of evolution states that today's organisms have arisen by descent and modification from more ancient forms of life." To paraphrase this sentence would be to state something like the following: "According to the theory of evolution, living beings have inherited changes over countless generations."

Summarizing   Summarizing is very closely related to paraphrasing in the sense that you are using your own words to express the author's main points. Summarizing is also similar to outlining or mapping in that it involves expressing all of the author's main points. However, a summary is unique in that it involves using your own words to restate all the author's main points—without the details and examples—in complete sentences and paragraphs in a way that reduces a longer passage to a much shorter version. A summary of a textbook chapter, for example, condenses the contents to one or two paragraphs that express the overall thesis and all the main supporting ideas. A summary does not include your personal reactions to the material or your opinions of the author's points. You are merely restating the author's thesis and main ideas in your own words.

When writing a summary, begin by paraphrasing the author's thesis or overall main point. Then write statements that paraphrase or sum up the essence of each of the major points in the same order in which they occur in the chapter. If you have carefully marked and annotated while you read, summarizing will be much easier. Also, perhaps the easiest way to summarize is to begin by outlining or mapping the material. Once you have a complete outline or concept map, all you need to do to summarize is to turn each point that you have listed into a complete sentence as part of a paragraph. The following example represents a summary based on the outline and map of the two biology textbook pages on pages 14 and 15.

Evolution is a major theory in the science of biology. Charles Darwin developed this theory to explain inherited changes. The theory of evolution is based on observations that organisms differ, that these differences are inherited, and that not all organisms reproduce. Two factors in inherited variations are natural selection and selective pressure. The process of evolution results in the adaptation of organisms to their environment, with only their best characteristics surviving.

Notice how this summary includes all of the points listed in both the outline and map from pages 18 and 19. This summary briefly paraphrases the author's main points from the textbook passage by condensing the two pages of original text into one paragraph. In a summary, the supporting details and examples are left out so that only the most significant points are included.

1g   Reading for Different Purposes

Rather than reading all text material in the same way, it makes more sense to apply specific reading strategies in certain situations depending on your purpose for reading. This could include varying how fast you read, using skimming or scanning strategies, or using other strategies to help you retain what you read. For example, the way you would read an encyclopedia article if you were reading to gain understanding would be very different than if you were trying to find a fact to help you complete a crossword puzzle. Similarly, reading a textbook chapter in preparation for an exam would require very different strategies used at a different reading rate than if you were simply searching for a date or a fact.

Varying Rate   Both the way in which you approach a reading task and the speed at which you read are determined by several factors, including your purpose for reading, the type of material you are reading, the difficulty of the material you are reading, and your own abilities as a reader. Reading rate is often referred to as the number of words read in a minute, or the *words per minute* (wpm). Your personal characteristics as a reader are determined by your general knowledge of vocabulary, your specific knowledge of the topic you are reading about, your physical and mental condition at the time you are reading, and your interest in the material.

There is no single correct reading rate because the speed should be adjusted according to the material read and the purpose for reading. The following table suggests how different reading material read for different purposes typically requires different reading strategies and different reading rates.

Type of Material	Purpose for Reading	Type of Reading	Reading Rate
Textbooks Argumentative essays Poetry Academic journals Library research	Analysis Critique Test Preparation Research report Complete understanding	Active reading	100–300 wpm
Newspapers Magazines Novels Personal interest nonfiction	Personal enjoyment Personal information	Casual reading	200–500 wpm
Reference material Nonfiction	Overview Location of facts	Skimming Scanning	More than 500 wpm

Skimming   Skimming is reading done to gain an overview of the material, very much like the previewing strategies discussed earlier in this chapter. When you are skimming, you are not reading every word. You are skipping words, sentences, paragraphs, indeed entire pages that seem unessential to a general understanding of the material. Sometimes you may use skimming to quickly examine an entire book to see if you want to read it or use it in a research paper or other project. To do this, you should look through the table of contents and any introductory chapters to get a brief overview of what the book contains and of the author's perspective on the topic. You might apply a similar technique to an article by skimming the title, introduction, headings, highlighted material, and conclusion. Skimming is thus a useful approach when all you want is a general sense of the main point.

Scanning   Scanning is even less like actual reading than skimming. Scanning is a process of searching for a single word or fact, and is thus more of a locating skill than an actual reading strategy. Scanning is used when looking up a word in a dictionary, finding a topic in an index, or locating a phone number in a telephone book. With textbook material, scanning might be used if your purpose is to find the answer to a question about the presidential election of 1864, which might first involve finding a date on a page. Scanning is often used together with skimming when researching a topic. You might first *scan* to locate relevant information then *skim* to get a general overview of the main idea.

Reading to Retain Information   As useful as skimming and scanning can be in certain situations, if your purpose is to gain a more complete understanding of the material, you must use other strategies, such as previewing, active reading, and reviewing, which are described earlier in this chapter.

These strategies utilize what cognitive research—studies of how people learn and remember information—has suggested will increase the retention of what you have learned. First, when you engage in previewing activities to gain an overview of what you will read, you are building up frameworks of understanding. By constructing a general sense of the main points that you will be reading about, you are establishing a context or mental framework that the information you will read will fit into. Second, when you engage in active reading strategies, such as marking and annotating, you are helping to reinforce the material that you give special attention to, which establishes aids to recalling the information later. Finally, when you practice reviewing strategies, you are engaging in activities that actually require you to recall the information, thus making it more likely to be added to your long-term memory and available for you to remember. These strategies are useful for many learning activities that are required of you in college courses, including reading to learn information you will be tested on later.

Taking Objective Exams   Reading in preparation for an objective test—one that includes multiple-choice, true–false, or matching questions—involves all the reviewing strategies discussed earlier. If you have highlighted or marked and annotated while you read the text material, it will be much easier for you to go back and study for a test. Since an objective test typically requires you to identify correct answers, you want to note information that could be stated in relatively short question-and-answer choices, such as statements of main ideas, key terms, definitions, facts, and names. Thus, reviewing what you have marked and annotated will be especially useful with an objective test.

On an objective test, you may encounter a passage that you must read in order to answer a question. Typically, exams that test your reading skills will have reading passages that the questions refer to. However, most tests you will take in your courses will only have questions that refer to reading assignments you will be expected to have completed in textbooks or other books before taking the test.

When taking a reading test with passages, it is best to read the passage quickly but carefully first to understand its main idea and how each paragraph contributes to the central point. Don't be too concerned with the details in a passage on your first reading. When you answer the questions, you can look back and scan for specific details if the question calls for it.

When answering each question, first make sure that you understand exactly what the question is asking. Then try to come up with what you think the answer should be before looking at the answer choices. Only after you do this, try to find the answer that most closely matches the one you have come up with. Finally, be sure you carefully consider each answer choice before making your final decision. Also, if there is a reading passage with the questions, be sure to refer back to the passage to confirm each of your answers.

Taking Essay Exams   Essay exams require a different sort of recall than the more information-specific objective tests. On an essay test, you are required to express your overall understanding of concepts or events that you have read about, how they relate to one another, and the significance they have.

To prepare for an essay exam, a useful strategy is to anticipate the types of questions that might be asked. A good way to proceed with this is to review the questions you formulated in your previewing and that you attempted to find answers to in your reading. Here your marking and annotations will be useful to review, as will any separate notes you took and any outlines or summaries you made. Also, any introductory questions or end-of-chapter questions should be considered as items that you could be asked to explain on a test. Read these carefully and look back at what you have marked and annotated to formulate answers. Writing out answers to these questions can help anticipate questions that may be asked and help formulate answers that you can give.

Then when actually faced with an essay question on an exam, you want to be sure that you understand exactly what the question is asking. A helpful strategy before writing your answer is to make a short outline of what you plan to say. This can both help you to recall information and establish a meaningful organization for your answer.

Chapter Review

Because college textbooks are usually structured to help students understand the information they are reading, being able to take advantage of these structural aids makes reading easier and more efficient. This chapter has thus considered the format or structure of textbooks, including graphic illustrations commonly found in textbooks; discussed some strategies for reading textbooks; and looked at ways to read for different purposes:

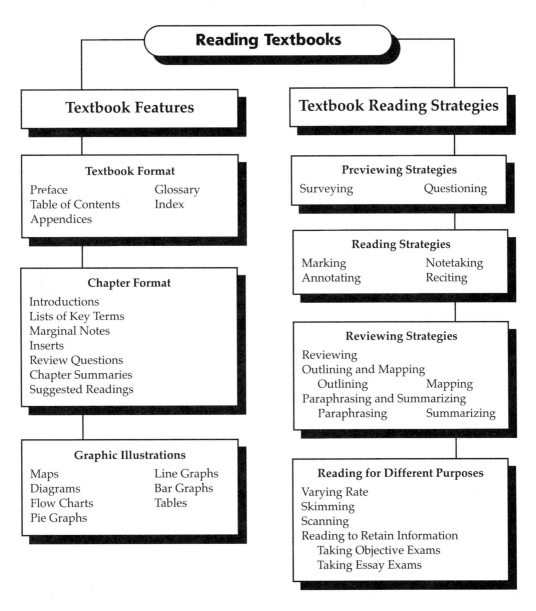

Reading Textbooks

Textbook Features

Textbook Format
Preface   Glossary
Table of Contents   Index
Appendices

Chapter Format
Introductions
Lists of Key Terms
Marginal Notes
Inserts
Review Questions
Chapter Summaries
Suggested Readings

Graphic Illustrations
Maps   Line Graphs
Diagrams   Bar Graphs
Flow Charts   Tables
Pie Graphs

Textbook Reading Strategies

Previewing Strategies
Surveying   Questioning

Reading Strategies
Marking   Notetaking
Annotating   Reciting

Reviewing Strategies
Reviewing
Outlining and Mapping
    Outlining   Mapping
Paraphrasing and Summarizing
    Paraphrasing   Summarizing

Reading for Different Purposes
Varying Rate
Skimming
Scanning
Reading to Retain Information
    Taking Objective Exams
    Taking Essay Exams

CHAPTER 2

Defining Words

When encountering an unfamiliar word while reading, many students might either just skip over the word, assuming that it is not essential to understanding the author, or dutifully look the word up in a dictionary. However, it is not always necessary to take the time to put down a book or magazine and refer to a dictionary. Instead, the context of the passage you are reading—the overall setting in which words are used in a sentence or paragraph—often provides clues to help you define an unfamiliar word. Also, the word parts—the root word and any prefixes or suffixes that compose the word—often make it possible to figure out the meaning of an unfamiliar word. However, if all else fails, or when you desire a more precise meaning than a context clue may suggest, remember that a good dictionary is a reliable, easy-to-use tool for locating the definition of virtually every word in the language.

Chapter Outline

Defining Words in Context

2a Definition

2b Explanation

2c Synonyms

2d Restatement

2e Antonyms

2f Examples

2g Surrounding Details

2h Mood

Defining Words through Word Analysis

2i Roots

2j Prefixes

  Amounts or Proportions
  Negative Meanings
  Directions or Relationships
  Time

2k Suffixes

  Adjectives
  Adverbs
  Nouns
  Verbs

2l Analyzing Words

Using a Dictionary

2m Sample Dictionary Page and Pronunciation Key

2n Guide Words

2o Main Entry

2p Pronunciation

2q Parts of Speech

2r Definitions

2s Synonyms

2t Related Word Forms

2u Labels

2v Word Origins

Defining Words in Context

When you come across a word with which you are unfamiliar or whose meaning is unclear to you, the *context* of the passage—the surrounding words in a sentence or paragraph—can often provide clues to help you figure out the meaning of this unfamiliar word. Sometimes an unfamiliar word will be directly defined or explained within a passage. In other cases, a word might be indirectly defined through the use of examples, by other words of similar or contrasting meanings, or through the overall meaning of the sentence in which the word is used or in the surrounding sentences.

Once you acquire the habit of trying to figure out the meaning of unfamiliar words by the context in which they are used, you will be surprised at how often you are able to do this. More often than not, you will be able to figure out the meanings of unfamiliar words by the surrounding words once you are aware of certain clues. The following is a list of different ways that you can use to figure out the meanings of unfamiliar words from context clues.

2a   Definition

A definition directly defines a word. On occasion, an author will give a direct definition for a term that he or she intends to introduce or that is essential in a discussion that is to follow. Direct definitions are often introduced by the word "is," as the following example illustrates.

> The Fourth Amendment insures that in most cases a law enforcement officer must obtain a warrant from a judge before making an arrest, seizing goods, or making a search. A <u>warrant</u> is <u>a written document issued by a court that allows a police officer to search a house or other building for suspected illegal goods</u>, such as drugs or stolen items, or to arrest a specifically named individual.

In this example, the word "is" clearly introduces the definition for the word "warrant." In other cases, the punctuation in a sentence—often commas or dashes—indicates that a definition is being given. If the author of the example above had used punctuation to indicate the definition of "warrant," it might have looked like this:

> The Fourth Amendment insures that in most cases before making an arrest, seizing goods, or making a search, a law enforcement officer must obtain a warrant, <u>a written document issued by a court that allows a police officer to search a house or other building for suspected illegal goods</u>.

In this sentence, the author uses a comma following the word "warrant" to lead into the definition.

2b   Explanation

An explanation provides details to explain the meaning of a word. Similar to a direct definition, an explanation usually follows a term with details, often using simpler words that are intended to clarify the meaning of the term. Explanations are typically longer than direct definitions and are often contained in more than one sentence. The following example explains what a "warrant" is without directly defining it.

> The Fourth Amendment insures that in most cases before making an arrest, seizing goods, or making a search, a law enforcement officer must first obtain permission from a judge in the form of a <u>warrant</u>. Once the <u>warrant</u> is issued, the officer has gained permission to search a house or other building for suspected illegal goods, such as drugs or stolen items, or to arrest a specifically named individual.

In this example, the word "warrant" is not defined, but it is explained by telling readers what permission has been granted to the officer by obtaining one. Without stating directly that a warrant is a written document, the explanation does make it clear that a warrant involves permission from a judge to search someone's private property for some suspected illegality or to make an arrest.

2c   Synonyms

A synonym is a word that has the same or similar meaning as another word. Sometimes a writer will include a word of the same or similar meaning in a sentence or in a nearby sentence that can make another word understandable. In the following sentence, look for a synonymous word or phrase for the word "ubiquitous."

> Whether one feels that <u>ubiquitous</u> popular culture represents a positive or negative influence on our society, it certainly seems clear that it is the <u>ever-present</u> reality for most of us.

In this sentence, there is a synonym for the word "ubiquitous" in the last clause. The sentence ends by stating that popular culture has become "ever-present" in our society, meaning that it is present everywhere; this means roughly the same as the adjective "ubiquitous" as it is used to describe popular culture in the first part of the sentence. Thus, "ubiquitous" means widespread, constantly encountered, or "ever-present."

2d   Restatement

A restatement states the meaning of a word in more readily understood words. Similar to the way that a synonym suggests a word's meaning, other words whose meanings are commonly known may accompany a word that an author feels might be less familiar to readers. For example, the idea expressed in the sentence in the above example could have been written to include a restatement clue as illustrated in the following example.

> Whether one feels that popular culture represents a positive or negative influence on our society, it certainly seems clear that it is the <u>ubiquitous</u> reality for most of us and is something that we <u>encounter at every turn</u>.

To say that popular culture is "something that we encounter at every turn" is not exactly the same as calling it "ubiquitous," but it certainly helps a reader understand what the more difficult word means— widespread or constantly encountered.

2e   Antonyms

An antonym is a word that has an opposite or contrasting meaning of another word. A writer may include a word or words of contrasting meaning in order to clarify another word. Transitional words such as "however" and "but" signal a reader that a contrasting idea is being introduced, which may include an antonym for a word before it. Read the following sentences and look for the antonym for the word "deleterious."

> Some social critics over the last decade have commented on the effects that popular culture has had on young people. Alan Bloom, for example, commented on the <u>deleterious</u> effects of rock music. Other commentators disagree and suggest that popular culture offers a <u>positive</u> contribution to our society.

Here the adjective "deleterious" is used to describe the effect Alan Bloom feels rock music has had on young people. In the sentence that follows it, the words "Other commentators disagree" suggest that a contrasting idea will follow. And indeed the word "positive" is then used to describe popular culture. It seems clear that "deleterious" means the opposite of "positive." Thus, to describe something as being "deleterious" means that it has a "negative" influence.

2f   Examples

An example is a single item, fact, incident, or aspect that is representative of a word or words. An author may follow a new word with specific examples in an attempt to illustrate the meaning of the word. The author here relies on the reader's experience. If the reader has personal experience with the example provided, it should clarify the meaning of the word in question. In the following sentence, examples are given to illustrate what is meant by "popular culture."

> When considering what <u>popular culture</u> includes, some obvious sources come to mind, including <u>television, radio, professional sports, various forms of popular music, general interest magazines, and the cinema</u>.

In this sentence, both the words "sources" and "including" suggest that examples will follow to illustrate what is meant by "popular culture." If a reader is familiar with these things, then it should be clear that "popular culture" refers to the shared information and forms of entertainment that people acquire through the most public forms of mass communication.

2g   Surrounding Details

Surrounding details often provide a general context for understanding the meaning of a word. If an author provides no obvious clues as to the meaning of a word with which you are unfamiliar, it may still be possible to infer its meaning. By using your understanding of the contents of the sentence in which the unfamiliar word is found and by noting other details in nearby sentences it is often possible to figure out what a word means.

> Previous to the time of the Greeks, forms of writing were more limited. Some cultures used extremely complex <u>ideographic</u> systems with hundreds of symbols, while others used syllabaries with symbols to represent the sounds of individual syllables. By developing an alphabet of signs that could be used to represent every sound in their language, including both consonants and vowels, the Greeks were able to simplify writing.

By understanding the general meaning of these two sentences, you can figure out the meaning of the word "ideographic." In these sentences, it is clear that an ideographic writing system is different from either a syllabary or an alphabet, both of which are explained in the passage. It seems that a syllabary is a writing system that uses symbols to represent different syllables, and an alphabet uses signs that stand for every sound in a language. If an ideographic system contains "hundreds of symbols" that represent neither syllables nor sounds, then they must represent something else. Because you are told that an ideographic system contains hundreds of symbols, you can infer that these symbols probably stand for entire ideas, objects, or whole words. This is in fact what an ideographic system of writing is—a writing system that uses a unique symbol or character to represent each concept.

2h   Mood

Mood is the predominant emotion of a sentence and can provide a context for undertanding a word. Sometimes in a sentence where there are no details or other clues that suggest the meaning for an unfamiliar word, the mood or tone of the sentence—the "feeling" created by the words the author uses—can suggest what it could mean.

> After my <u>miserable</u> attempt at an apology, Judith turned slowly toward me, her eyes watering so I could barely see them. I felt her gaze pour through me as I sank into the floor and hoped the words I feared would come next would not.

In this sentence, the word "miserable" is used differently than it is perhaps most often used. The word is usually used to mean sad or unhappy, but here that definition would not really make complete sense. Although the author—or the character the author is portraying—probably does feel unhappy, the context suggests that he feels more than this. An examination of how the author feels suggests the meaning of "miserable" as it is used here. The author seems to have hurt Judith's feelings by something he has just said or done, and he feels so ashamed that he "sank" figuratively "into the floor." His apology does not seem to be much consolation for Judith, nor does it make him feel any less guilty. Thus, the adjective "miserable" must mean at least "inadequate" and probably even "shameful," which is exactly what it does mean in this context. Your experience with feelings similar to those expressed in this sentence helps you to define the word "miserable" as it is used in this context.

Defining Words through Word Analysis

Even though the context often provides clues to help you figure out the meaning of an unfamiliar word, this is not always the case. Sometimes there is very little or nothing at all in the sentence or in surrounding sentences that suggests a meaning for a certain word, or sometimes you may lack experience with clues that are provided. In such cases, the meaning of a word can often be figured out by understanding the word parts that make it up—*roots*, *prefixes*, and *suffixes*.

Every word in English is composed of at least one root or core word that gives it its central meaning. Many words also have one or more prefixes or suffixes, word parts added to the beginning or ending of a word that contribute to the word's meaning. Some words are formed out of several word parts and combine roots, prefixes, and suffixes, all of which contribute to their meanings.

For example, the word "incontrovertible" begins with two prefixes—"in," meaning "not," and "contro," meaning "against." Then the root word "vert" follows which means "turn"; finally the suffix "ible" means "capable of" and makes the word an adjective. Putting these meanings together would literally result in something like "not against turn capable," which makes very little sense. However, when considered in the context of a sentence, it is possible to see how the word parts suggest the meaning: "The evidence suggesting his innocence is incontrovertible." Even though in this example the context alone cannot tell you what the word means, when the word parts are considered within the meaning of the sentence, it seems clear that "incontrovertible" means something like "not capable of being turned against." In other words, if something is described as "incontrovertible," it is unquestionable or impossible to dispute.

This method of defining a word by the meaning of its word parts is known as *word analysis.* A knowledge of the meaning of common roots, prefixes, and suffixes will enable you to figure out the meanings of many otherwise unfamiliar words that you encounter in your reading. The following is a list of some of the most common English roots, prefixes, and suffixes; definitions for each; and examples of words containing each word part.

2i   Roots

A root is the stem or most basic part of a word. It is the main part of a word that either gives it its basic meaning or, if combined with another root, helps determine its meaning.

Root	Meaning	Examples
anthro	human	anthropoid, anthropology
aqua	water	aquarium, aquatic
aud, audi	hear	audio, audit, audition
auto	self	autograph, automatic, automobile, autonomous
bene	good	benediction, benefactor, beneficial, benefit
bio	life, living	biodegradable, biography, biology, biosphere
capt, cept, ceive	take, sieze	accept, captivate, captive, capture, receive, reception
cede, ceed, cess	go, move, yield	access, cessation, precedent, proceed, process
chron, chrono	time	chronic, chronicle, chronological, synchronize
civ	citizen	civic, civilization, civilize

Root	Meaning	Examples
corp	body	corpse, corporation, incorporate
cred	believe	credence, credential, incredible
demo	people	democracy, demographic
derm	skin	dermatologist, dermatitis
dic, dict	say, tell, speak	dictate, diction, dictator, predict, verdict
du, duo	two	dual, duet, duplicate, duplex
duc, duct	lead, take, fashion, make	deduct, induce, conduct, educate, introduce, induct
equ	equal	equal, equate, equitable
fac, fact	do, make	facilitate, facsimile, factory
fer	carry, bear	ferry, refer, referee, transfer
geo	earth	geography, geology
graph, gram	write, written	autograph, graphics, monograph, telegram
grat	please, thank	congratulate, grateful
gress	go, move	aggression, progress, regress
ject	throw	eject, project, reject
man	hand	manual, manuscript
miss, mit	send, let go	mission, missile, permit, transmit
morph	form, shape	amorphous, morphology
mort	death	immortal, mortal, mortuary
mob, mot, mov	move	mobile, motion, movement
nom, nym	name	nominate, nominal, pseudonym, synonym
path, pathy	feeling	apathy, empathy, sympathy
ped, pedo	child	pediatrician, pedophile
ped, pod	foot	biped, pedal, podiatrist
pel, puls	push, drive, force	compel, expel, propulsion
pend, pens	hang	pendulum, suspend, suspense
phon, phono	sound	microphone, phonograph, phonetic, telephone
port	carry	import, portable, transport
pos	place	deposit, impose, position
prim	first	prime, premiere, primitive
psych	mind	psyche, psychic, psychology
rupt	break	disrupt, rupture
script, scrib	write	describe, inscribe, manuscript, scribble, scripture
sect	cut	dissect, section
sist	stand	consist, desist, insist, resistance
spec	look	inspect, spectacular, spectator
tain, ten	have, hold	detain, detention, entertain

Root	Meaning	Examples
tele	distance	telepathy, telephone, television
tend, tens	stretch	extend, tension
the, theo	god	atheist, pantheism, theology
tract, trac	draw	contract, distract, retract, trace
vers, vert	turn	aversion, convert, revert
vid, vis	see	television, video, visible, vision
voc, vok	call, voice	evocative, evoke, vocal, vocalist, vocalize

2j Prefixes

A prefix is a word element or group of letters added at the beginning of a word or root to form a new word that is related in meaning to the original word or root. A prefix can indicate amount, quality, direction, or time.

Prefixes Referring to Amounts or Proportions   The following list provides commonly used prefixes that refer to amounts or proportions, their meanings, and some examples of words using them.

Prefix	Meaning	Examples
ambi-	both	ambidextrous, ambivalent
bi-	two	biceps, bicycle, bimonthly
mini-	small, reduced	miniature, minimum, minivan
mono-	alone, one	monopoly, monogamous
multi-	many	multicultural, multicolored
poly-	many, more than one	polygon, polytheism
semi-	half, partial	semicircle, semiconscious, semifinal, semimonthly
tri-	three	triangle, tricycle, trinity, triple
uni-	one	unicycle, unite, universe

Prefixes with Negative Meanings   The following are some common prefixes with negative meanings and examples of each.

Prefix	Meaning	Examples
a-, an-	not, without	amoral, anarchy, atypical
anti-	against	antibiotic, antifreeze, antisocial
contra-, contro-	against	contraception, contradict, contrary, controversy

Prefix	Meaning	Examples
dis-	apart, away, not	discourage, disfavor, distract
il-, im-, in-, ir-	not	illegal, immobile, inexact, irreplaceable
mal-	bad	malady, malcontent, malformed
mis-	badly, wrong	mischief, misconduct, misery, misplace, mistake
non-	not	nonfat, nonreturnable, nonstop
pseudo-	false	pseudonym, pseudoscience
un-	not	unfamiliar, unhealthy, unknown, unpredictable

Prefixes Referring to Directions or Relationships   These prefixes all refer to some direction or relationship, which suggests the meaning of each example provided.

Prefix	Meaning	Examples
ab-	away, from	absent, absolve, absorb
ac-, ad-	to, toward	accede, accord, accost, admit, advance, advantage
ante-	before	anterior, anteroom
arch-	chief, main, great	archdiocese, archenemy, architect, archway
circum-	around	circle, circuit, circumference
co-, col-, com-, con-	together, with	collateral, collect, commit, company, conduct, connect, coordinate, coworker
de-	away, down, from	deport, defrost, demystify, descend, detachment
ex-	out, away from	exaggerate, exceed, exception, exclude, exhaust, extract, exit
extra-	beyond, more than	extraordinary, extrasensory, extraterrestrial, extravagant
in-, im-	into, within	inborn, implant
inter-	among, between	international, intercept, intersection
intra-	within	intramural, intravenous
intro-	inward	introduce, introspection, introvert
mid-	middle	middle, midterm, midwife
per-	by, through, throughout	perception, perfume permit, permeate, perennial

Prefix	Meaning	Examples
pro-	in place of, for, favoring, forward	pro bono, pro-choice, pronoun, progress, propeller
re-, retro-	again, back	recall, recede, remove, retroactive, retrospect
sub-	under, below	submarine, substandard, subheading, subway
super-	above, superior	superimpose, superfine, supersonic, supervisor
trans-	across, over, beyond	transcend, transcontinental, transition, transmit

Prefixes Referring to Time   The prefixes in this list all indicate some time reference, which can be seen in the examples for each.

Prefix	Meaning	Examples
ant-, ante-	before	antecedent, antedate, anticipate
post-	after, behind, later	postdate, posterior, posthumous, postpone
pre-	before	precede, preface, prelude, predispose, preliminary
pro-	before, earlier	probation, progenitor

2k   Suffixes

A suffix is a word element or group of letters added at the end of a word to form a different part of speech. A suffix might change a word into an adjective, an adverb, a noun, or a verb.

Suffixes Used to Form Adjectives   The following is a list of commonly used suffixes that change a root word into an adjective, the meaning of each, and examples containing them.

Suffix	Meaning	Examples
-able, -ible	able to be, capable of	agreeable, changeable, defensible, edible, manageable
-al	of, relating to, characterized by	directional, fictional, practical, radical, social

Suffix	Meaning	Examples
-ant, -ent	causing, promoting or performing	absorbent, benevolent, conversant, expectant
-ant, -ent	in a condition of	different, efficient, expectant
-ary, -ory	of, relating to, characterized by	advisory, cautionary, judiciary, stationary
-en	made of	earthen, oaken
-eous, -ious, -ose, -ous	full of, having the qualities of	atrocious, comatose, hilarious, plenteous, verbose
-ful	full of, having the qualities of	beautiful, bountiful, eventful, peaceful, masterful, wishful
-ic	of, relating to, characterized by	horrific, hypodermic, mythic, patriotic, specific
-ile, -il	relating to, capable of	agile, civil, docile, fragile, infantile, volatile
-ine	of or pertaining to	asinine, crystalline, marine
-ish	belonging to, having the qualities of	bookish, English, oldish, reddish, sweetish
-less	without	careless, childless, harmless
-ly, -y	having the qualities of, characterized by	daily, dreamy, grouchy, hourly, juicy, lovely, lucky, saintly

Suffixes Used to Form Adverbs

This suffix forms an adverb when added to words, such as the examples in the following list.

Suffix	Meaning	Examples
-ly	in a way that is, in the manner of	gladly, gradually, momentarily, partly, secondly, slowly

Suffixes Used to Form Nouns

This list shows common suffixes used to form nouns when added to verbs or other nouns, such as in the words that illustrate each one.

Suffix	Meaning	Examples
-ance, -ence	a state, condition, action, or process	emergence, reference, performance, resistance
-ant, -ent	one that causes, performs, or is characterized by	accident, coolant, defendant, deodorant, lubricant, precedent, stimulant
-arch	chief, highest	matriarch, monarch, patriarch
-ary, -ery, -ory	a place or practice	aviary, bakery, observatory, slavery, snobbery

Suffix	Meaning	Examples
-ation, -cion -ion, -ition,	a state, condition, action, or process	celebration, expedition, separation, suspicion, union
-ency	a state or condition	consistency, complacency, dependency, emergency
-er, -or	an agent or person who is or does	carpenter, projector, southerner, tailor, tractor, trailer
-hood	a condition or state	childhood, motherhood, priesthood
-ie, -y	a person characterized by, or a condition of	cabby, cheepie, cookery, groupie inquiry, jealousy, laundry
-ism	a practice, condition, or belief system	alcoholism, Buddhism, criticism, humanism, plagiarism, shamanism
-ist	one who does, is, or believes in	Buddhist, cyclist, geologist, novelist, pacifist
-log, -logue	speech, discourse	catalog, dialogue, monologue, travelogue
-logy	science, study	geology, neurology, zoology
-ment	an action, condition, product, or means	entanglement, entertainment, fragment, government
-ness	a condition or quality	darkness, kindness, sickness
-ship	a quality, condition, or skill	friendship, penmanship, statesmanship
-tomy	the act of cutting	appendectomy, lobotomy

Suffixes Used to Form Verbs   These suffixes form verbs out of nouns or adjectives that they are attached to, as the following examples show.

Suffix	Meaning	Examples
-en	to become, cause, or resemble	fasten, harden, lengthen, strengthen, sweeten
-ize	to make, express, or represent	Americanize, apologize, baptize, computerize, dramatize, sterilize, tyrannize

2I   Analyzing Words

Now read the following sentences containing words with one or more word parts. Notice how each word can be defined according to the meaning of the combined word parts.

To <u>predict</u> an event is to announce or "tell" about it "before" it happens.

When Japan <u>export</u>s a car to the United States, it moves or "carries" the car "out" of its country to ours.

If two houses are <u>adjac</u>ent to one another, they are "characterized by" a nearness "to" each other.

A <u>malevol</u>ent action is one that "causes" something "bad" to happen.

An <u>autograph</u> is one's own name "written" by "oneself."

To <u>voca</u>lize something is to "cause" it to be expressed with the "voice."

A <u>move</u>ment is an act or "action" of "moving."

A message that is <u>transmittable</u> is "able to be" "sent" from one place "across" to another.

If something is <u>reversible</u>, it is "capable of" being "turned" "back" to the way it formerly was.

To present something <u>visuall</u>y is to show it "in a way that is" able to be "seen."

A <u>specta</u>tor is a "person" who watches or "looks" at something.

A <u>distraction</u> is a situation or "action" that "draws" one's concentration "away."

Using a Dictionary

When you are unable to use either the context or the word parts to help you define an unfamiliar word, or when you want more precise information than you can figure out for yourself, you can always consult a dictionary. By providing a relatively simple-to-use resource for defining words, a dictionary is certainly a reader's best friend. However, in addition to providing word definitions, a good dictionary also contains spellings, pronunciations, parts of speech, word origins, and various word forms. Many dictionaries also contain biographical and geographical information on significant historical and contemporary persons and places, as well as photographs and illustrations for many entries.

All the features of a dictionary are illustrated on the sample dictionary page that follows. Further explanations of these features are offered in this section.

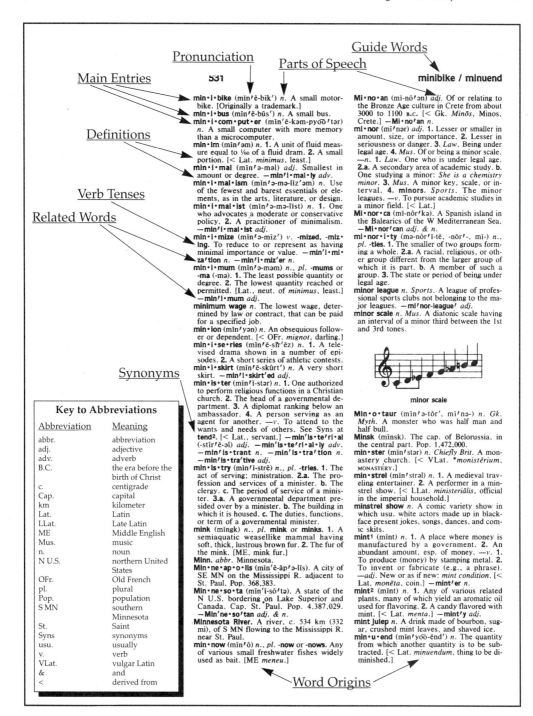

Main Entries

Pronunciation

Parts of Speech

Guide Words

Definitions

Verb Tenses

Related Words

Synonyms

Word Origins

531   minibike / minuend

min·i·bike (mĭn′ē-bīk′) n. A small motorbike. [Originally a trademark.]
min·i·bus (mĭn′ē-bŭs′) n. A small bus.
min·i·com·put·er (mĭn′ē-kəm-pyōō′tər) n. A small computer with more memory than a microcomputer.
min·im (mĭn′əm) n. 1. A unit of fluid measure equal to ⅟₆₀ of a fluid dram. 2. A small portion. [< Lat. *minimus*, least.]
min·i·mal (mĭn′ə-məl) adj. Smallest in amount or degree. —**min′i·mal·ly** adv.
min·i·mal·ism (mĭn′ə-mə-lĭz′əm) n. Use of the fewest and barest essentials or elements, as in the arts, literature, or design.
min·i·mal·ist (mĭn′ə-mə-lĭst) n. 1. One who advocates a moderate or conservative policy. 2. A practitioner of minimalism. —**min′i·mal·ist** adj.
min·i·mize (mĭn′ə-mīz′) v. -mized, -mizing. To reduce to or represent as having minimal importance or value. —**min′i·mi·za′tion** n. —**min′i·miz′er** n.
min·i·mum (mĭn′ə-məm) n., pl. -mums or -ma (-mə). 1. The least possible quantity or degree. 2. The lowest quantity reached or permitted. [Lat., neut. of *minimus*, least.] —**min′i·mum** adj.
minimum wage n. The lowest wage, determined by law or contract, that can be paid for a specified job.
min·ion (mĭn′yən) n. An obsequious follower or dependent. [< OFr. *mignot*, darling.]
min·i·se·ries (mĭn′ē-sîr′ēz) n. 1. A televised drama shown in a number of episodes. 2. A short series of athletic contests.
min·i·skirt (mĭn′ē-skûrt′) n. A very short skirt. —**min′i·skirt′ed** adj.
min·is·ter (mĭn′ĭ-stər) n. 1. One authorized to perform religious functions in a Christian church. 2. The head of a governmental department. 3. A diplomat ranking below an ambassador. 4. A person serving as an agent for another. —v. To attend to the wants and needs of others. See Syns at **tend²**. [< Lat., servant.] —**min′is·te′ri·al** (-stîr′ē-əl) adj. —**min′is·te′ri·al·ly** adv. —**min′is·trant** n. —**min′is·tra′tion** n. —**min′is·tra′tive** adj.
min·is·try (mĭn′ĭ-strē) n., pl. -tries. 1. The act of serving; ministration. 2.a. The profession and services of a minister. b. The clergy. c. The period of service of a minister. 3.a. A governmental department presided over by a minister. b. The building in which it is housed. c. The duties, functions, or term of a governmental minister.
mink (mĭngk) n., pl. mink or minks. 1. A semiaquatic weasellike mammal having soft, thick, lustrous brown fur. 2. The fur of the mink. [ME. mink fur.]
Minn. abbr.
Min·ne·ap·o·lis (mĭn′ē-ăp′ə-lĭs). A city of SE MN on the Mississippi R. adjacent to St. Paul. Pop. 368,383.
Min·ne·so·ta (mĭn′ĭ-sō′tə). A state of the N U.S. bordering on Lake Superior and Canada. Cap. St. Paul. Pop. 4,387,029. —**Min′ne·so′tan** adj. & n.
Minnesota River. A river, c. 534 km (332 mi), of S MN flowing to the Mississippi R. near St. Paul.
min·now (mĭn′ō) n., pl. -now or -nows. Any of various small freshwater fishes widely used as bait. [ME *meneu*.]

Mi·no·an (mĭ-nō′ən) adj. Of or relating to the Bronze Age culture in Crete from about 3000 to 1100 B.C. [< Gk. *Mĭnōs*, Minos, Crete.] —**Mi·no′an** n.
mi·nor (mī′nər) adj. 1. Lesser or smaller in amount, size, or importance. 2. Lesser in seriousness or danger. 3. Law. Being under legal age. 4. Mus. Of or being a minor scale. —n. 1. Law. One who is under legal age. 2.a. A secondary area of academic study. b. One studying a minor: *She is a chemistry minor.* 3. Mus. A minor key, scale, or interval. 4. minors. Sports. The minor leagues. —v. To pursue academic studies in a minor field. [< Lat.]
Mi·nor·ca (mĭ-nôr′kə). A Spanish island in the Balearics of the W Mediterranean Sea. —**Mi·nor′can** adj. & n.
mi·nor·i·ty (mə-nôr′ĭ-tē, -nŏr′-, mī-) n., pl. -ties. 1. The smaller of two groups forming a whole. 2.a. A racial, religious, or other group different from the larger group of which it is part. b. A member of such a group. 3. The state or period of being under legal age.
minor league n. Sports. A league of professional sports clubs not belonging to the major leagues. —**mi′nor-league′** adj.
minor scale n. Mus. A diatonic scale having an interval of a minor third between the 1st and 3rd tones.

minor scale

Min·o·taur (mĭn′ə-tôr′, mī′nə-) n. Gk. Myth. A monster who was half man and half bull.
Minsk (mĭnsk). The cap. of Belorussia, in the central part. Pop. 1,472,000.
min·ster (mĭn′stər) n. Chiefly Brit. A monastery church. [< VLat. *monistērium*, MONASTERY.]
min·strel (mĭn′strəl) n. 1. A medieval traveling entertainer. 2. A performer in a minstrel show. [< LLat. *ministeriális*, official in the imperial household.]
minstrel show n. A comic variety show in which usu. white actors made up in blackface present jokes, songs, dances, and comic skits.
mint¹ (mĭnt) n. 1. A place where money is manufactured by a government. 2. An abundant amount, esp. of money. —v. 1. To produce (money) by stamping metal. 2. To invent or fabricate (e.g., a phrase). —adj. New or as if new: *mint condition.* [< Lat. *monēta*, coin.] —**mint′er** n.
mint² (mĭnt) n. 1. Any of various related plants, many of which yield an aromatic oil used for flavoring. 2. A candy flavored with mint. [< Lat. *menta*.] —**mint′y** adj.
mint julep n. A drink made of bourbon, sugar, crushed mint leaves, and shaved ice.
min·u·end (mĭn′yōō-ĕnd′) n. The quantity from which another quantity is to be subtracted. [< Lat. *minuendum*, thing to be diminished.]

Key to Abbreviations

Abbreviation	Meaning
abbr.	abbreviation
adj.	adjective
adv.	adverb
B.C.	the era before the birth of Christ
c.	centigrade
Cap.	capital
km	kilometer
Lat.	Latin
LLat.	Late Latin
ME	Middle English
Mus.	music
n.	noun
N U.S.	northern United States
OFr.	Old French
pl.	plural
Pop.	population
S MN	southern Minnesota
St.	Saint
Syns	synonyms
usu.	usually
v.	verb
VLat.	vulgar Latin
&	and
<	derived from

2m   Sample Dictionary Page

The sample dictionary page, shown in the right-hand side of the illustration, is typical of one from a good paperback dictionary. As this sample shows, a dictionary contains many features in addition to definitions. On the left-hand side of the illustration, you will see a list of abbreviations used in the sample dictionary page. These and many other abbreviations used within word entries are defined for you on a page near the beginning of your dictionary. As this sample shows, a dictionary contains many features in addition to definitions.

There are many dictionaries on the market published by many publishers. Unabridged dictionaries include virtually every word in the English language and are available only in large hardcover editions. Abridged college editions are shorter versions of unabridged dictionaries and have been designed to include information that should be adequate for most students' needs. For home use, a hardcover college edition is especially useful because of its larger size and durability. For classroom use, abridged dictionaries are more useful because their availability in smaller sizes and paperback covers makes them less expensive and more portable. Whichever dictionary you use, you are sure to find it a most valuable tool. Though dictionaries vary in how the information in each word entry is organized, all the major dictionaries contain the same basic features.

2n   Guide Words

Guide words are found at the top of a dictionary page. They indicate the first and last entries on the page.

In the sample dictionary page, the guide words "minibike/minuend" indicate that every word on the page falls alphabetically between these two words. Guide words make it easy to locate a word quickly, assuming you know approximately how it is spelled. (If you have difficulty with spelling, you might find it useful to pick up a misspeller's dictionary that lists words according to common misspellings.)

2o   Main Entry

The main entry is the word that is defined. Main entries are usually listed in bold print and are followed by the definitions and other information indented slightly from the margin. Each main entry is divided into syllables and is only capitalized if it is a proper noun.

Names of persons are listed alphabetically by the last name. Words with identical spellings but with different meanings and origins will often have separate entries. This is the case with the two entries in the sample dictionary page for "mint." The first entry for "mint" derives from the Latin word for coin (*moneta*), and the second entry derives from the Latin word referring to a certain plant (*menta*).

2p   Pronunciation

Directly following the main entry, pronunciation symbols and stress marks indicate how to pronounce the word. This is one of the most valuable features of a dictionary. You can find out the exact pronunciation for every word in the English language once the relationship between the pronunciation symbols and the pronunciation key is understood. The pronunciation for a word is typically provided within parentheses right after the main entry. The pronunciation shows some consonants and all vowels as symbols according to how they are pronounced. A pronunciation key is needed in order to know how to interpret these symbols. All dictionaries include a full pronunciation key in the front of the book before the word entries begin. Many hardcover dictionaries also include partial keys at the bottom of every page or every facing page, while most paperbacks only include a key in the front of the book. For example, notice the pronunciation symbols for the vowels in "minibike" can be interpreted by referring to a pronunciation key. A dictionary pronunciation key would show you something like the following:

/ē/   **bee;**   /ĭ/   **pit;**   /ī/   **pie, by.**

The vowel symbols in the entry word are thus pronounced the same as they are in the example words in the pronunciation key.

2q   Parts of Speech

Following the pronunciation, the part of speech for the main entry is indicated by an abbreviation. If a word can be used as more than one part of speech, each one will be listed and indicated somewhere in the entry. For example, the first entry for the word "mint" above (*mint¹*) includes noun (*n.*), verb (—*v.*), and adjective (—*adj.*) usages. The definition of the noun is listed first. The definition of the verb begins on the third line of the entry, and the definition of the adjective begins on the sixth line. Dictionaries typically define the different parts of speech only if the definition changes slightly for each one. In paperback editions, the different parts of speech are usually listed without definitions at the end of the entry.

Note that the parts of speech are abbreviated in the dictionary. A list of the abbreviations used in the dictionary will be included in its introductory pages.

2r   Definitions

The definitions include all the possible meanings of the main entry. The meanings of a word are typically numbered in boldface print. Usually, a dictionary lists the most important or frequently used meanings first. However, in some dictionaries, the oldest meaning will be listed first. Notice above how the listing for the word "minister" includes four numbered definitions for the noun usage, then lists a definition for the verb usage. Also notice that for the word "ministry," both the second and third definitions are divided into three related definitions (**2.a.**, **b.**, and **c.**; **3.a.**, **b.**, and **c.**)

2s   Synonyms

A synonym is a word that has the same or a similar meaning as another word. Synonyms are sometimes listed as part of the definition of a main entry. For example, in the above definition for the verb form of "minister," you are told to "See Syns at **tend²**." This tells you to refer elsewhere in the dictionary to the second main entry for the word "tend," which is a synonym for the verb "minister" and where a list of other synonyms is provided. Indeed, if you were to look up this second definition for "tend," you would see something like the following, which ends with a list of synonyms ("Syns"), including "minister":

> **tend²** (tend) v. **1.** To care for or watch over. **2.** To attend to or service: *tend a fire.* **3.** To give one's attention or attend [ME *tenden,* ATTEND.] *Syns: attend, care, minister, watch* **v.**

2t   Related Word Forms

Related word forms are variant forms of an entry word. They include irregular verb tenses and past participles, unusual plural spellings, and related words formed by adding various word parts.

Irregular verb tenses and unusual plural spelling are usually listed right before the definitions begin. Various forms of the word are usually listed at the end of the entry along with their parts of speech. Notice above in the entry for the word "minister" how five related words are listed after the definitions. Also, notice how the entry for the verb "minimize" indicates the spelling for both past and present participles (**-mized**, **-mizing**) right after the part of speech, showing how the "e" at the end of "minimize" is dropped when the "ed" and "ing" endings are added. For the word "mink," notice how the plural forms (*pl.*) are listed, telling you that either of two spellings ("mink" or "minks") is acceptable.

2u   Labels

Labels are identifications for words used in restricted ways, such as nonstandard or slang expressions, words limited to certain geographic areas or fields of knowledge, or words no longer in common usage. A dictionary usually includes labels, usually in italics, that indicate that a word is normally used only in some limited way. For example, notice in the entry for the word "minor" that definitions are listed for both the adjective and noun forms, and that labels are provided to show that a definition applies only to a particular professional, artistic, or athletic field: law (*Law*), music (*Mus.*), and sports (*Sports*).

2v   Word Origins

Word origins provide the history of the main entry. Information concerning the historical roots of a word, its etymology, are included either near the beginning or at the end of an entry. Many English words have their origins in Latin or Greek words, but many also come from French or old versions of English. In the entry for the word "minnow" in the sample dictionary page, the bracketed information at the end of the entry, "ME *memeu*" tells you that the word derives from Middle English, the version of the language used from about 1100 to 1500 C.E. In the entry for "minuend," you are told within the brackets at the end that the word comes from ("<") the Latin ("Lat.") word *minuendum*, which means "thing to be diminished." Remember that these and other abbreviations are defined for you on a page near the beginning of your dictionary.

Chapter Review

When you come across an unfamiliar word while reading, there are a few effective stategies for defining the word, short of looking it up in a dictionary. One way is to consider the context—the sentence and overall situation in which the word is used. Another way is to consider the word parts—the root and any prefix or suffix that combine to form the word. But of course when these strategies do not help you to figure out the definition to your satisfaction, a dictionary contains, among other important features, the definitions for most of the words you will read in English. Exceptions may include technical words, which are often included in the glossary if you are reading a textbook, or recently coined words, which may require you to use your imagination.

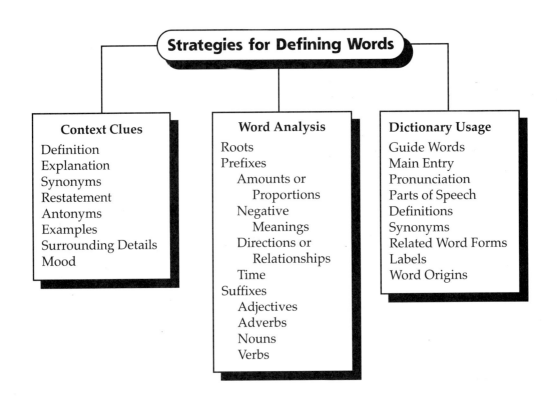

Strategies for Defining Words

Context Clues
Definition
Explanation
Synonyms
Restatement
Antonyms
Examples
Surrounding Details
Mood

Word Analysis
Roots
Prefixes
  Amounts or
    Proportions
  Negative
    Meanings
  Directions or
    Relationships
  Time
Suffixes
  Adjectives
  Adverbs
  Nouns
  Verbs

Dictionary Usage
Guide Words
Main Entry
Pronunciation
Parts of Speech
Definitions
Synonyms
Related Word Forms
Labels
Word Origins

CHAPTER 3

Recognizing Main Ideas

There is perhaps nothing more important in understanding what you read than being able to identify an author's main point. This is especially true when reading nonfiction and textbook material, and involves both the recognition of stated main ideas and important details and the inference of significant unstated points. The *main idea* is the central or most important idea of a single paragraph, a series of related paragraphs, or an entire passage. It sets the direction and states the main point, and it often suggests the purpose. The main idea is an umbrella idea that encompasses all the details related to it. The *supporting details* explain the main idea or elaborate upon it. To grasp the essence of an author's meaning, it is essential to be able to distinguish between the main ideas and supporting details by understanding the general points and by seeing how the more specific supporting points explain them. Recognizing main points and significant details often involves *inference,* the ability to figure out something that an author wants readers to understand but does not directly state. Astute readers are thus able to recognize main points and infer suggested ideas.

Identifying Main Ideas and Supporting Details

A paragraph or passage is usually about a certain *topic* or general subject and has a *main idea* that represents the point made about the topic. The main idea may be either stated or implied. An author will often state the main idea in a sentence that is more general than the supporting details and that summarizes the point of the details. Even though an author will not always come right out and directly state what the main point is, you want to be able to grasp the central point that is being made. This is not as difficult as it may seem, once a few strategies are understood. To get a sense of the topic of a passage, ask yourself "who" or "what" it is about. Then to figure out the complete main idea, ask yourself, "What point is the author making about the topic?" or "What aspect of the topic is the author's main concern?"

The supporting details of a passage consist of specific facts, examples, or reasons that directly explain, illustrate, or support the main idea. In a longer selection, the main ideas of each paragraph become the supporting details for the *thesis* statement, the overall main point of the entire passage or essay. If a paragraph or passage contained only general statements, such as the topic sentence and thesis statement, the writing would not only be short but also quite uninteresting. It is the specifics that add life and interest to a piece of writing and make the reader able to fully understand what is being discussed, often through vivid images that allow readers to visualize what is being described. Also, it is in recognizing the specifics and seeing how they relate to the main idea that reading becomes a means of both acquiring understanding and enjoying oneself.

Sometimes the supporting details explain or clarify the main idea. This is often done by providing concrete examples and illustrations. If a passage or an article is an *argument*—an attempt to persuade readers to agree with the author's opinion—the supporting details provide the evidence to support the main point and make it convincing. In a *narrative*—a retelling of events that occurred in time—the supporting details portray the events and tell specifically what happened. Supporting details often describe by trying to show how something looks, sounds, smells, or feels. For whatever purpose supporting details are used, they add interest and help readers understand as fully as possible the point an author is making.

3a   Identifying the Core Idea of a Sentence

Identifying the core idea of a sentence is like paraphrasing, which was discussed in Chapter 1. Paraphrasing is using your own words to express an author's essential meaning; thus, when you paraphrase, you are reducing complicated sentences to their core meanings, which is what you do to formulate the main idea of a paragraph or longer passage. In a sentence, the core idea is formulated in the subject, verb, and object. Supporting details are used to add description to or expand upon the core ideas. Supporting details are modifying words and phrases—such as adjectives, adverbs, prepositional phrases, and restrictive clauses—that fill out the core idea by adding descriptive or explanatory details. By identifying the subject, verb, and object in a sentence, and by eliminating descriptive or modifying words and phrases, it is possible to grasp the core meaning of a sentence. For example, the following sentence highlights the subject, verb, and object.

> <u>Americans</u> once <u>assumed</u> that American <u>Indians</u>, like so many European immigrants, <u>would assimilate</u> into the American melting pot.

To identify the main idea, the sentence can be paraphrased as "Americans assumed Indians would assimilate." The following steps outline this process of paraphrasing.

1. First, identify the subject and verb of the sentence. In this sentence, the subject is "Americans," and the main verb, or the word that suggests what "Americans" do, is "assumed."

2. Once the subject and verb are identified, then look for what it is that Americans assumed. The sentence suggests that Americans assumed that Indians "would assimilate." The modifying phrase "like so many European immigrants" suggests that Americans thought Indians should behave the same as immigrants. And the prepositional phrase "into the American melting pot" indicates that this expected behavior was for Indians to assimilate into the mainstream of society, just as it was thought everyone else had. These are supporting ideas that make the core idea of the sentence—the subject, verb, and object—more understandable.

3. If you leave out the modifying phrase "like so many European immigrants" and the prepositional phrase "into the American melting pot," leaving in the connecting word "that," a shortened paraphrasing of the sentence would thus be "Americans assumed that Indians would assimilate."

The example sentence above is written in the active voice, where the subject performs the action. In a sentence written in the passive voice, where the subject performs no action, it becomes a little more complicated to formulate the core idea.

It was once assumed that American Indians, like so many European immigrants, would be assimilated into the American melting pot.

This sentence means the same thing as the previous example, but here the subject is "It." The subject "It" could refer to certain scholars, politicians, or the American people in general. If you assume that "It" refers generally to "Americans," and you revise the verb "was assumed" and the phrase "would be assimilated" into their active voice versions—"assumed" and "would assimilate"—you will then arrive at the same paraphrase as before: "Americans assumed that Indians would assimilate."

3b   Identifying the Main Idea of a Paragraph

A paragraph is a group of related sentences that all address the same general topic. The *topic* of a paragraph is the general subject, and the *topic sentence* is a statement in the paragraph that expresses the main point made about the subject. Every paragraph has a topic or subject, but not every paragraph has a topic sentence. Sometimes an author does not directly state the main idea of a paragraph. In such cases, a reader is left to infer, or figure out, the main idea from the details.

In a paragraph, an author typically uses supporting details to expand upon the main idea. In fact, because a topic sentence is usually no more than one sentence, most of a paragraph consists of supporting details. However, these supporting details are not all of equal importance. Similar to the way that the topic sentence is more general than the supporting details, some details are more general than others.

Identifying the Topic of a Paragraph   The topic of a paragraph or passage is what that paragraph or passage is about in a very general sense. The topic is the subject and could serve as an adequate title of a passage. Thus, when identifying a topic, it is usually stated as a phrase or an incomplete sentence, rather than as a completely formed sentence. The topic of a passage is similar to the subject of a sentence in the sense that it is generally who or what is responsible for any action taking place or who or what is receiving attention in the passage. Asking yourself the question, "Who or what is this about?" will help you to identify the topic.

Identifying the Topic Sentence and Major Details of a Paragraph
Identifying the topic sentence and major details of a paragraph is like outlining, which was discussed in Chapter 1. A paragraph is a group of sentences that are all on one topic. Often the main idea of a paragraph is not directly stated, but when there is a sentence that states the main point it is called the topic sentence. The topic sentence of a paragraph states the main or controlling idea in a way that limits the general topic. The topic sentence of a paragraph in a longer passage probably states one narrow aspect of the broader topic in a way that is manageable within a single paragraph.

The details that directly support the topic sentence or main idea of the paragraph are called the *major supporting details.* The supporting details that only indirectly support the main idea, but directly support the major details are called the *minor supporting details.* To identify the major details in a paragraph, first determine the main idea or topic sentence. Key words in the topic sentence may suggest the nature of the details that will follow. Then look for the major points made in support of the main idea. Often, *transitions*—words or phrases that indicate how ideas are related to one another—will be used to introduce the major supporting details.

A useful way of thinking about the difference between main ideas and supporting details is to remember that the main point is a *general statement* and the supporting details are *specific information* that explains, describes, or expands upon the main idea. A topic sentence is thus a general statement of what the specific details add up to. In the following example of a paragraph about prehistoric cave art, consider the difference between the general topic sentence and the more specific details.

Prehistoric cave artists used a variety of tools and methods to create their art. These ancient artists used stones to flatten out the surfaces of uneven cave walls. When drawing, they typically worked with red and yellow rocks. They used this same rock for painting but ground it up and mixed it with animal fat. Prehistoric painters used flat bones for palettes and made brushes from reeds or bristles. When putting pigments onto hard-to-reach surfaces, these artists would blow through hollow reeds filled with pigment. The mixture of saliva and the pigment allowed it to stick onto the surface of the cave.

Notice how the first sentence, the topic sentence, mentions very generally the "tools and methods" used by cave artists. The rest of the sentences in the paragraph describe some of these specific tools—flattening stones, flat bone palettes, reed or bristle brushes, hollow reeds—and specific methods—flattening cave walls with stones, mixing ground up rocks with animal fat, blowing pigment mixed with saliva onto the walls. Thus, the general topic sentence states the main idea, and the supporting details explain this idea with more specific information.

Read the following paragraph trying first to identify the general topic. Then notice the topic sentence, the sentence that states the main idea, and the major supporting details.

Historical factors have not only discouraged assimilation but have actually contributed to the endurance of traditional Indian values and cultures. One factor that has contributed to the cultural persistence of the Indians is that defeated tribes were usually isolated on reservations. This practice of physical separation worked against assimilation by isolating tribes from mainstream influences. In addition, government policies of forced acculturation deliberately tried to eliminate traditional cultures and languages, often by separating children from their families and sending them to government-run boarding schools. Such attempts often caused individuals to resent and reject white influences. Another factor contributing to the persistence of Indian values is that white Americans have historically tended to consider any non-Caucasian ethnic groups to be fundamentally inferior. With opportunities for social and cultural mobility denied, or at least made very difficult, many Indians have sought to retain their identities through the reaffirmation of traditional values.

In this paragraph, the topic in the most general sense is the American Indians. More specific to this paragraph, the topic could be expressed as "Historical Factors and Indian Traditions" or "The Endurance of Indian Cultures." Either of these could serve nicely as a title for this paragraph. Now, you want to decide which sentence in the paragraph expresses the main point made about this topic in the paragraph. This will be the topic sentence. In this case, the first sentence is the topic sentence because it states generally what the paragraph goes on to explain in more detail—historical factors have contributed to the endurance of Indian cultures.

The topic sentence is followed by a sentence beginning with the phrase "One factor," which introduces the first major detail: "defeated tribes were usually isolated on reservations." The third sentence is not a new major detail but expands upon the first one by explaining a little more about how this isolation worked. The fourth sentence then introduces the second major detail with the words "In addition." The second major detail—"government policies of forced acculturation"—is then further supported with a minor detail in the next sentence about the resentment that often resulted. The final major detail is introduced by the phrase "Another factor" about how "white Americans have historically tended to consider any non-Caucasian ethnic groups to be fundamentally inferior." This is followed by a final minor detail about the effect of denied opportunities.

An *outline* of the paragraph would begin with the main idea then indicate the organization of the major and minor details. An outline is generally written as an organized list of short phrases or single words that merely suggest the points made in the paragraph. An outline of the paragraph would look something like this.

Historical factors discouraging the assimilation of Indians (main idea)
A. Isolated on reservations (major detail)
     away from mainstream (minor detail)
B. Government policies of forced acculturation (major detail) resentment (minor detail)
C. American racism (major detail) opportunities denied (minor detail)

Location of the Topic Sentence   As in the previous example, you will often find that authors begin a paragraph with the topic sentence, frequently as the very first sentence. This is often done in textbooks where a conscious effort is made to make it as easy as possible for students to understand the material. However, it is not always that simple. Sometimes a paragraph will begin with introductory information to provide background that leads into the main idea. In this case, the topic sentence introduces the main idea of the paragraph. Sometimes the topic sentence will be stated in the middle of a paragraph with supporting details before and after it, in which case it ties the parts of the paragraph together into a statement of the main point. Sometimes a paragraph will end with the main idea in the form of a concluding sentence to summarize what the supporting details have been suggesting. In any case, the topic sentence serves a similar purpose: It sums up the contents of the paragraph and states the overall main idea.

Read the following paragraph, which is a continuation of the previous example; notice the topic sentence that, in this case, is not the first sentence:

> The anthropologist Joseph Epes Brown has suggested that where Indians have been able to live in areas less disturbed by urban development, they have often been able to form identities in relation to nature and to the tribal group. These identities revolve around traditional rites and spiritual attitudes that have provided Indians with a sort of screening mechanism in the acculturation process. According to Brown, this has been the Indians' strongest aid in maintaining their own values and cultures. Certainly serious social problems that plague reservation life such as alcoholism, poverty, and illness work against this cohesion. But traditional practices create a strong social bond that helps Indian families offset these powerful disintegrative forces. <u>Thus, many Indian people have been able to maintain a sense of group identity where traditional practices have remained strong.</u>

In this paragraph, the emphasis is on Indians who have been able to maintain a group identity. The paragraph begins with one factor that contributes to this, namely the remote location of reservations. Second, traditional rites and attitudes are mentioned that Brown feels are the Indians' most important asset or "strongest aid." Finally, the author mentions that traditional practices can counter the effects of other "disintegrative forces." The author ends with what is essentially a summary statement, introduced by the transitional word "thus." In this example, the final sentence summarizes in a general sense what the details in the paragraph had led up to—traditional practices help maintain a group identity.

Inferring an Unstated Main Idea in a Paragraph   Inferring an unstated main idea in a paragraph is like summarizing, which was discussed in Chapter 1. When a paragraph does not contain a topic sentence that states the main point, there is usually a main idea that is implied or suggested in the details. In this case, your task is to *infer* or figure out the point made by the supporting details. To do this, you need to first ask yourself, "What are the details about?" Then, to infer the main point, ask yourself "What point do the details make?" What you are essentially doing in this case is *summarizing* the contents of the paragraph, or stating in your own words the core meaning of the paragraph.

The skill of summarizing is one of the most important things you can learn as a beginning college student. Summarizing is involved in writing answers to questions on essay tests and in writing up information gathered from various sources for research papers. When trying to infer an unstated main idea, you are essentially summarizing what the details are all about. You are taking the specific details and generalizing from them a statement of the main idea. To *generalize* means to formulate a general statement that accounts for all the specific details. This is the essence of summarizing, and the essence of formulating a main idea statement suggested by the details.

Read the following paragraph, and try to infer or figure out from the details first the topic and then the main idea.

Einstein conceived of a universe of space filled with stars and other matter, all moving in relation to one another. He reasoned that with everything in the universe in motion, there could be no stationary location that could provide a vantage point superior to any other. Einstein also reasoned that even though the earth is moving rapidly through space, we are able to experience ourselves and other objects on earth as being stationary only because we are all also moving through space at the same rate as the earth. He concluded that our experience of movement only seems fast or slow in relation to the speed of other objects. If I walk past a tree planted solidly in the ground, I experience myself to be moving past a stationary object. However, in reality both the tree and I are hurtling through space on a planet in orbit around a star, in a solar system in movement through a galaxy.

When you ask yourself "What are the details about?" you can see a few repeated ideas: Einstein, space, movement. It seems that the paragraph is discussing Einstein's ideas concerning space and movement. The topic then, stated as a title, could be something like "Einstein's Theory of Movement in Space." If you then ask what point the author is making about this topic, it seems that there is a contrast made between what a person's "experience" is and what "in reality" is taking place. When you read that "there could be no stationary location that could provide a vantage point superior to any other" and that motion "seems fast or slow in relation to the speed of other objects," it seems that Einstein believed our experience of movement to be "relative" to our location. Thus, to the question "What point do the details make?" you could answer as follows: "Einstein believed that movement is experienced only in relation to the movement of other objects." This is basically a one-sentence summary of what the paragraph is about, and a statement of the implied main idea of the paragraph.

Identifying Main Ideas in Longer Passages

As you saw above, the general subject of a paragraph is referred to as the topic, and a statement of the main idea is referred to as the topic sentence. However, most pieces of writing are composed of more than one paragraph. In most nonfiction writing, you will typically encounter paragraphs of several related sentences that share a main idea that is frequently stated in a topic sentence. However, you will occasionally read pieces that are composed of several very short paragraphs. This is especially common in newspaper articles where paragraphs are often only one sentence long. In cases like this, several paragraphs will be about one main idea, which may or may not be stated directly. In any case, a topic sentence is essentially a summary statement of what the details in the paragraph or related paragraphs suggest. Consider the following excerpt from a newspaper article about some violent incidents in Mexico. In the article, several short paragraphs support a single main point and share a common topic sentence.

Now violence has erupted. Just <u>two weeks ago,</u> <u>two peasant activists were shot to death</u> in a remote village as they left a political meeting and headed home to get ready for a march in protest of an earlier attack on farmers.

In another village, a group of men who identified themselves as police shot and killed 12 people, including four children, on July 5. Police denied responsibility and blamed the deaths on a family feud.

And in the most publicized incident, police shot and killed 17 farmers and wounded 14 in a bus outside the village of Aguas Blancas, north of Acapulco, on June 28.

Authorities charged 10 police officers with homicide and abuse of power in the Aguas Blancas case.

But a debate is still raging in Mexico over who ordered the hundreds of police to this remote area and why.

On July 20, about 40 survivors and relatives of the dead, including black-garbed widows and weeping mothers, gathered at the schoolhouse in nearby Atoyaquillo to give testimony to four members of the government-run National Human Rights Commission.

They said that about 45 peasants were crowded in the cattle truck that served as a bus on the region's deeply rutted roads, heading for shopping and to Atoyac de Alvarez for a protest over the disappearance of a political activist.

The driver stopped the bus in a gulch near Aguas Blancas, where the police were gathered, and the firing began.

"They were ambushed," said Maria Casteljon, whose 14-year-old son Sergio survived the attack. The police came because someone sent them. Only the government can tell us why."

Jane Bussey, "Death, Misery in the Mountains of Mexico."

The first four paragraphs of this passage list the shooting incidents that have taken place and state that several police officers have been charged with crimes for their involvement. The fifth paragraph states the overall point of the passage: that there is a controversy concerning who ordered the police to carry out these violent acts. The next four paragraphs recount some of the testimonies of witnesses to these shootings, who suggest that the government is ultimately to blame. In this case, the topic sentence ties together the points made in the first and second sets of paragraphs—the violent acts and the testimonies of witnesses. This passage represents an example of what you will commonly see when reading newspaper articles—a series of several one- or two-sentence paragraphs containing details supporting the same main point.

3c   Identifying the Thesis Statement

In a longer passage—such as an article, an essay, or a book chapter—the subject is still referred to as the topic, but the overall main idea is referred to as the *thesis*, and an author's statement of the main idea is called the *thesis statement*. The process outlined above for identifying a topic sentence of a paragraph is similar to what you need to do when identifying the thesis of a longer passage. Like the details in a paragraph that support a main idea, in a longer selection entire paragraphs support the thesis. The main ideas of the supporting paragraphs are thus actually the major details in an essay or article.

A logical place to look for the thesis statement is in the introduction and in the conclusion, particularly in the last sentence of an introduction and the first sentence of a conclusion. These are the places where an author is most likely to summarize the main point. However, an introduction is not always limited to the first paragraph, and in fact may often consist of several paragraphs. Similarly, a conclusion may begin several paragraphs before the end of a passage. Nonetheless, try to identify these parts of the passage when looking for a sentence that may state the thesis.

To figure out the thesis, ask the same questions as you would to identify the main idea of a paragraph—"What are the details about?" and then "What point do the details make?" With these questions in mind, read the following passage, and first try to identify its topic. Then notice the thesis statement in the introductory paragraph, and the major and minor supporting details in each paragraph. Also, note how each supporting paragraph directly supports the thesis.

> Although most personal communication still takes place orally, in modern cultures the written word has taken precedence as the primary means of communicating formal information. Of course, this has not always been the case. Several crucial developments have taken place over the centuries that have led to the dominance of the written word, including the development of paper by the Chinese in 105 C.E. and the invention of the printing press in Germany in 1450 C.E. *But perhaps the most significant development of all was the evolution by the ancient Greeks of a system of vowel signs that when added to consonant signs formed the first true alphabet.*
>
> Some scholars believe that <u>the development of alphabetic writing by the Greeks in the sixth and fifth centuries B.C.E. made possible much of the civilization</u> that has been so admired ever since, including their

philosophy, history, and science. <u>Previous to the time of the Greeks,</u> <u>forms of writing were limited to extremely complex</u> ideographic systems with symbols for representing entire objects or concepts, or to syllabaries that used symbols to represent the sounds of individual syllables. <u>By developing an alphabet</u> of signs that could be used to represent every sound in their language, including both consonants and vowels, <u>the Greeks were able to simplify writing</u>. This made written language much easier for people to use and understand and allowed writing to spread as never before. In this way, <u>the Greeks were the first</u> <u>to develop a complete alphabet and were thus the first to become a</u> <u>truly literate society</u>. According to the scholar Walter Ong, this literacy enabled the Greeks to record complex, abstract ideas in writing for the first time in such a way that allowed them to organize and explore their thoughts in intellectual forms that were not possible before.

In a <u>modern literate culture</u> such as the United States, most informal communication may still be oral, and there may be dialects that are still based more on speech than on writing, such as various rural or street dialects. However, what is referred to in this country as <u>standard English</u>—the version of the language used in business, professional, academic, and other public situations—<u>is based on written forms</u> and on the printed word. <u>This dependence on print-based language in modern</u> <u>Western societies is a direct legacy of the alphabet first developed by</u> <u>the Greeks more than 2500 years ago</u>.

In this passage, the author begins with an introduction that first mentions the importance of writing in modern cultures, then lists a couple significant historical developments in written communication. The author ends the first paragraph with a statement expressing the view that the Greek alphabet is "perhaps the most significant development of all." This statement expresses the author's opinion, which is then supported by the information in the following two paragraphs. First, the author discusses the significance of the alphabet for the Greeks, then ends with comments concerning how the alphabet has influenced modern life. It seems clear that the topic of this short essay is the Greek development of the alphabet, and that the last sentence in the introductory paragraph states the point the author wants to make about the topic. The last sentence in the introduction is the author's thesis statement, the statement of the main idea.

The following is an outline of this passage that first paraphrases the thesis then indicates how the major and minor supporting details are organized.

The development by the ancient Greeks of a true alphabet was perhaps the most significant event in the history of writing. (thesis)

    A. Alphabetic writing and Greek civilization (main idea, first supporting paragraph)
        1. Previous forms of writing (major detail)
            a. ideographic systems (minor detail)
            b. syllabaries (minor detail)
        2. Greeks simplified writing (major detail)
            a. easier to use and understand (minor detail)
            b. spread as never before (minor detail)
        3. First truly literate society (major detail)
            a. able to record complex ideas (minor detail)
            b. organized thoughts in new ways (minor detail)
    B. Modern literate cultures and Greek legacy (main idea, second supporting paragraph)
        1. Standard written English (major detail)
        2. Dependence on print (major detail)

You will notice that in this outline the thesis is expressed in slightly different words than in the passage, and the wording of the listed details is also a little different. It is important to remember that when outlining and summarizing, you are expressing the main points and significant supporting details *in your own words*. When you can do this while retaining the same meaning as in the passage, you can consider yourself to have successfully demonstrated your comprehension of what you have read.

3d   Inferring an Implied Thesis

Sometimes an author will not state the thesis directly but perhaps prefers for the reader to draw his or her own conclusion based on the supporting details or evidence provided. In this case, you need to first identify the subject or topic by asking yourself, "What is this passage about?" Then to formulate a thesis, ask the question, "What point is the author trying to make about the topic?" A thesis statement will thus have two parts: the topic and the point made about the topic. When inferring a thesis, you are basically composing a concise one-sentence summary of the contents of the entire passage.

Sometimes it is difficult to identify the main idea of a passage because it may seem that there is more than one point suggested by the supporting ideas. In a case like this, the main idea may express the relationship between the supporting ideas, or how different aspects of the supporting evidence are related to one another. Read the passage below, and try to figure out the topic and the unstated thesis.

> Some social critics over the last decade have commented on the negative effects that popular culture has had on young people. Alan Bloom, for example, commented on the deleterious effects of rock music. Neil Postman has similarly pointed out the negative effects of television on literacy and thinking skills.
>
> Other commentators disagree and suggest that popular culture offers a positive contribution to our society. For example, Robert Pattison has suggested that popular forms such as rock music represent a new vitality in English language use. Indeed, Camile Paglia has suggested that critics of television and other media have failed to recognize that, like it or not, popular culture *is* our culture. Similarly, the historian Lawrence Levine has shown that over the last century there has been a coming together of high and popular cultures in new forms, such as jazz, that are both intellectually challenging and have mass appeal.
>
> Whether one feels that popular culture represents a positive or negative influence on our society, it certainly seems clear that it is the ever-present reality for most of us. But exactly what does this ubiquitous popular culture include? Some obvious forms come to mind: television, radio, professional sports, various forms of popular music, general interest magazines, the cinema.
>
> So how many Americans plan their evening hours around their favorite television programs, rather than sitting around in conversation? How much more excited do we get over the latest NBA championship, than over the latest Nobel Prize for literature? And how often do we choose to listen to the radio or watch a video rather than curl up with a book? I'd wager that for most of us, it is most of the time. Indeed, when most people hear the name "Madonna," I'm pretty sure they think of the "material girl" rather than the Virgin Mary. And I would guess that people are more interested in David Letterman's move from NBC to CBS than they are in Alexander Solzhenitsyn's move from the United States back to Russia.
>
> So how does a middle-aged community college teacher feel about all of this? Well, let me put it this way: I may prefer National Public Radio to Power 98 and Ted Koppel to Jay Leno; but whether it's waking up to *Morning Edition* or going to bed after *Nightline,* I'm still listening to the radio and watching TV, rather than reading *The New York Times* over morning coffee or falling to sleep with *War and Peace* on my chest.

In this passage, there is a repeated reference that is pretty obvious: popular culture. It is safe to say that this is the topic of the passage. The question then becomes, "What point is the author making about popular culture?" The answer to this question will be the author's thesis or main idea. In the first two paragraphs, the author contrasts those who point out the "negative effects" of popular culture with those who feel that it makes "a positive contribution to our society." The author then goes on in the third paragraph to say that no matter how one feels about it, it seems that there are many forms of popular culture all around us. Next, the author mentions what he feels are a few examples that illustrate most people's preference for popular culture. The author then ends with a conclusion that is meant to suggest how he feels "about all of this."

The question then is "What *does* the author feel? This will get at the main idea. Without coming right out and saying it, it seems that the author is suggesting that he himself is influenced by the popular media in his choices of entertainment and information. Thus, the thesis could perhaps be stated something like this: "Though not liked by everyone in all its forms, popular culture pervades our society and is extremely attractive for most people." Or, as the author might say: "Even though most popular culture is only of mediocre quality, I have to admit that it is a preference that I share with most other people."

Chapter Review

Perhaps the most basic factor in understanding what you read is being able to recognize the main ideas. Whether the main ideas are directly stated or merely implied, an effective reader can recognize an author's most significant points by answering a few simple questions:

To determine the **topic** ask yourself,
  "Who" or "What" is the passage about?

To determine the **main idea** ask yourself,
  "What aspect of the topic is the author stressing?" or
  "What point is the author making about the topic?"

Recognizing the main ideas is not always easy, especially in long, complex readings. However, with practice and attention, you can surely improve your comprehension by applying the strategies discussed in this chapter.

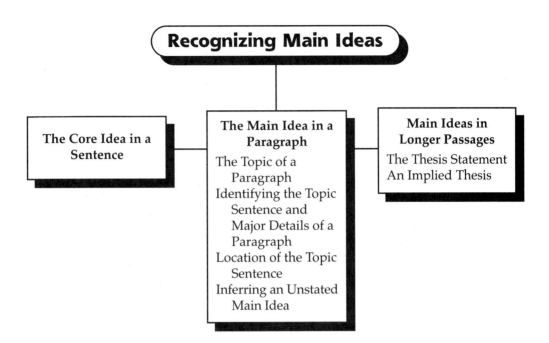

Recognizing Main Ideas

The Core Idea in a Sentence

The Main Idea in a Paragraph
The Topic of a Paragraph
Identifying the Topic Sentence and Major Details of a Paragraph
Location of the Topic Sentence
Inferring an Unstated Main Idea

Main Ideas in Longer Passages
The Thesis Statement
An Implied Thesis

CHAPTER 4

Identifying
Organizational Patterns

Whether you are reading for information, understanding, or pleasure, it is important to recognize that writers do not place ideas in random order, but deliberately structure passages for clarity and effect. As you have seen, a typical nonfiction essay, article, or other passage begins with an introduction, proceeds with supporting paragraphs, and ends with a conclusion. Narrative fiction also tends to follow a similar sequence by establishing a setting or situation, describing the action, and culminating with a resolution of some sort. The purpose of this familiar structure is to make the piece of writing as understandable as possible by connecting ideas in a logical way. Words or short phrases used to connect specific ideas within a passage are called *transitions,* and the overall way that the ideas are structured within the passage is called the *pattern of organization.*

Understanding Transitions

The sentences within a passage are organized in support of a main idea, but they also exist in relation to one another. Transitions are words and phrases used by writers to indicate specific relationships between ideas and to create a coherence or logical connectedness between the ideas in a passage. Even single sentences often contain more than one idea. When this is the case, the relationship between the ideas may be indicated by a coordinating or subordinating conjunction or by some other connecting word that reflects the type of relationship. Knowing the meanings and functions of transitions will help you to understand how ideas are related to one another in sentences, paragraphs, and longer passages.

Transitions, or connecting words, can offer clues to the relationships between the ideas. Below is a list of transitions. For each type of transition listed below, you will find a definition, a list of some common examples, and a sentence that illustrates how a transition is used. You will notice that some transitional words can be used to indicate different relationships. For this reason, you cannot be too literal in thinking that a certain word always reflects the same relationship. Sometimes you must rely on the context—the logic and meaning of the sentences—to determine how ideas are related and how transitions reflect relationships.

4a   Addition

Addition words indicate a continuing thought or that one idea is simply being added to another. Examples of addition words are as follows: and, in addition, also, furthermore, moreover, besides, first of all, one, second, third, next, lastly, finally, too.

> Artists' conceptions of our pre-human ancestors usually depict them living in caves <u>and</u> show them covered entirely with hair.

4b   Time Order

Time order words signal a time sequence or steps in a process. Examples of time order words include the following: first, second, third, next, last, finally, after, before, lately, until, soon, since, often, now, while, during, immediately, frequently, previously, presently, subsequently, then.

> Apparently, eons of evolution have reduced what may have <u>previously</u> been a generous endowment of hair to what <u>presently</u> remains as a few patches.

4c   Location

Location words show spatial relationships or the location of things. Examples of location words include the following: above, below, beneath, inside, outside, around, near, nearby, close, far, distant, further, adjacent to, opposite, beyond, behind, in front, on top, on the bottom.

> It seems that now our hair growth is limited to a few strategic locations, most noticeably <u>on the top</u> of the head.

4d   Definition

Definition words introduce the meaning of a word or an idea. Examples of definition words include the following: means, is, or, can be defined as, is the same as, like, refers to.

> The color of our hair depends on the type of pigment in each follicle <u>or</u> individual strand of hair.

4e Clarification

Clarification words introduce a restatement or a discussion intended to make something clearer or more understandable. Examples of clarification words follow: evidently, in fact, obviously, indeed, clearly, in other words, of course, too.

> A single hair is stronger than a similarly sized piece of copper wire. In fact, if a rope were to be made from 1000 hairs, it would be strong enough to hold up a large adult.

4f Emphasis

Emphasis words stress something or make a strong statement about something in order to draw the reader's attention. The following are examples of emphasis words: indeed, in fact, certainly, definitely, without a doubt, undoubtedly, admittedly, unquestionably, truly.

> Indeed, human hair is surprisingly strong.

4g Classification

Classification words indicate categories or different types of objects, ideas, or events. Examples of classification words include the following: various, categories, types, fields, ranks, groups, aspects, features, parts, characteristics.

> Different types of head lice have adapted their claws to be able to grab onto different hair shapes, so that a black person cannot catch head lice from a white person, and vice versa.

4h Comparison

Comparison words show similarities or likenesses. Comparison words include the following: similarly, likewise, like, just like, just as, in a similar fashion, as well, in the same way, as, in like manner, compared with, equally.

> Our hair is so elastic that a wet hair can be stretched by more than half its length. Similarly, our hair is so flexible that it can be bent in any way without breaking.

4i   Contrast

Contrast words indicate differences. They include the following: but, although, however, nevertheless, yet, nonetheless, while, whereas, on the one hand, on the other hand, in contrast, contrary to, conversely, on the contrary, at the same time.

> While everyone's hair has certain things in common, other features vary from person to person.

4j   Cause and Effect

Cause and effect words indicate reasons or results. The following are examples of cause and effect words: as a result, because, for, thus, consequently, accordingly, affect, hence, then, therefore, determined by, if . . . then.

> The shape of each hair follicle is determined by genetic factors unique to the race of the person.

4k   Illustration

Illustration words introduce an example meant to illustrate a more general statement; they reflect a progression from a general idea to specific details. Examples of illustration words include the following: for example, for instance, to illustrate, namely, specifically, such as, including.

> Human hair is truly a subject of fascination. For instance, the hair on our head grows about six inches a year, a much faster rate than any of our other bodily parts.

4l   Summary

Summary words introduce a summary statement or a condensation of what had come before in more specific detail, moving from specific details to a general idea. Summary words include the following: in conclusion, in short, to sum up, thus, in sum, in brief, on the whole, to conclude, in summary.

> Thus, while most of us have gotten along just fine combing, brushing, spraying, or doing whatever else we do to our hair without knowing much about it, a little knowledge can only serve to increase appreciation for something that some of us have watched gradually disappear as the years go by.

Recognizing Patterns of Organization

The pattern of organization of a passage is the principal method an author uses to develop ideas. A passage may be developed by one single method, or it may be developed by a combination of methods. When trying to determine the overall organization, first look for a statement of the main idea with some wording in it that may suggest the pattern. Then look for the major supporting details and for transitional phrases that introduce them. Just as transitions reflect how ideas are related to one another in sentences, they also reflect how supporting details are organized within and between paragraphs. However, sometimes the main idea and transitional elements will not make the pattern of organization clear to you. For this reason, you should always attempt to verify your assessment of the pattern of organization by understanding the general meaning of the passage.

In a paragraph or longer passage, you will often find several types of transitions indicating several types of relationships between ideas. To determine the overall pattern of organization, you must decide which scheme provides a framework, consisting of the main idea and the major supporting details. The minor supporting details will then be presented within this broader pattern. The following is a list of common patterns of organization, including explanations and paragraphs that illustrate each one.

4m   List Patterns

The presentation of information as a list could include nearly anything—items, places, events, reasons, or consequences. However, when an author simply lists a series of ideas, facts, or other details in a passage without any particular sequence or other logical relationship involved, the pattern is called *simple listing*. When the list is in the form of categories, classes, kinds, or types, the pattern is called *classification*. In either case, the listed items could be presented in any order without changing the meaning. The organization of ideas in more complex relationships, such as cause and effect and order of importance, will be discussed separately later on.

Simple Listing or Enumeration   Simple listing, or *enumeration,* is a pattern that lists information as a series of facts, ideas, or other details, the order of which could be changed without changing the meaning. The pattern may be suggested by transitions indicating "addition." However, be aware that words such as "first" and "second" could either reflect enumeration or time sequence, depending on the meaning of the passage they are in. Thus, you must consider the context as well as the transitional words when determining the organizational pattern.

> In the years since the guarantees against unreasonable searches and seizures became part of the Constitution, the Supreme Court has interpreted the Fourth Amendment to allow some important exceptions and to include some significant extensions. For example, it has ruled that a warrant is not needed to enter the home of a person who is under arrest. Also, police do not need a warrant if they have witnessed a crime or are in pursuit of a criminal. Nor does a police officer need a warrant to search a car, which could disappear in the time it would take to obtain one. In addition, the Supreme Court has interpreted the Fourth Amendment to imply the general right to privacy, which has been extended to include a woman's right to have an abortion. These interpretations continue to be controversial, especially for liberals who see the erosion of civil rights in the name of fighting crime and for conservatives who feel that the right to abort a pregnancy is extending the guarantee of privacy too far.

When the topic sentence states that some "exceptions" and "extensions" have been made to the Fourth Amendment, it is suggesting that these will be explained. The transition "for example" introduces the first major detail, an exception to the warrant requirement. Next, the word "also" leads into another exception concerning warrants for moving vehicles. Finally, "in addition" introduces the extension made by the Supreme Court of the right to privacy to include abortion. The final sentences discuss some public responses to these exceptions and extensions. In this example, the major details have been listed and discussed in an order that could have been changed without changing the meaning. Sometimes an author may list the points in such as way as to lead from the least to the most important (or vice versa); but in most cases, the order of the items in an enumeration pattern is not crucial to the meaning.

Classification   A classification pattern is very similar to simple listing, but differs in that it specifically lists categories, classes, kinds, branches, divisions, parts, elements, or types of something. This pattern is suggested by transitions that indicate classification. Like simple listing, the items listed in a classification pattern can usually be changed without affecting the meaning.

Art schools offer specialized education for students who are dedicated to pursuing careers in the visual arts. The <u>branches of the visual arts</u> are usually separated into <u>different departments</u> depending on the media or on the purpose for which the art will be used. <u>Two-dimensional arts</u> include drawing, painting, printmaking, and photography, and deal with line, tone, perspective, and color, all realized on flat surfaces. These arts tend to stress expressive, aesthetic, and topical content, and are usually termed fine art. <u>Three-dimensional studies</u> include work that involves building structures out of wood, metal, fibers, or ceramics. Like the two-dimensional arts, these arts tend also to emphasize personal and aesthetic purposes and are also considered fine art. <u>Design departments</u> incorporate many of the same elements as the two-dimensional and three-dimensional arts, but with a different purpose. Design work is typically for commercial uses, such as advertising, illustration, packaging, or construction. The commercial arts include architecture, graphic design, and illustration. Finally, other areas such as film, video, and computer animation, which some art schools now offer, are sometimes referred to as <u>time arts</u> or <u>four-dimensional arts</u>. These areas incorporate elements of the visual arts along with the performing arts, and may be oriented toward either commercial or noncommercial ends.

Here the main idea is that art schools organize the "branches of the visual arts" into "different departments." The word "branches" is used to mean something like parts or categories, and the word "departments" reflects a similar meaning. The paragraph then goes on to list and briefly describe four departments, each housing a different branch of the visual arts. Even though you can see examples of enumeration within this paragraph, particularly in the list of two-dimensional arts, the overall pattern is a classification: two-dimensional, three-dimensional, design, and time or four-dimensional art departments.

4n   Order Patterns

These patterns are similar to list patterns in the sense that they also present lists of things. However, the difference is that the items in an order pattern must either appear in a certain sequence for the passage really to make sense or must be organized with some other logical progression. Perhaps the most common order pattern is *chronological order,* where events are listed in time sequence. Another similar pattern of this type is a description of a *process order,* or a series of steps carried out in a procedure or stages occurring in some function or development. A final order pattern is *spatial order,* which involves a discussion of size, place, location, or geographical area. While with a spatial order, the order may be less important than with chronological or process patterns, there will usually be some logic to the sequence of descriptions.

Chronological   Most fiction and some types of nonfiction—including biography, autobiography, history, and some news accounts—describe events that have occurred in time. This type of writing is called *narrative* and portrays events in a way that is similar to the way all of us experience the events in our lives—as events occurring one after another in time. This organizational pattern is called chronological order, a pattern that indicates a time sequence. Time order transitions are commonly used in this pattern.

> At the turn of the century, a German scientist named Alzheimer discovered certain types of brain lesions that cause the symptoms that we have come to know as Alzheimer's disease. At the time, it was thought that the disease was rare. And for years, there was not much research conducted. Now we know that it is much more common than was once thought. There are approximately 4 million sufferers of the disease in this country now, a disease that will affect nearly 50 percent of those over the age of eighty-five.

In this paragraph, several transitional phrases are used that indicate a time sequence: "At the turn of the century," "At the time," "for years," and "Now" in the last two sentences. The discussion shows how scientists' views of Alzheimer's disease have changed from the beginning of the twentieth century to the present. This is done in chronological order.

Process   A process pattern is a description of a series of steps, stages, or changes that are necessary in doing or making something, in proceeding toward some end result, or in carrying out some procedure. This pattern may be in the form of directions that must be followed in order to carry out some activity, or it may describe how some phenomenon occurs. A description of a process is likely to include time order transitions.

> Rarely occurring before the age of forty, Alzheimer's disease robs in small degrees, until memory and personality are completely gone.

About nineteen million people are watching someone in their family going through what is usually a slow <u>process</u> that can take between three and thirty years. <u>In the early stages</u>, people begin to forget recent events but can still recall past events clearly. These minor memory losses can often be compensated for by writing notes to oneself as memory aids. <u>As the disease progresses</u>, the loss of memory gradually increases until such important functions become seriously impaired, including judgment, speech, and muscle coordination.

This paragraph briefly describes the "process" of developing Alzheimer's disease. The transitional phrases "In the early stages," and "As the disease progresses," lead into two stages patients go through in this disease. These stages are listed in sequence to show how the disease progresses in severity.

Spatial   Spatial order is a pattern in which an author describes something by its size or location. This pattern is usually very descriptive and could be used to describe a place or geographical area. Location transitions will probably be used in spatial order descriptions.

The afternoon sun poised <u>near the top</u> of a Royal Palm and shone clearly around lengthening shadows on the descending arc of its passage over a backyard in Biscayne Shores. Gray-brown dirt showed in spots through the unmowed grass <u>behind</u> a white clapboard house. Four old tires formed soccer goals <u>at either end</u> of a solid patch of lawn along a white wooden fence <u>on the south side</u> of the house. A playhouse filled with items for the next yard sale stood in the shade of a mango tree at the <u>far end of the yard</u>. Its door squeaked back and forth like a huge leaf moving in response to an occasional touch from an unseen hand.

Here a backyard is described, with several location transitions used to indicate different spots: "near the top" of a palm tree, "behind" the house, "at either end" of a lawn, "on the south side" of the house, and on the "far end" of the yard. These clearly indicate a spatial pattern.

4o   Exemplification Patterns

Illustration transitions usually appear in an exemplification pattern. In this pattern, authors attempt to define or clarify something through concrete details. In a *definition,* an author usually begins by defining the general meaning of a term or concept, then goes on to provide specific details to make the meaning clearer. While a definition can indeed involve any or all of the different organizational patterns, the use of examples is quite common, especially to clarify a meaning through concrete illustrations. An author also frequently uses examples in a *clarification* pattern to make it easier for readers to understand a point, but rather than defining a term, clarification explains something. In either case, authors commonly use concrete, specific details so that readers can more easily visualize or understand the topic in terms that relate to real life experiences.

Definition and Example   A definition is an attempt to explain the meaning of a word or concept. In this pattern, examples are usually provided to help readers understand what the term or idea really means.

> Alzheimer's disease <u>is</u> a brain disorder that causes the loss of memory and judgment. Most sufferers are elderly, who are frequently diagnosed only after family members begin to notice their increasing difficulty remembering simple things. This short-term memory loss is an early symptom that a doctor may recognize as a sign of the onset of the disease. <u>For example</u>, a doctor may sit with an elderly man whose forty-year-old daughter has brought him in for a "check up." The doctor asks him to remember three words—a rose, an orange, and a horse—that he will be asked to recall a little later in their session. The man repeats the three words back to the doctor and assures her that he will have no trouble remembering them. After a few minutes, the doctor asks her patient, "A minute ago, I asked you to remember three things. Do you recall what they are?" to which he responds, "I'm sorry, but I wasn't paying a bit of attention." The doctor assures him that he doesn't need to be sorry, but she suspects that her patient may have Alzheimer's.

This paragraph begins with a brief definition of Alzheimer's disease, with the word "is" leading into the definition. After a couple of sentences about how the disease is first recognized, the transitional phrase "for example" introduces an extended illustration meant to show how early symptoms suggest to a doctor that a patient may have the disease. The example is meant to illustrate the early stages of memory loss associated with Alzheimer's.

Clarification through Example   Similar to a definition, a clarification pattern attempts to clarify and explain. However, rather than discussing the meaning of a term or idea, the purpose of a clarification is more to explain or discuss a general topic through specific examples.

> Albert Einstein theorized that as speed increases, time slows down. In our everyday experience, the speed differences between things we are familiar with are so insignificant that time differences are not apparent. However, it is possible to imagine a situation in which speed differences could have noticeable effects. <u>For instance</u>, if a spaceship were to travel to the nearest star and back at close to the speed of light, the astronauts would experience the journey to take several years. However, time on earth would have passed at such a different rate that no one who was alive when the astronauts left would be alive when they returned. Because of their incredible speed, the passage of time would have slowed down for the astronauts relative to the passage of time on earth.

In this paragraph, Einstein's theory of time is discussed, with an example provided in an attempt to make a very abstract idea more concrete. The transitional phrase "For instance" leads into the futuristic example of the space travelers, which is intended to show how the passage of time could vary. The example is here used to clarify Einstein's theory.

4p   Comparison/Contrast Patterns

A comparison pattern deals with similarities, and a contrast pattern discusses differences between two or more things. Authors often discuss two or more things by showing what they share—comparison—or in terms of how they differ—contrast. These organizational patterns are likely to incorporate comparison and contrast transitions. Sometimes an author will discuss two things or ideas by both comparing and contrasting them in the same passage. In such cases, the pattern is called comparison/contrast.

> Every time we see something familiar, hear music we like, or taste food we enjoy, we naturally assume that these things exist outside of us, independent of whether or not we happen to be around. <u>Nevertheless</u>, science suggests a very different explanation of what our common sense tells us about what we perceive. <u>Contrary to</u> what we may think, there are no colors, sounds, or tastes that exist independently of our ability to perceive them. In fact, the world around us is filled with many types of electromagnetic energy waves that stimulate the sense

organs and that are interpreted by the brain. Thus, the details of our everyday experience are in a very real sense more constructions of the brain than reflections of what exist outside of us.

The last sentence in this paragraph states the main point, that what we experience is really an interpretation made by the brain rather than a pure picture of what is in our environment. In two other places, the paragraph mentions this difference between our common sense and what science has found, and the transitions "nevertheless" and "contrary to" reflect this contrast.

Analogy   In a certain type of comparison called an analogy, an author attempts to make one thing understandable by comparing it to something that is in reality different from it but that shares something in common with it. For example, if in an article an author compares the human brain to a computer, this comparison is not meant to be taken literally. A bodily organ is obviously very different from a mechanical device. However, because the author feels that they do share some characteristics in common, she might compare the organ that we never see to a device that we have all seen as a way to clarify the one in the light of the other. This is an attempt to make one thing understandable in terms of something perhaps more familiar. When an author uses a comparison of this sort throughout a paragraph or an entire passage, it is called an analogy, and it can be considered a type of comparison pattern.

> The function of the human eye can be understood once it is thought of as <u>similar to</u> a camera. <u>Like</u> the lens of a camera, the cornea and lens of the eye focus light images that pass through them. The focused light is then projected onto the back of the eye cavity, very <u>much like</u> in a camera where the light image is focused onto the film. There an image is formed, but in both the eye and in a camera this image does not fully reflect reality. The image on film is in negative form and needs processing in order for it to appear as the familiar objects or people eventually seen in a photograph. <u>Similarly</u>, the image on the retina needs to be sent through nerve fibers to the brain where it is interpreted and made comprehensible.

In this paragraph, the functioning of a camera is used to help explain the functioning of the human eye. This comparison to a camera is meant only to clarify how the eye works, and not to suggest they are alike in every way. They share enough characteristics so that the comparison is useful. This is an analogy that is meant to explain or clarify. The transitions "similar to," "like," "much like," and "similarly" clearly indicate that a comparison is being made.

4q   **Cause and Effect Patterns**

A cause and effect pattern asks the question "Why?" or "With what results?" The words "why" or "what" might not be used directly in a topic sentence or thesis statement, but in a cause and effect pattern the question is at least implied. Sometimes an author begins with a statement of the main idea that identifies a cause or a reason, and then goes on to identify the effects or results. In this case, the passage in effect is answering the question "What are the results?" In other instances, an author might begin with an effect or result, and then proceed to explain the reasons or causes. In this case, the passage answers the question "Why has something happened?" In either case, transitions that reflect cause and effect relationships will probably be used to introduce the major details and to link the ideas in the passage together. The purpose of a cause and effect pattern is to discuss the reasons or results of some occurrence and to offer explanations.

> As Alzheimer's disease progresses, the <u>effects</u> become more debilitating, often having terrible <u>consequences</u> for the sufferers and their families. The loss of memory, the loss of one's personality, indeed the dreadful experience of losing control of one's life, can have disintegrating <u>effects</u> on the ties that bind a family together. Sufferers may experience sudden outbursts of rage or sorrow with no apparent <u>cause</u>. In severe cases, patients have lost not only much of their memory but also their ability to care for themselves. But what may be the most terrifying <u>result</u> of this disease is the personality loss that accompanies severe cases. This can be devastating, not only for the patients, but also for their relatives, who are forced to watch the person they love gradually slip away.

Here the paragraph is answering the question "What are the results?" by describing some of the "effects" of Alzheimer's disease. The first sentence—the topic sentence—clearly indicates that this will be a discussion of the "terrible consequences" of the disease. The transitional words "effects," "cause," and "result" are used in association with the major supporting details, which show some of the effects of Alzheimer's on patients and their families.

Problem / Solution   A type of cause and effect pattern where an author introduces a problem and then offers one or more solutions is called a problem/solution pattern. In this pattern, an author will usually begin with a statement of the problem as the main idea. Then some causes or effects of the problem might be listed. Finally, the author will probably offer one or more solutions to the problem. In a problem/solution passage, you may or may not notice cause and effect transitions, but the main idea and major details will likely include words such as "problem," "difficulty," "answer," or "solution":

> Unfortunately, <u>the sufferers of Alzheimer's have not benefited from much scientific research</u>. In fact, the very <u>nature of the disease has confounded research efforts</u>. By the time an individual is diagnosed as having Alzheimer's, their memory loss is often so severe that information important to studying the onset of the disease may have been lost. <u>Another problem</u> is that there are <u>not enough brains to study</u>. Scientists have lots of brains of people who have died with Alzheimer's, but there is a serious lack of brains from healthy people to compare them with. <u>People are often reluctant to donate their brain</u> for research, partly because they tend to find the idea of removing the brain to be distasteful, but also perhaps because many people believe that the brain is the seat of the soul.
>
> These <u>problems</u> in the study of Alzheimer's had not been <u>overcome</u> until <u>Dr. David Snowden</u>, an epidemiologist at the University of Kentucky, <u>arrived at what he thought might be a solution</u>. While trying to locate a clearly defined group of elderly people willing to be studied, and more importantly willing to donate their brains to research after they die, Dr. Snowden realized that such <u>an ideal group might be found in a convent</u>. He found such a convent in Minnesota, where the nuns average eighty-five years of age, have led <u>well documented lives</u>, and are perfectly <u>willing to be</u> <u>subjects</u> <u>of study while they are alive, and even after they die</u>. Since this first group of nuns was located, more than five hundred sisters from Baltimore to the Mississippi have signed up to participate in the study.

In this passage, the author begins with a statement of the problem—the lack of research into Alzheimer's disease. He then goes on to explain why there have been problems studying the disease. First, he mentions that patients' memory loss has "confounded" or made it difficult to research the disease. Then he mentions "Another problem," the problem of finding people willing to donate their brains for research studies. The second paragraph then describes Dr. Snowden's solution to this problem. Thus, the passage progresses from a statement of the problem to some causes of this problem to a solution that has been found. This is clearly a problem/solution pattern of organization.

4r   Mixed Patterns—General and Specific, Order of Importance

As you know, not all problems have easy solutions, and not all issues are easily analyzed. Similarly, it is not always a simple matter to identify the pattern of organization of a passage. Sometimes, a paragraph or passage does not fit neatly into one of the categories that have been identified above. A passage may indeed combine several different patterns in a discussion of a topic.

However, in such cases you may be able to discern a broad structure to the discussion that will arrange ideas in relation to one another according to their relative importance. Perhaps the passage proceeds from *general to specific*—from a general main idea to specific details. Or perhaps the author begins with the details and ends with a concluding statement of the main idea, and has thus gone from *specific to general*. You will also frequently see authors employ a rhetorical technique called *order of importance,* in which the most important point—the point the author wants the reader to remember most—will be emphasized by either locating it first, followed by lesser points, or by placing it as the last thing discussed, preceded by lesser points. Consider the following passage in terms of these and the other patterns previously discussed.

> *After three years of study and the examination of over one hundred brains, the research into Alzheimer's has begun to arrive at some interesting findings.* The value of having nuns as subjects lies in the degree to which they have documented their lives. Baptismal records, birth certificates, and autobiographies have been invaluable in investigating the types of lives led by the sisters, some of whom eventually developed Alzheimer's disease and some of whom did not.
>
> <u>The researchers examined autobiographies written by the sisters in their youth before they entered the convent.</u> The research team analyzed the nuns' vocabulary as a way to measure complex thinking and

intelligence. They then compared these findings with their rates of Alzheimer's. Early findings show that those nuns who tended to have the lowest intelligence were about ten to fifteen times more likely to develop Alzheimer's or some other type of cognitive impairment in old age.

The implications of this research are profound. These findings suggest that how well the mind and brain develop in childhood and youth plays a key role in whether or not an individual develops Alzheimer's disease later in life. The studies show that although 40 percent of the nuns get Alzheimer's, about the same rate as everyone else, the sisters tend to develop the disease later in life and with less severe symptoms than other people. The researchers believe that the active life in the convent, while not preventing Alzheimer's, has postponed the onset of the disease for the nuns.

Other researchers are confirming the findings of the studies done with the sisters. Dr. Marian Diamond, a biologist at the University of California at Berkeley, has shown that the outer structure of the brain can be increased in dimension by enriched environments, and conversely can be decreased in deprived environments. Other research done with human brains by Arnold Sheibel, Director of the UCLA Brain Research Institute, has shown that the brains of individuals who have had more education developed more branches on their nerve cells than individuals with less education. Dr. Sheibel believes that enrichment and stimulating interaction with the environment builds up a more complex brain, which is better protected against debilitating diseases such as Alzheimer's. Similarly, the work of Dr. Diamond suggests that an individual can actually protect oneself from Alzheimer's by taking up hobbies and learning new things. Her work with rats has shown that if they are given the same toys week after week, their brains actually reduce themselves over time.

An implication of these studies is that a person who has received less education and has involved herself in activities with few new experiences is more likely to develop Alzheimer's later in life than a person who has been better educated and who has had a more active, creative life. Dr. Sheibel believes that since the nerve cells in the brain are designed to be stimulated, it is essential to provide them with new input. He feels that all the research with both animals and humans shows that it is never too late to begin stimulating activities to offset diseases such as Alzheimer's.

There is a lot going on in this passage. However, it is possible in a general sense to identify general to specific patterns in each individual paragraph and a broad specific to general pattern in the passage as a whole, as well as the use of order of importance.

In each paragraph we can see a similar pattern—from general to specific, a progression from a general statement of the main idea to specific details that explain it. The topic of the passage is clearly stated in the first sentence—"the research into Alzheimer's has begun to arrive at some interesting findings." The first paragraph then goes on to list (*exemplification*) a few things that were important about the study done with the nuns. The second paragraph explains the steps the researchers followed in time sequence (*process*), showing how they "examined autobiographies written by the sisters" and what this research found. The third paragraph begins by stating that the "implications of this research are profound" and then goes on to explain (*clarification*) what these findings suggest. The fourth paragraph introduces "Other researchers" who "are confirming the findings" of those who studied the nuns. The details of the paragraph explain the work of Dr. Diamond and Dr. Sheibel (*exemplification*) and point out their similar findings (*comparison*). The final paragraph first introduces a major "implication of these studies" concerning the importance of education and living "a more active, creative life" in preventing Alzheimer's, then goes on to explain (*clarification*) why this is so.

When the entire passage is considered in terms of an organizational pattern, it is apparent that several patterns have been used in the different paragraphs, with the "interesting findings" introduced in the first paragraph and discussed in the following three paragraphs leading to the conclusion in the last that "a person who has received less education and has involved herself in activities with few new experiences is more likely to develop Alzheimer's later in life than a person who has been better educated and who has had a more active, creative life." In this sense, with various patterns used within the different paragraphs, the passage as a whole is organized from specific to general, from the main points made in the first four paragraphs to an overall conclusion in the final paragraph.

Finally, from paragraph to paragraph, the author moves from a description of a research study to the implications of the study. This strategy of ending with the implications, especially the suggestion in the final paragraph that "it is never too late to begin stimulating activities," seems to be a way to emphasize through order of importance that there is hope, which is apparently the point the author wants to leave you with.

Chapter Review

Writers use transitional words and short phrases to connect ideas within a passage, which often also reflect the overall pattern of organization or the way that the ideas are structured within the passage. When attempting to determine the organizational pattern of a passage, the following steps will help.

1. First look for a statement of the **main idea** which may include some wording that suggests the pattern.
2. Then look for the **major supporting details** and for **transitional phrases** that introduce them.

Sometimes, as you have seen, a passage may be quite complicated and may include several organizational patterns, which make it very difficult to identify any single one. In such cases, you should always consider the general meaning of the passage when trying to determine the pattern of organization.

Recognizing Patterns of Organization

Transitions:
Words and phrases that indicate relationships between ideas

Addition	Clarification	Contrast
Time order	Emphasis	Cause and effect
Location	Classification	Illustration
Definition	Comparison	Summary

Organizational Patterns:
Ways that main ideas and supporting detail are organized and presented

List Patterns
Simple Listing or Enumeration
Classification

Comparison / Contrast
Analogy

Order Patterns
Chronological
Process
Spatial

Cause and Effect
Problem / Solution

Exemplification Patterns
Definition and Example
Clarification through Example

Mixed Patterns
General and Specific
Order of Importance

CHAPTER
5

Using Inference

In order to fully grasp what an author means, it is often necessary to understand more than the printed words on a page. It is sometimes necessary to use your *inferential* ability to fully understand what an author means, tries to accomplish, or feels but does not come right out and say. To do so, you must sometimes draw upon your personal knowledge and experience, your logic, and your imagination to read "through" an author's words or to *infer* what he or she may merely suggest. This chapter will first look at *inference* in general and will then concentrate on two specific aspects of critical reading that involve inference: recognizing authors' *purpose*—their reason for writing—and *tone*—the attitude with which they write.

Recognizing Implied Meaning

Whenever you make a guess, an estimate, or a judgment about something or someone that is based on factual information or observation, but that goes beyond that information, you are *making an inference* or *drawing a conclusion.* In such cases, you are using what you know to be true to *infer* or *conclude* what you suspect is also probably true.

For example, Sir Arthur Conan Doyle in the story "The Red-Headed League" describes how his fictional character Sherlock Holmes infers that a certain Mr. Jabez Wilson had recently done a good deal of writing: "What else can be indicated by that right cuff so very shiny for five inches, and the left one with the smooth patch near the elbow where you rest it upon the desk?" Though Mr. Wilson had no intention of advertising his writing habits, to a master detective like Holmes, it was quite obvious.

In writing, authors sometimes leave subtle hints for readers about things they would rather not come right out and say. A writer may do this because it is sometimes more effective to communicate a message with a suggestion than with a literal statement, or because it is sometimes easier to influence readers with subtle references than with direct assertions. When a reader is aware of these writing strategies and is reading to understand implied meanings, he or she is often said to be "reading between the lines."

When you are using your knowledge, your experience, your logic, and your awareness of writers' techniques to interpret meanings that extend beyond literal statements, you are *making inferences*. When you are inferring implications, consequences, or courses of action from the details of an author's discussion, you are *drawing conclusions*.

5a   Making Inferences

Most of the information you receive in the course of your life comes to you without any explanations. You are constantly using your inferential powers to make sense of all the experiences you have, based on your ability to make interpretations consistent with logic and with everything you know. You do the same thing when you read, especially when you read things that by design require a good deal of inference.

Frequently in poetry, fiction, or forms of artistic or creative non-fiction, writers depend upon readers' inferential ability. Requiring the reader to infer certain things can be effective and is often used to create humorous, ironic, or suspenseful situations or moods. Read the following paragraph, inferring what you can about what the author is suggesting in this description of a family.

> Cold has a thousand shapes and a thousand ways of moving in the world: on the sea it gallops like a troop of horses, on the countryside it falls like a storm of locusts, in the cities like a knife-blade it slashes the streets and <u>penetrates the chinks of unheated houses.</u> In Marcovaldo's house that evening <u>they had burned the last kindling,</u> and the family, <u>all bundled in overcoats,</u> was <u>watching the embers fade in the stove,</u> and the <u>little clouds rise from their own mouths at every breath.</u> They had stopped talking; the little clouds spoke for them: the wife emitted great long ones like sighs, the children puffed them out like assorted soap-bubbles, and Marcovaldo blew them upward in jerks, <u>like flashes of genius that promptly vanished.</u>
>
> Italo Calvino, *Marcovaldo*

Obviously, this writer is describing a family that is sitting together in the cold of winter in a house in a city. Without saying so, the references to the cold that "penetrates the chinks of unheated houses," to the family "all bundled in overcoats," and to their breath rising like "little clouds . . . from their own mouths," makes it clear that this is taking place in the winter. We know it is in a city because the example in the first sentence of the cold "in the cities like a knife-blade" is the last one listed by the author, leading into the next sentence that introduces Marcovaldo's house and family. By reading that the family members "had burned the last kindling" and were "watching the embers fade in the stove," it seems that this must be taking place either in a past time or in a country where wood-burning stoves are used to heat city houses. It also would be safe to guess that the family must be too poor to buy enough wood for their stove; otherwise, they probably would not be sitting in the cold watching the last of their heating fuel burn up. Also, by describing Marcovaldo's breath as like "flashes of genius that promptly vanished," the author seems to be suggesting that he, presumably the husband and father, is perhaps an impractical dreamer, or at least someone whose good ideas never seem to amount to much. This much can be inferred from the details of the paragraph.

As this example shows, writers often leave things unstated that they want their readers to understand but that they don't want to have to come right out and say. The next passage is another example of a writer expecting readers to infer what is not stated directly but is meant to be obvious.

> Spaniards lived in the fortress city of St. Augustine and across the drier top of the peninsula to Pensacola, with various priests scattered about the hammocks and barrier islands of the coastlines south to Miami. Nowhere else in their empire were the Europeans so diffident, so tentative, so unrewarded. <u>The whole story of their enterprise can be compressed into a moment on the Gulf coast beach</u> where Father Luis Cancer, convinced that he had gained the Indians' trust, knelt down before them on the sand and was promptly knocked off with conch shells.
>
> John Rothchild, *Up for Grabs.*

This excerpt from a humorous history of Florida pokes fun at the Europeans' early attempts to settle the state. The author apparently feels that the story of Father Cancer is representative of the "whole story of their enterprise." If this is the case, then the author seems to be suggesting that the Europeans failed to establish an effective colony in Florida because, like Father Cancer, they estimated their environment very poorly.

Now read the following opening paragraph from a book about the American Revolutionary War, in which the author expects readers to know what all the references mean without having to explain them.

> White puffs of gun smoke over a turquoise sea followed by the boom of
> cannon rose from an unassuming fort on the diminutive Dutch island
> of St. Eustatius in the West Indies <u>on November 16, 1776.</u> The guns of
> Fort Orange on St. Eustatius were returning the ritual salute on entering
> a foreign port of an American vessel, the *Andrew Doria,* as the ship came
> up the roadstead, flying at her mast the red-and-white-striped flag of
> the Continental Congress. In its <u>responding salute</u> the small voice of St.
> Eustatius was <u>the first officially to greet</u> the largest event of the cen-
> tury—the entry into the society of nations of <u>a new Atlantic state</u> des-
> tined to change the direction of history.
>
> Barbara Tuchman, *The First Salute.*

The date provided in this paragraph—November 16, 1776—
makes it clear that the author is writing about an event that occurred
near the beginning of the American Revolution. According to the author, it was customary for an incoming ship and a fort to acknowledge
one another by firing cannon shots. She suggests this in her opening
sentence by referring to the cannon fired by the ship as "White puffs
of gun smoke over a turquoise sea" and to the cannon fired in return
as "the boom of cannon" from the "unassuming fort." The author
makes it clear that this event had historical significance by describing
the "responding salute" from the fort as "the first officially to greet"
the "new Atlantic state." What she is implying is that the cannon-fire
salute from the fort at St. Eustatius was the first foreign recognition of
the new nation of the United States of America. Though the author
does not state any of this directly, she intends readers to infer it from
what she does say. In this case, a reader's background knowledge is
important in recognizing the references included by the author.

5b   Drawing Conclusions

A conclusion is an inference concerning the author's implied consequences, implications, suggestions, or recommendations. When a
reader infers prescriptions for future action or consequences that
may result from what an author describes, he or she is drawing conclusions. Like any inference, a conclusion extends understanding beyond an author's words and must always be based on what the
author says. In order for a conclusion to be reasonable or acceptable,
it must be supported by information provided by the author. A logical conclusion is one that is suggested by a series of details in a text
and is consistent with the reader's knowledge or experience.

For example, in the following paragraph, the author tells you about how what people say affects how others perceive them, but she leaves unstated a broader conclusion that attentive readers can pick up on their own.

> <u>Getting credit often depends on the way you talk.</u> For example, a woman tells me she has been given a poor evaluation because <u>her supervisor feels she knows less than her male peers.</u> Her boss, it turns out, reaches this conclusion <u>because the woman asks more questions:</u> She is seeking information without regard to how her queries will make her look.
>
> <u>The same principle applies to apologizing.</u> Whereas <u>some women</u> seem to be <u>taking undeserved blame</u> by saying "I'm sorry," <u>some men seem to evade deserved blame.</u> I observed this when a man disconnected a conference call by accidentally elbowing the speaker-phone. When his secretary re-connects the call, I expect him to say, "I'm sorry; I knocked the phone by mistake." Instead he says, "Hey, what happened?! One minute you were there, the next minute you were gone!" Annoying as this may be, there are certainly instances in which people improve their fortunes by covering up mistakes.
>
> Deborah Tannen, "And Rarely the Twain Shall Meet."

The author states quite directly two points that these two examples illustrate: She begins by stating that "Getting credit often depends on the way you talk," and she ends by telling us that "people improve their fortunes by covering up mistakes." However, in the first example, a woman receives a poor evaluation because, as the author tells us, she "asks more questions," which suggests to her boss that she lacks knowledge of her field. In the second example, while, according to the author, a woman would tend to accept responsibility for a mistake by saying, "I'm sorry," a man avoids the blame for hanging up on someone by saying, "One minute you were there, the next minute you were gone!" as if something just happened on its own. In the first example, the woman was straightforward and lost out, while in the second the man was devious and avoided blame. These examples suggest that even though women seem less concerned with appearance, it is appearance that is rewarded most in the workplace. Thus, a couple of conclusions that can be drawn from this are that generally the difference between the ways men and women conduct themselves leads to men getting more credit and less blame than women and that, more specifically, it seems to pay to be devious. Though none of this is stated directly, the author wants us to draw these conclusions for ourselves.

Thus, writers often leave conclusions unstated on the assumption that their readers will understand for themselves without having to be told. The following is another example in which a writer expects readers to infer what is not stated directly but is meant to be obvious.

> The great religions of the East, Hinduism and Buddhism, which stretched human vistas into vast and endless cycles far beyond the seasons and the years of an individual life or a generation, brought a refuge from these cycles by helping the individual merge into the All. The Hindu promise was *samsara* (Sanskrit for "migration"), escape from the endless round, not by "life everlasting" but by dissolving the individual into an unchanging anonymous Absolute. Buddhism, too, offered its escape from the "weary reiteration" of life toward *nirvana* (Sanskrit for "blowing out"), the merging of the self into the Universe.
>
> The great religions of the West, also seeking to escape from the animal world of Again-and-Again, found an opposite path. While Hindus and Buddhists sought ways *out of* history, Christianity and Islam sought ways *into* history. Instead of promising escape from experience, these sought meaning in experience. Christianity and Islam were both rooted in Judaism, and all three revealed <u>a dramatic shift from a world of cycles to a world of history.</u>
>
> Daniel J. Boorstin, *The Discoverers.*

In this passage, the author refers to the "great" religions of the East and West—Hinduism, Buddhism, Christianity, and Islam—which are indeed the world's four most popular religions. Judaism is mentioned here as the source religion of both Christianity and Islam. The author points out the difference between the religions of the East and West in that Hindus and Buddhists seek ways to "escape from the endless round" of "a world of cycles" while Christians, Muslims, and Jews represent "a dramatic shift" and seek "meaning in experience" in "a world of history." By stating that this difference represents a "dramatic shift from a world of cycles to a world of history," the author is suggesting that a very important change in world views has taken place in the relatively recent emergence of the historical religions of the West. Thus, without saying so directly, the author is implying that the Western religions represent an advancement over the ancient religions of the East. He implies that by considering worldly experience meaningful in and of itself, Christians, Moslems, and Jews have been able to be more conscious of life as "a world of history," or as an unfolding of historical events.

Now read another paragraph in which an author describes Malcolm X's trip to Mecca and the realization he had at that time.

Malcolm set out alone on a pilgrimage to Mecca, and afterwards he claimed to have discovered that the Black Muslim racial dogma had all along been an eccentric aberration, and no part of true, classical Islamic theology. At the airport in Cairo, among a multitude of other pilgrims headed for Mecca, he removed his Western apparel and wrapped his waist and shoulders in two white cloths, his long rusty-skinned legs now extended bare and ostrichlike below, and he had shoved his large feet into sandals. On the flight to Jedda, he told Haley, <u>he was awed</u> to find the plane crammed with "white, black, brown, red, and yellow people, blue eyes and blond hair, and my kinky red hair—all together, brothers." On the verge, as it were, of <u>a second release from a captivity</u>—this one a release he had never anticipated—he was filled with exhilaration to note that "the whole atmosphere was of warmth and friendliness." He said, "The feeling hit me that there really wasn't any color problem here." Upon reaching Mecca, he found himself eating "from the same plate . . . with fellow Muslims, whose eyes were the bluest of blue, whose hair was the blondest of blond, and whose skin was the whitest of white." In all his life, he said afterwards, it was "the first time I had ever stood be-fore the Creator of All and felt like a complete human being."

Marshall Frady, "The Children of Malcolm."

In this passage, the author is trying to convey to us the conver-sion in his thinking that Malcolm X went through during his trip to Mecca. The author begins by telling us exactly what Malcolm real-ized about the teachings of the Black Muslims concerning race, that it "had all along been an eccentric aberration, and no part of true, classical Islamic theology." Then by describing how Malcolm was "awed" by seeing fellow pilgrims of all races on the airplane and by describing this as "a second release from a captivity," the author is suggesting that Malcolm's experience led to a personal change in his thinking that had previously been bound by racial stereotypes but that now was more accepting of all races. This interpretation is not stated directly but is implied through a description of what Malcolm went through on this eventful trip. Thus, through inference, you can draw the conclusion that the trip changed Malcolm's thinking in im-portant ways.

Recognizing Author's Purpose

Everything in print has been written for some reason and expresses a particular attitude or approach. For example, journalists write for a living, and they may have been given an assignment to investigate and write objectively about, or they may have been asked to express their opinions in an editorial or op-ed column. Freelance writers also try to use writing as a livelihood or to supplement their income by trying to find periodicals or publishing houses to publish their work. On the other hand, authors who are also professors at a college or university are often required to publish regularly in order to be eligible for tenure or promotion. Publication in academic journals or with academic presses is not generally done for profit as much as for the prestige of having one's work read and taken seriously by colleagues. In any event, whatever it is you are reading, there is a person behind it with very human motivations and feelings.

In addition to the very real human motives behind an article or book, a written work is usually composed with a specific rhetorical purpose, or a particular effect that the writer wishes to have on the reader. Being able to identify this purpose is crucial in gaining a full understanding of what you are reading.

However, readers sometimes confuse an author's purpose with the effect a passage may have. For example, an objective news account of a ghastly murder may be intended to inform readers about something that happened, but the effect on some readers may range from disgust to fright. Here, an author's purpose should be thought of as a best guess at what he or she is trying to accomplish, rather than as a reader's personal reaction to the details of the writing.

In poetry, authors try to convey ideas or experiences through imagery and powerful uses of language, which may range from descriptions of experiences or feelings to philosophical or spiritual reflections. In fiction, authors present imaginative narratives or descriptions in story form that are meant to involve readers through identification with the characters or situations presented. Authors of these types of imaginative literature may write for reasons ranging from entertainment to inspiration.

In nonfiction, including everything from advertisements to newspaper articles to college textbooks, writers attempt to present credible discussions of topics and want readers to accept and believe whatever information or explanation is being presented. Some forms of nonfiction are intended to entertain, amuse, convince, or even shock. Others are intended to inspire, as in the case of patriotic pieces, or to eulogize, as in the case of pieces that remember a late personality or public figure. You will sometimes also read pieces that have more than one purpose, such as an article meant to both inform readers about some issue and persuade them to take a particular view toward it.

However, most of the writing you will come across will typically fall into one of three broad categories: writing meant to *entertain, inform,* or *persuade.* Entertaining writing is intended to amuse or provide readers with a pleasurable experience. Informative writing is meant to explain or instruct, or simply to tell readers about something. Persuasive writing is meant to convince readers to believe in some idea or to take some course of action.

In any case, being able to understand an author's purpose will greatly increase the meaning that a piece has for you. When trying to determine an author's purpose, you should look for any hints in the title, in any headings or subheadings, or in an introductory or concluding statement. Sometimes in nonfiction, the main idea of a piece may suggest, or in some cases even state, the author's purpose. However, because authors rarely state their purpose directly, in most cases you will need to determine an author's unstated purpose through inference.

5c   Entertaining Writing

Writing to entertain is intended to amuse readers or to provide them with a pleasurable or enjoyable reading experience. Writing that is meant to be enjoyable may appear in the form of poetry, fiction, or nonfiction. Sometimes humorists write to amuse readers with funny stories or situations. Sometimes authors may entertain by simply telling a good story. The following is an example of a passage clearly meant to amuse.

> When it comes to sports I am not particularly interested. Generally speaking, I look upon them as dangerous and tiring activities performed by people with whom I share nothing in common except the right to trial by jury. It is not that I am totally indifferent to the joys of athletic effort—it is simply that my idea of what constitutes sport does not coincide with popularly held notions on the subject. There are a number of reasons for this, chief among them being that to me the outdoors is what you must pass through in order to get from your apartment to a taxicab.
>
> Fran Lebowitz, *Metropolitan Life.*

While you may or may not share this author's definition of sports or of the outdoors, you must admit that she makes her opinion amusingly clear: She does not like sports and does not feel much in common with those who do. This may indeed be a serious thing for this urban author, but she has chosen to express her view through humor.

Now read another example of writing meant to entertain, this time from a mystery novel by a very successful storyteller.

> In the high, dry mountains of the Colorado Plateau, fog is out of its element. It forms as part of a climactic accident, produced when a cold front crosses a mountain range and collides with warmer air on the opposite slope. And it survives no longer than a fish out of water. By dawn, when the four of them reached the place of Hosteen Begay, the fog had already lost its character as a solid blinding cloud. Now it survived only in pockets, as patches and fragments. Chee stood at the edge of one such fragment, exactly where Sharkey had told him to stand—on the slope west of the meadow where Begay had built his hogan. His role was to make sure that if Gorman tried to escape he would not escape in that direction. Chee rested a hip against a boulder. He waited and watched. At the moment, he watched Deputy Bales, who stood beside a ponderous pine, right hand against the tree trunk and his left holding a long-barreled revolver, its muzzle pointing at the ground. The bottom of the tree trunk and Bales's lower legs were obscured by the mist, making—in the dim light—man and tree seem somehow detached from solid earth. Over the meadow, the fog was almost solid, frayed only here and there by the very beginning of a cold dawn breeze. Chee glanced at his watch. In eleven minutes it would be sunrise.
>
> Tony Hillerman, *The Ghostway.*

This is a description of a stake-out in a novel where the main character, Sergeant Jim Chee of the Navajo Tribal Police, solves a mysterious murder. Readers may find stories such as this satisfying for various reasons, but in the end they are made from the fertile imagination of authors who intend to provide their readers with the pleasure of a suspenseful tale.

5d   Informative Writing

Authors who intend to inform their readers try to present information clearly so readers can understand the material as easily as possible. Writers of informational pieces may attempt in an objective or neutral way to describe, summarize, explain, instruct, present, or portray information. Various patterns of organization may be used to present factual information, observations, or explanations to support main ideas. Examples of informative writing include news articles, instructional manuals, college textbooks, encyclopedias, business reports, and research reports. Read the following passage, thinking of the author's intention as you do.

> Vitamins and minerals are nutrients that are essential to life. They are so-called "micronutrients" because, in comparison with the other nutrients—carbohydrates, proteins, fats, and water—we need them in relatively small amounts.
>
> Vitamins function by and large as *coenzymes.* Enzymes are catalysts or activators in the chemical reactions that are continually taking place in our bodies. Vitamins are a fundamental part of the enzymes, the way your muscles are a fundamental part of your arms and legs. Most people are aware that we have enzymes to help us digest our food. But enzymes do more than help us digest food. They are at the very foundation of *all* our bodily functions. Enzymes are what make things happen, and happen faster.
>
> Shari Liebeman & Nancy Bruning, *The Real Vitamin & Mineral Book.*

These authors are informing you about vitamins. In the first paragraph, they mention how necessary vitamins are for life. Then in the second paragraph, the authors briefly explain why vitamins are so essential. The authors here are trying to inform readers about the importance of vitamins in the healthy functioning of the human body.

Now read another passage also meant to inform. This one is a little more complex in that it reports the results of scientific research by briefly summarizing a theory developed by the author and a colleague.

> Everyone knows that behavior is transmitted by culture, but culture is a product of the brain. The brain in turn is a highly structured organ and a product of genetic evolution. It possesses a host of biases programmed through sensory reception and the propensity to learn certain things and not others. These biases guide culture to a still unknown degree. In the reverse direction, the genetic evolution of the most distinctive properties of the brain occurred in an environment dominated by culture. Changes in culture therefore must have affected those properties. . . .
>
> We were looking for the basic process that directs the evolution of the human mind. We concluded that it is a particular form of interaction between genes and culture. This "gene-culture coevolution," as we called it, is an eternal circle of change in heredity and culture. Over the

course of a lifetime, the mind of the individual person creates itself by picking among countless fragments of information, value judgments, and available courses of action within the context of a particular culture. More concretely, the individual comes to select certain marital customs, creation myths, ethical precepts, modes of analysis, and so forth, from among those available. We called these competing behaviors and mental abstractions "culturegens."

Edward O. Wilson, Naturalist.

In this passage, the author briefly describes the conclusions he and a colleague arrived at after years of scientific study. He is reporting here their theory of "culturegens," the idea that the "basic process that directs the evolution of the human mind" is the "interaction between genes and culture." The author begins by stating the common understanding that "behavior is transmitted by culture." He then goes on to state that culture and biology affect one another. Though the author is stating a theory, he is merely informing us of that theory.

5e   Persuasive Writing

In the broadest sense, almost all writing is persuasive in that authors want readers to identify with a topic under discussion and want to convince readers to believe the words or ideas as they are presented. However, for the sake of this discussion, persuasion will be defined more narrowly as those pieces of writing that are meant to influence a reader's belief in an idea or to move one to perform some specific action. Authors of persuasive pieces attempt to engage readers in discussions in order to obtain some desired response.

Persuasion may take the form of criticism or *satire*—a form of social commentary that portrays public figures or current events in absurd or ridiculous ways—or may attempt to arouse a sense of identification, sympathy, or pity. Examples of persuasive writing include editorials, book or movie reviews, advertisements, articles in favor or against a political candidate, and other articles meant to convince readers of some idea. In whatever form, persuasive writing attempts to make a case through appeals to a reader's intellect, values, or emotions.

Read the following passage, noticing that the main point is an opinion and that the details are provided to present convincing support.

Opponents of affirmative action, including many liberals, genuinely believe in their stance's righteousness. Others want nothing more than to maintain white privilege. Both are obstacles to progress.

They can't understand that setting aside a small percentage of jobs, contracts, and university admissions for minorities isn't about preferential treatment or reverse discrimination; it's about including us in a mix.

For minorities the issue is not whether there should be a level playing field, but whether we'll make it to the field. Under affirmative action, if 20 percent of a city's contracts are set aside for minority firms, 80 percent could go to white firms. The same equation could apply to job and university slots. So I ask, who's getting preferential treatment?

Affirmative action has helped many minorities escape dire beginnings. But even today, the vast majority remain isolated and trapped in poverty and pathological self-destruction.

Angelo Figueroa, "Must Fight Back on Affirmative Action."

By stating that opponents of affirmative action "are obstacles to progress," that minorities merely want to be included "in a mix," and that the issue for minorities is being able to "make it to the field," the author makes clear his support for affirmative action. Then with the question "who's getting preferential treatment?" at the end of the second paragraph, the author implies that whites are still getting much more than minorities, even with affirmative action quotas. In the last paragraph, by stating that affirmative action programs have "helped many minorities escape dire beginnings" and that most minorities "remain isolated and trapped in poverty and pathological self-destruction," the author suggests his main point. The author's purpose is thus to convince readers that affirmative action programs are absolutely necessary for minorities.

Now read another attempt at persuasion. In this case, not only is there an attempt to convince readers to agree with a certain point, but there is also a case made that a specific action should be taken.

Charged with redesigning America's entitlement programs to ensure their soundness and equity, the commission [the federal Bipartisan Commission on Entitlement and Tax Reform] has completely shut out the group that will be most affected by its recommendations—the 130 million Americans under 35.

It is this post-Boomer cohort that will inherit the tab for Uncle Sam's current fiscal irresponsibility. It is these so-called Generations X and Y who face sharp tax increases and big benefit cuts if entitlement programs are not restructured to reflect changing demographic and economic realities. Current trends, for example, indicate that today's 27-year-old will pay $203,000 more in taxes than he receives in government benefits, compared with a 72-year-old, who will receive $98,600 more in benefits than he paid in.

Why such disparity? In 1939, when Social Security was created, there were 50 active workers to pay for each retiree. That ratio dropped to 20 to 1 by 1950 and will plummet to just 2 to 1 by 2025. To support this upside-down pyramid—and the more generous benefits of the past 50 years—workers born after 1960 can expect up to 40% of their future salaries to go to payroll taxes.

Despite the massive generational implications of our current system—and the changes contemplated in the health-care debate—the 32-member commission includes not a single member under 40. More than one-third of the members are over 60, and seven already qualify for Social Security. Members' average age is 57.

Jon Cowan and Rob Nelson, "Age Discrimination—Against the Young."

These authors express the opinion that it is unfair for older Americans to recommend entitlement reforms that are likely to affect younger Americans more. They point out the fact that under the current system, older Americans benefit far more and have to pay less than will younger people because of "changing demographic and economic realities." These conditions are described in the third paragraph to show the disparity between generations. Then in the final paragraph, the authors describe the make-up of the commission showing that there is "not a single member under 40." Assuming that the data provided by the authors are accurate, they present a compelling argument that young people should be allowed to participate in changing the entitlement system, specifically by having members on the commission responsible for suggesting reforms. The author's purpose here is clearly to persuade readers to agree that this should be done.

5f   Combined Purposes—Dominant Purpose

You will often read passages that may do more than one thing and accomplish more than one purpose. For example, an author may try to inform readers of something as a way to make a convincing point, or may try to inform readers in an entertaining way. In any case, an author usually has one dominant purpose in mind that is accomplished by whatever else may be going on in the piece. Consider the following passage as an example of such writing.

> I think the most interesting change in America since 1954 is the way in which attitudes about "life station" have evolved. When I was born, in 1947, the American dream was essentially defined in terms of the capacity of white males to challenge the capacity of the social and economic class into which they had been born and to participate in a fluid class structure that was based on notions of a meritocracy. Women, blacks, the disabled, and gays and lesbians were for all intents and purposes "invisible people" and were considered the "exceptions" to the American dream. That is no longer the case. The combined effects of the "movements" for civil rights, for gender equity, for freedom of choice for abortion, for disability rights, and for gay rights all have altered irrevocably the notion of "station" and have given new meaning and breadth to the parameters of the "American dream." No longer are some Americans consigned to limitations on the basis of the circumstances of birth; today the notion of a meritocracy is more inclusive than it was in 1954. This development has far-ranging consequences, reflected in the work force and otherwise, but it may well represent the most fundamental redefinition of American life of this century.
>
> Carol Moseley-Braun, "How Have We Changed?"

In this paragraph, the author expresses her opinion that "the most interesting change in America" since the 1950s involves increased opportunities for social mobility. This is stated clearly in the first sentence. She then describes certain changes that have occurred in her lifetime that support this conclusion. She says that attitudes toward "life station" have changed as a result of social movements that "have altered irrevocably the notion of 'station' and have given new meaning and breadth to the parameters of the 'American dream.'" She expresses the view that formerly marginal minority groups and women are now able to "participate in a fluid class structure . . . based on notions of a meritocracy" as white men have always been able to. It is clear that the author feels it is a good thing that some Americans are no longer "consigned to limitations on the basis of the circumstances of birth." It is also clear that she wants readers to understand and accept this view. Thus, by informing readers of these changes, the author is trying to convince them to agree with her interpretation of them. While the passage is informational, its main purpose is persuasive.

Recognizing Author's Tone

While an author's purpose is closely related to the main idea and can often be inferred from the main idea and the way in which the details are presented, the tone of a piece of writing is a little more elusive. The tone of a paragraph, an article, or another piece of writing refers to the author's attitude toward the topic under discussion. Stated another way, the tone refers to the mood or feeling reflected in the writing.

In addition to indicating an author's attitude toward the subject, the tone can often suggest something about the author's purpose: If the tone of an article is objective or straightforward, then the author's purpose is probably to inform; if the tone of an article is angry, critical, sarcastic, appreciative, or sympathetic, then the purpose is probably to persuade.

While the idea of an author's tone may seem somewhat vague, attentive readers can infer the tone of a piece of writing from the words chosen to describe or present ideas. The tone is often indicated by the words a writer chooses and by the way ideas are presented. The tone is the feeling you think the author has toward his or her topic. Below is a list of words identifying some common tones.

5g   A List of Some Common Tones

The following list of common terms is arranged alphabetically. If some of the terms listed are unfamiliar to you, a good dictionary will help you to understand their meanings.

Ambivalent	Enthusiastic	Irreverent
Angry	Fearful	Joyous
Apathetic	Gloomy	Loving
Appreciative	Grim	Melancholy
Arrogant	Happy	Miserable
Authoritative	Hateful	Mocking
Bitter	Hopeful	Nostalgic
Comic	Horrifying	Objective
Compassionate	Hostile	Optimistic
Condescending	Humorous	Outraged
Critical	Hysterical	Pessimistic
Cynical	Impassioned	Respectful
Defensive	Indignant	Reverent
Depressing	Insulting	Righteous
Detached	Intimate	Sad
Disapproving	Ironic	Sarcastic

Satiric   Sorrowful   Threatening
Scornful   Sincere   Tragic
Serious   Straightforward   Vindictive
Solemn   Sympathetic   Wondering

5h   Descriptions of Some Common Tones

What follows are definitions and brief examples for a few of the more common tones.

Critical   When an author makes an unfavorable analysis, evaluation, or judgment, the tone is critical.

> There's a whole lot of sharing going on out there, and just one of the interesting things about it is it doesn't seem authentic—i.e., the secrets people are sharing don't seem like real secrets but like narrative constructed to give us a claim on the national microphone. One wonders also, Who's listening? Who is learning, being heartened, instructed, shocked? Hemingway once said: Do not confuse movement with action. We are becoming a people who confuse chatter with communication.
>
> Peggy Noonan, "How Have We Changed?"

This author is critical of the American people who, she feels, talk too much about mundane matters but communicate little of importance. The reference to "the national microphone" refers to radio and television talk shows that she apparently feels epitomize a preoccupation with empty talk. The author clearly states that she feels this talk "doesn't seem authentic." The author is thus critical of those of us who, she feels, "confuse chatter with communication."

Impassioned   An impassioned tone is expressed by warmth, passion, or intensity of feeling.

> He was dreaming of her arms around him strong, when the rain on the tin roof woke him up. But the feeling he had, the love he felt from her, remained. The wet earth smell came in the window that Robert had propped open with an old shoe the night before. He was overwhelmed by the love he felt for her; tears filled his eyes and the ache in his throat ran deep into his chest. He ran down the hill to the river, through the light rain until the pain faded like fog mist. He stood and watched the rainy dawn, and he knew he would find her again.
>
> Leslie Marmon Silko, *Ceremony.*

In this passage, the author is describing the intense feelings of both love and longing that a man is having for a woman whom he has just dreamed about, with "her arms around him strong," and whom he apparently misses very much but knows he will "find her again." By stating that Robert "was overwhelmed by the love he felt for her" and that "tears filled his eyes and the ache in his throat ran deep into his chest," the author is expressing the very passionate feelings that this man has for the woman he is remembering.

Indignant   An indignant tone is expressed through anger over something unjust, unworthy, or mean.

> These two cartoon imbeciles, so ill-drawn as to resemble doodles done by a 4-year-old, so plotlessly adrift, so one-and-a-half-dimensional, so idly malicious, so tooth-grindingly repetitious, so inert and soulless that owl dung seems wise by comparison—these two soiled mannequins have laid hands on my youngsters' minds. I could scream.
>
> Michael Browning, "A Pox upon MTV Bozos for Debasing Our Civility."

Referring to the two MTV cartoon characters Beavis and Butthead, this author is clearly upset about the influence that watching them on television has had on his children. He expresses his anger first by ridiculing the cartoon characters and finally by showing that he is so upset that he "could scream."

Ironic   An ironic tone expresses irony. Irony is used where an author wants to make a point, often with subtle humor, by saying the opposite of what he or she really means. This definition can also be extended to include descriptions of events when an author may point out or describe the contrast between what is and what one would expect, as in the following example.

> Our own era has perfected the systematic use of cultural technology to fabricate the dominant icons of political protest: King and Malcolm X, the Jacob and Esau of black America. . . .
>
> But, as always in history, what is forgotten is as crucial as what is remembered. It has been convenient to airbrush out the more radical aspects of King's later, post-Nobel years: his antiwar political protests; his recognition that the battle for equality was passing from the realm of civil rights to that of economic justice. In Memphis the night before his assassination, King was speaking not to a civil-rights rally but in support of a garbage workers' strike. As for Malcolm, his all-too-brief final

period, marked by a cosmopolitan embrace of a color-blind humanism, has been almost completely erased from the popular culture's memory banks. In its place, the man who launched a million "X" caps. As with King's image, Malcolm's proved more resilient than its owner: Malcolm may have adopted the stance of transracial humanism toward the end of his life, but most people—not least the political heirs he had decided to disinherit—felt free to ignore such vagaries.

King and Malcolm, both murdered at thirty-nine, were both destined to be used by many who had never read them to justify a host of political programs they had either abandoned or never embraced. In this sense, they have come to resemble each other more in death than they ever did in life. The complexities of both men are incompatible with the simplicities of heroism. Simplify, simplify—that is the imperative of the hero industry.

Henry Louis Gates, Jr., "Heroes, Inc."

In this passage, the author is pointing out the irony that people "who had never read them" are now using Martin Luther King, Jr., and Malcolm X "to justify a host of political programs they had either abandoned or never embraced." The author tries to show how the beliefs that both King and Malcolm X did embrace near the end of their lives—King's "antiwar political protests" and "his recognition that the battle for equality was passing from the realm of civil rights to that of economic justice"; and Malcolm X's "cosmopolitan embrace of a color-blind humanism"—have been nearly forgotten by those who claim to represent them. He ends with the suggestion that King and Malcolm X "have come to resemble each other more in death than they ever did in life" by being misrepresented and used as heroic symbols for other people's purposes. The author intends to convey the feeling that this is indeed sadly ironic.

Objective   An objective tone is used when a writer tries to make clear, straightforward statements without expressing emotion, opinion, preference, or bias.

Most immigrants have had to learn a new language, and as a national language English has acted as a powerful force in their assimilation. This is not to suggest, however, that other languages have not played a part in the development of American society. American Indians spoke about three hundred different languages when the first European explorers came to the New World. During the colonial period settlers spoke Spanish, French, German, Russian, Swedish, and Dutch as well as English. Nineteenth- and early twentieth-century immigrant languages included Italian, Polish, and Yiddish.

An important facet of American culture and education from the colonial period, bilingualism remains a controversial and emotional issue. Many groups assert their children must be educated not only in English but also in their "native" language if they are to maintain their cultural traditions and heritages. Critics of bilingualism maintain that a common language (English) provides the most effective means of drawing together the diverse ethnic and cultural groups that constitute the American people.

Eugene F. Provenzo, Jr., *An Introduction to Education in American Society.*

In the first paragraph, the author begins by introducing the idea that while America has from the beginning been a land of many languages, most immigrants have had to learn English as part of the assimilation process. Examples of the many languages spoken by Americans are then listed. In the second paragraph, the author begins by stating that "bilingualism remains a controversial and emotional issue." He then goes on to briefly tell us how the two opposing sides in this controversy see this issue. Though the author uses the words "powerful" to describe the assimilating effect he feels English has on immigrants and "important" to describe the role played by bilingualism throughout the history of American education, he in no way expresses or even implies his own opinion of bilingual education, except to make it clear that it continues to be a significant issue in American education and culture. Thus, the author remains objective in his discussion of this topic.

Optimistic An optimistic tone expresses the view that the most favorable outcome is likely, or it stresses only the positive aspects of something.

Genuine politics—politics worthy of the name, and the only politics I am willing to devote myself to—is simply a matter of serving those around us: serving the community, and serving those who will come after us. Its deepest roots are moral because it is a responsibility, expressed through action, to and for the whole, a responsibility that is what it is—a "higher" responsibility—only because it has a metaphysical grounding: that is, it grows out of a conscious or subconscious certainty that our death ends nothing, because everything is forever being recorded and evaluated somewhere else, somewhere "above us," in what I have called "the memory of Being"—an integral aspect of the secret order of the cosmos, of nature, and of life, which believers call God and to whose judgment everything is subject.

Vaclav Havel, Summer Meditations.

In this passage, the President of the Czech Republic expresses his view of politics as "serving the community, and serving those who will come after us" out of a sense of social responsibility and spiritual understanding. He says about political life that "Its deepest roots are moral" and that a politician's actions are accountable to "the secret order of the cosmos, of nature, and of life." This author is expressing no cynicism about politics but seems to see it as a noble calling. This is certainly a positive, optimistic view.

Pessimistic   Pessimistic tone is the opposite of optimistic tone. It expresses the view that the most unfavorable outcome is likely, or it stresses the most negative aspects.

Think of the code words that whites have for blacks: minority, urban, criminal, crime rate, social programs, inner city, qualified candidate, welfare mother. Then listen to the black codes for whites: suburban, Republican, conservative. Each group sees the other as "them."

In this polarized climate our so-called leaders have lost the will to do more than simply condemn our problems. Even worse, they have lost the imagination to do more than censure the victims and blame the victimizers.

We are left with the discouraging idea that my interests and I are incompatible with you and your rights. We justify, in the name of winning all, the total disparagement of those who then lose all.

Lani Guinier, "To Heal the Nation, We Must Talk."

Here the author expresses the view that American blacks and whites see each other as "them," as alien and different from one another. She sees the nation's leaders as lacking the will to do any more about this "polarized climate" than "censure the victims and blame the victimizers," or avoid responsibility by blaming others. She feels that people "are left with the discouraging idea" that these are incompatible differences and that those who succeed rationalize "the total disparagement of those who then lose all." This is indeed a very negative, pessimistic view of racial relations.

Respectful   A respectful tone expresses appreciation, respect, high regard, esteem, or consideration.

I remember the moment when it dawned on me that my father did not impress the world at large as a powerful figure. We were at a camera store . . . in Kansas City. I don't remember how old I was, but it was old enough, at least, to be using a camera. We were standing at a counter waiting to be helped, but nobody seemed to be paying much attention. My father was standing quietly, with a faraway look in his eye, and it struck me that he was not one of the people in the world who would noisily demand service or one of the people whose very presence would command attention. He was not powerful in the way that most people use that word—although in those days I suspect that he and Uncle Maish together might have gone a long way toward lifting the end of a car off the ground.

In novels of American strivers, the sort of realization I had in that camera store can cause the hero to become disillusioned with his father or to resolve that he himself will, at any cost, be a person who commands attention. I didn't have that sort of reaction. I do remember the precise counter we stood at and precisely the direction we were facing—but it was not a moment that changed my opinion of my father or changed the way I thought about myself. That may have been because in his own world he was a figure of such strength. It may have been because his values were so deeply embedded—he had such stubborn confidence in their rightness—that it would have seemed trivial to put much weight on how the world of less certain human beings might respond to him.

Calvin Trillin, "Messages From My Father."

In this passage, the author describes a childhood experience in which he realized for the first time that his father "did not impress the world at large as a powerful figure." He noticed that his father was ignored by the salespeople in a camera shop and was not someone "whose very presence would command attention." Although this realization seems to have been somewhat of a surprise to the author, it in no way changed his opinion of his father. The author recognized that in his own world, his father "was a figure of such strength" who possessed deeply held values. For the author, his father's moral integrity and strength of character far outweighed "how the world of less certain human beings might respond to him." The author clearly admires and respects his father.

Tragic   A tragic tone is expressed when some regrettable, sorrowful, or disastrous situation or event is described or discussed, or when an author shows pity for a tragic turn of events.

There was silence all round now, broken only by groans. In front of the block, the SS were giving orders. An officer passed by the beds. My father begged me:

"My son, some water. . . . I'm burning. . . . My stomach. . . ."

"Quiet over there!" yelled the officer.

"Eliezer," went on my father, "some water. . . ."

The officer came up to him and shouted at him to be quiet. But my father did not hear him. He went on calling me. The officer dealt him a violent blow on the head with his truncheon.

I did not move. I was afraid. My body was afraid of also receiving a blow.

Then my father made a rattling noise and it was my name: "Eliezer."

I could not see that he was still breathing—spasmodically.

I did not move.

When I got down after roll call, I could see his lips trembling as he murmured something. Bending over him, I stayed gazing at him for over an hour, engraving into myself the picture of his blood-stained face, his shattered skull.

Then I had to go to bed. I climbed into my bunk, above my father, who was still alive. It was January 28, 1945.

I awoke on January 29 at dawn. In my father's place lay another invalid. They must have taken him away before dawn and carried him to the crematory. He may still have been breathing.

There were no prayers at his grave. No candles were lit to his memory. His last word was my name. A summons, to which I did not respond.

I did not weep, and it pained me that I could not weep. But I had no more tears. And, in the depths of my being, in the recesses of my weakened conscience, could I have searched it, I might perhaps have found something like—free at last!

Elie Wiesel, *Night.*

In this passage, the author describes a horrible experience in a Nazi concentration camp near the end of the Second World War. The events described are clearly tragic, not only because of his father's brutal death, but also because the author failed to respond to his father's call out of fear of his being beaten by the Nazi guard. We can only imagine the author's pitiable state of mind at this time, as he "had no more tears" to shed for his father, who he realized may have been burned alive in the crematory. The author of this passage expresses feelings of physical and mental pain inflicted by brutal treatment in a situation where the victims are unable to escape or fight back; this is indeed tragic.

Chapter Review

Making inferences and drawing conclusions requires the use of personal knowledge, logic, and imagination to determine what an author may be indirectly suggesting but not coming right out and stating. This inferential reading is often necessary to understand things that an author assumes you will recognize or may want you to grasp but prefers not to directly say.

Two very important elements that are necessary to fully understand a passage and that usually need to be inferred are the author's purpose—the reason for writing—and the tone—his or her attitude toward the topic. When trying to determine an author's purpose and tone, you should look for the following:

When **making an inference**, use your
>   knowledge,
>   experience,
>   logic, and
>   awareness of writers' techniques

to figure out an author's meanings that are not stated directly but that are suggested by what is said.

When **drawing a conclusion**, consider the
>   implications,
>   consequences, or
>   courses of action

suggested by the details of an author's discussion.

To determine the author's **purpose**, look for hints in the
>   title,
>   headings or subheadings,
>   introductory or concluding statement, and
>   main idea or thesis.

To determine the author's **tone**, try to figure out the feeling you think the author has toward his or her topic by looking for hints in the
>   words chosen to describe or present ideas, and
>   way ideas are presented.

Using Inference in Reading

Implied Meaning

Making Inferences
Drawing
   Conclusions

Author's Purpose

To Entertain or
   Amuse
To Inform or Explain
To Persuade or
   Convince
Combined Purposes

Author's Tone

Critical
Impassioned
Indignant
Ironic
Objective
Optimistic
Pessimistic
Respectful
Tragic

CHAPTER

6

Interpreting Language

Writers often choose their words very carefully in order to have certain desired effects. This is possible not only because subtle differences in the meanings of words can reflect subtle meanings that an author intends, but also because the meanings of words can change according to the context. If each word had only one meaning, a meaning that could be looked up in a dictionary and that never changed, reading would perhaps be less difficult, but it would also be much less interesting. However, the English language is considerably richer than that, and authors select words for their emotional, suggestive meanings and also sometimes use words in imaginative, unconventional ways to make impressions and create vivid images. This chapter will thus concentrate on understanding the *connotative* meanings of words and on interpreting the *figurative* use of language. The ability to understand the subtle and imaginative uses of language makes reading not only more meaningful but also more pleasurable.

Understanding the Suggested Meanings of Words

Every word has a literal meaning that can be read in a dictionary. This literal, dictionary definition of a word is its *denotation.* A word's *connotation,* on the other hand, refers to the emotional or suggestive meaning that some words are understood to have when used in certain contexts or in certain ways. A word's connotation can be either positive, negative, or neutral, depending on how it is used.

6a   Connotations

Each of us probably has certain words we associate with experiences we have had and that have personal meanings for us that are not necessarily shared by everyone in the same way. For example, if you grew up near the ocean, the word "beach" might elicit memories of sunny days in the water and on the sand. However, for those of us without such experiences, the word *beach* is more abstract, known only perhaps from photographs or television. In addition to the many personal associations each of us has with certain words, there are many words with public or cultural meanings that are shared by most people in our society. It is thus possible to learn much about an author's purpose and attitude from the words he or she uses.

For example, we all know that a lemon is a yellow citrus fruit with a somewhat sour taste. This word has neither a positive nor negative connotation. However, if we were to call a car a lemon, we would not be referring to it literally as a type of fruit; in this context, we would be using the word "lemon" with a negative connotation to mean an automobile of poor quality. Similarly, the word "cool" literally means "moderately cold." However, if a person is described as being cool, we do not mean to say that he or she has a low temperature; by using the word "cool" in this context, we probably mean to say that the person has desirable qualities.

In addition, some words are very similar in their denotative meanings but have subtle differences in connotation, and the choice of one word over another indicates the point that an author wants to make. For example, the words "confident," "cocky," and "arrogant" have similar denotative meanings: They all describe someone who is self-assured and has self-confidence. However, the word "confident" is the most positive and suggests that the person has faith in him- or herself. The word "cocky," on the other hand, is less positive and suggests that the person referred to is annoyingly overconfident. The word "arrogant" definitely has a negative connotation and suggests that the person is obnoxiously full of himself to the point of being domineering and overbearing. So the choice of one of these words over the others in a description of a person would suggest how an author would want to portray that individual.

In another example, before the 1960s, the terms "Negro" and "colored" were the respectable words for Americans of sub-Saharan African decent. However, during the civil rights movement, these words were replaced with the word "black," which was felt to be free of the old associations with slavery and domination that the other terms held. Most recently, the more ethnically descriptive term "African-American" has for many people become the most preferred reference. Clearly, the choice of one of these terms over another can make a great difference in the impression an author wants to make, and in the reaction he or she wants to get.

Words with Negative Connotations   Authors often write not only to communicate but also to arouse some emotion or make readers respond to their ideas or suggestions. Carefully chosen words can be very effective in accomplishing these purposes, and a careful reader can recognize how words are used for certain effects. Authors assume that the words they choose for their suggestive, connotative meanings will be understood by their readers. For this reason, the shared connotative meanings of words are not explained. To know what they mean, we must rely on our background knowledge of such words and on our inferential ability to figure out what an author means in a given context.

Read the following passage, paying careful attention to the connotative meanings of certain carefully chosen words that are meant to convey a certain message.

> Living in a land so transformed by the <u>burdens</u> we brought, we find it almost incredible that North America was not long ago an <u>unscarred</u> place of overpowering beauty and fecundity, where the hand of humankind was dark, aboriginal, and mythologically bound, so that it <u>brushed but lightly</u> its environment. Traveling the <u>cancerous</u> stretch of the eastern seaboard, from the English outposts in Massachusetts, down through the Outer Banks of North Carolina, and on into the Island of Flowers, Florida, where Soto and Narvaez <u>trudged off</u> on their <u>nightmare</u> errands, we have some trouble imagining either beauty or fecundity. The old chronicles that tell of these seem travelers' tales to us now, though we have no doubt that we are in the presence of tremendous industry and power. Nothing less could have changed this landscape so totally from what it once was that even with our narrative guides we are at a loss to find vestiges of that old New World.
>
> Frederick Turner, *Beyond Geography*.

In this passage, the author discusses the transformation of North America from the "unscarred place of overpowering beauty and fecundity" in which the Indians lived, to "the cancerous stretch of the eastern seaboard" created by the Europeans. The author uses the word "burdens" to describe what the Europeans brought (including the author in his reference to "we") and the word "cancerous" to describe the effect they have had; and by referring to the land before then as "unscarred" and "brushed but lightly" by the aboriginal inhabitants, the author is suggesting that the Europeans ruined what the Indians had preserved. Also, by saying that the Spanish explorers Soto and Narvaez "trudged off" on "nightmare errands," the author emphasizes their insensitivity and the disastrous effect they had. The words the author has chosen to use here clearly suggest that he feels the European influence in the New World has not been especially positive.

Words with Positive Connotations   Now read another passage, which is also about the European presence in North America. However, this passage is from a different point of view, reflected by a different choice of words.

Before American society could be created by the settlers, America had to be transformed. The forest had to <u>give way</u> to the fields, the plow, the draft ox, the mule, the sheep, the goat, the wheel, gunpowder, steel had to <u>make possible</u> a new life in which tens of millions could live a<u>bun-dantly</u> where a few hundred thousand <u>savages</u> had been living <u>precari-ous</u> and <u>poverty-stricken</u> lives. America had to be <u>made</u> before it could be lived in, and that making took centuries, took extraordinary energies and bred an attitude toward life that is peculiarly American.

D. W. Brogan, *The American Character.*

This author also discusses the European transformation of America. However in this case, the author suggests a positive impact by stating first that the forests had to "give way" to the settlers' influence, suggesting that the new land was willing to "make possible a new life." Then by using the word "abundantly" to suggest how the settlers lived, and the words "savages," "precarious," and "poverty-stricken" to describe the Indians and their lives, the author makes it clear that the way of life brought by the European settlers was an improvement over what had existed before. Finally, the author suggests that "America had to be 'made' before it could be lived in," indicating his view that not much of value existed before the settlers created it. Again, the author's choice of words clearly reflects his point of view. In this case, the author makes it clear that in his opinion the European settlers brought a better life to this land than had existed before.

6b   Euphemisms

Sometimes unpleasant or embarrassing situations are referred to in polite-sounding words to lessen the impact of a harsh or sensitive reality that a more direct word might reveal. These terms are called *euphemisms* (pronounced "u'-fe-mizm") and are often chosen for their milder, more acceptable connotations. The purpose of a euphemism is to try to make an offensive or embarrassing reality seem as tame as possible. For example, a frequently used euphemism for laying off employees is the technical-sounding word "downsizing." Other common examples include "sleeping together" to mean the act of sexual intercourse and "putting to sleep" to mean the killing of a pet.

Understanding Idioms

Every language has certain characteristic ways of expressing ideas that are considered normal. The commonly used expressions of a language are called *idioms* and are learned by users of that language through repeated exposure and use, by listening, reading, and paying attention to the special phrases and expressions that are heard and seen.

Some *idiomatic* expressions are as common as the use of one preposition instead of another, something that often drives non-native speakers crazy. For example, the sentence "I went *to* sleep *at* midnight" states that the author began sleeping at 12:00 A.M., but says it with prepositions that may seem arbitrary; indeed, why not say "I went *into* sleep *on* midnight"? These choices are less grammatical than they are customary, or idiomatic, English usages.

Some idioms are composed of commonly used figurative expressions that use words in ways that differ from how they are usually used and that cannot be understood by defining their individual meanings. These idioms only make sense if they are understood as ways to visualize something in order to make it clear. For example, if someone were to ask an English-speaker, "How do you do?", she would not ask in return, "How do I do what?" She would understand that this idiom is not as much an actual question as it is a respectful greeting that means "I hope you are feeling well."

Now read the following passage, taken from a newspaper gossip column, that includes several common idioms.

> Who knew the Donald <u>had a</u> chivalrous <u>bone in his</u> pampered <u>body</u>? Trump <u>came out swinging</u> in defense of the perky princess of morning talk, Kathie Lee Gifford. He's "very angry" at how people are <u>trashing</u> her.
>
> Yonette Joseph, "The People Column."

In this little piece, Donald Trump is described as having "a chivalrous bone in his pampered body." To say that "someone doesn't have a (you fill in the adjective) in his body" means that the person totally lacks that quality. Here the expression indicates the author's surprise that Donald Trump has shown such chivalrous behavior that he "came out swinging," another idiom meaning that he aggressively came to the defense of Kathie Lee. Finally, to say that people are "trashing" Ms. Gifford means that she is being severely criticized.

6c   A Few Examples of American English Idioms

These are examples of commonly used figurative expressions, or idioms, that you will see used quite frequently.

Idiom	Meaning
It is <u>raining cats and dogs</u>.	There is a severe rain storm.
It has <u>come in handy</u>.	It has been useful.
He <u>caught</u> her eye.	She noticed him.
It <u>caught</u> fire.	A fire has ignited.
<u>Act</u> your age.	Behave with more maturity.
We <u>struck</u> a bargain.	We agreed on a transaction.
I was <u>taken in</u>.	I was deceived.
She <u>takes after</u> her mother.	She resembles her mother.
I will <u>look up</u> an old friend.	I will locate and visit an old friend.
Last night he <u>kicked the bucket</u>.	He died last night.
He <u>carried out</u> the order.	He obeyed the order.
She <u>blew her top</u>.	She got very angry.
He is <u>behind the eight ball</u>.	He is in trouble.

Interpreting Figurative Language

In addition to choosing words according to their connotations and using common idioms to express ideas, writers sometimes use language in original ways that depart from common usage. This is called using figurative language. Authors use figurative language to express a point or to clarify an idea through imaginative comparisons or with words used in unusual, suggestive, or symbolic ways. Figurative language often enhances meaning by representing abstract ideas in more concrete, vivid images.

For example, in the following sentence, the author uses the verb "echoed" in an unusual way to make a point that is perhaps more effective than if he had said literally what he meant: "The melody echoed in my mind long after the song had ended." The author does not mean literally that he continued to hear the sound of the music long after the song was over. What he means is that he remembered the tune after hearing it. The word "echoed" in this sentence suggests that the melody made such an impression on him that he could not help but remember it. This is an example of figurative language called *metaphor*, an implied comparison whereby one thing is spoken of as if it were something else.

The use of figurative language is so common both in writing and in everyday speech that most of us are often unaware when an expression is used figuratively. For example, how many times have you heard the expressions "It's raining cats and dogs" or "It takes two to tango"? These are both figurative expressions meant to make a point but not intended to be taken literally.

To understand figurative expressions, you must first recognize which words are being used figuratively and are not meant to be taken literally. Then you must try to see the quality that the writer is trying to indicate by using the comparison or reference. Finally, you must infer what the figurative expression means in the context of the sentence. For example, if you read that "Susan walked into the oven called Room 1372," you should recognize that the word "oven" is being used figuratively. Since the word "oven" suggests great heat, and since a room—perhaps a classroom—is mentioned, you would be safe to interpret this sentence to mean that "Susan walked into a very hot Room 1372." It is thus necessary for you to understand figurative expressions in order to grasp and appreciate the frequent use authors make of imaginative language in their attempts to communicate ideas and experiences.

There are many types of figurative language that you regularly encounter, but the most frequently used are *similes, metaphors, hyperboles, personification, symbolism,* and *irony.*

6d   Simile

A simile is a figurative expression that directly compares two unlike things that have some quality in common. A simile uses the words "like" or "as" to indicate the comparison. For example, in the following sentence, notice the use of a simile to describe a person's cheeks.

> On this cold winter morning, your cheeks are **like** ripe tomatoes.

In this sentence, someone's cheeks are apparently flushed from the cold and are being compared to the red color of ripe tomatoes.

Read the following example of a simile used in an attempt to make a point about an abstraction by comparing it to something concrete.

> After a month of walking the ancient road to Santiago, Spain, a pilgrim loses his mind—not in the psychiatric sense, but **like an obsolete appliance.**
>
> Jack Hitt, "How a Pilgrim Progresses."

Here the author compares his mind to "an obsolete appliance." What he seems to be suggesting is that after walking for an entire month on a pilgrimage, he has no use for his intellectual mind. In fact, the author goes on in the article from which this sentence has been taken to explain his simile by saying, "It's useless and unnecessary, but should its function ever be needed again, you can always retrieve it."

Now read a fairly long sentence in which an author uses two similes to describe something she has observed in the Florida Everglades.

> The live oaks, **like** dim giants crowded and choked by a thrusting forest of younger hardwoods, made that great Miami hammock, the largest tropical jungle on the North American mainland, which spread south of the Miami River **like a dark cloud** along that crumbling, spring-fed ledge of rock.
>
> Marjory Stoneman Douglas, The Everglades: River of Grass.

First the author compares the live oaks to "dim giants," apparently referring to their subdued color and their huge size. She then compares the Miami hammock to a "dark cloud," suggesting that it is covered by thick vegetation that makes it appear as a mass.

6e   Metaphor

Like a simile, a metaphor also compares two unlike things that share some common quality. However, when a metaphor is used, there are no words such as "like" or "as" that suggest the comparison. In a metaphor, the comparison is implied, and two unlike things are spoken of as if they were actually the same. Notice in the following sentence how a metaphor is used to express an idea.

> In our progress toward equality of opportunity, the potholes of racial inequity will not go away. We must fix them, rather than simply drive around them.

Here the author compares racial inequality to potholes in a road, suggesting a constant reminder of neglect and potential danger. He then goes on to say that these "potholes" must be fixed rather than avoided, suggesting that racial inequity must be dealt with rather than ignored.

Read the following example of an author's use of a metaphor to describe falling rain and to create a certain mood.

There were storms to the south and masses of clouds that moved slowly along the horizon with their <u>long dark tendrils trailing</u> in the rain.

Cormac McCarthy, All The Pretty Horses.

In this sentence, the author speaks of the rain seen falling from clouds at a distance as "long dark tendrils." The word "tendrils" is used metaphorically and literally refers to the long, threadlike parts of a climbing plant such as a grape used to attach itself to a fence or a tree for support. This metaphor creates an image that is recognizable by anyone who has ever seen rain falling as long streams from a dark cloudy sky, as if they were the tendrils of a huge plant trailing behind it as it moved across the sky.

Now, notice how in the following passage an author attempts to communicate his perception of America through the use of metaphors.

In order to show you America I would have to take you out. I would take you to <u>the restaurant</u>—OPEN 24 HOURS—alongside a freeway, any freeway in the U.S.A. The waitress is a blond or a redhead—not the same color as her last job. She is divorced. Her eyebrows are jet-black <u>migraines</u> painted on, or relaxed clownish <u>domes</u> of cinnamon brown. <u>Morning</u> and <u>the bloom of youth</u> are painted on her cheeks. She is at once antimaternal—the kind of woman you're not supposed to know—and supramatenal, the nurturer of lost boys.

She is the <u>priestess</u> of the short order, <u>curator</u> of the apple pie. She <u>administers</u> all the consolation of America. She has no illusions. She knows the score; she hands you <u>the Bill of Rights</u> printed on plastic, decorated with an <u>heraldic</u> tumble of French fries and drumsticks and steam.

Your table may yet be littered with the bitten toast and spilled coffee and a dollar tip. Now you will see the greatness of America. As one complete gesture, the waitress pockets the tip, stacks dishes along one strong forearm, produces a damp rag soaked in <u>lethe</u> water, which she then passes over the Formica.

There! With that one swipe of the rag, the past has been obliterated. The Formica gleams like new. You can order anything you want.

Richard Rodriguez, Days of Obligation.

The author here compares America to a roadside restaurant. He describes the waitress with contradictory cosmetic adornment in "migraine" eyebrows, "domes" of hair, with "morning" and "bloom of youth" cheeks. This apparently shows characteristics that are both threatening and inviting, suggesting perhaps that America offers both something "you're not supposed to know" and a nurturing shelter. By describing the waitress, who represents America as a "nurturer of lost boys," the author reminds us of the promise engraved on the Statue of Liberty: "Give me your tired, your poor, your huddled masses yearning to be free." Then by describing the waitress as a "priestess" and a "curator" and as one who "administers" a "Bill of Rights" menu, he seems to suggest that she represents the essence of what America itself offers—an opportunity to erase the past with "one swipe of the rag" as she cleans off the table, ready to start over for someone else. Also, the reference to "damp rag soaked in lethe water" that the waitress used to clean off the table is metaphorical. The adjective "lethe" is a reference to "Lethe," the river of forgetfulness in Greek mythology, suggesting a clean sweep, a new beginning free from the past. It seems that Rodriguez sees America as a place of impermanence where there is the constant opportunity to start over and begin anew, a place where "You can order anything you want." This is communicated almost entirely through metaphors, but is communicated quite effectively.

6f Hyperbole

Sometimes writers use exaggeration to emphasize a point or to have some desired effect. When this is done through hyperbole (pronounced "hi-per'-bol-ee"), or overstatement, the author is relying on the reader's being able to understand that there is indeed a contrast between what is said and what is actually the case. A hyperbole is a statement that seems stronger or more extravagant than the situation calls for. Consider the following example in which a British writer comments on his visit to the American Midwest.

> Out in the Midwest, the word "Johnson" is constantly on my case. Everyone is called Johnson. I am reminded of the old loggers' song quoted by Kurt Vonnegut:
>
> My name is Yon Yonson
> I come from Wisconsin. . . .
>
> Everyone is called Johnson. And everything is called Johnson. Everywhere is called Johnson: streets, creeks, forts, bridges."
>
> Martin Amis, "Buy My Book, Please."

This author doesn't mean that everyone and everything in the Midwestern states are literally named Johnson. There may indeed be many people and places with this name, but the author is obviously exaggerating to make a point. He seems to suggest that he has noticed a certain sameness in the Midwest, with what he feels are apparently people and places with distinctive Scandinavian characteristics. In any event, the author is using hyperbole to make his rather humorous point.

6g Personification

Personification is a figurative use of language that attributes human characteristics to nonhuman things or concepts. When an object, animal, or idea is given human qualities or attributes, personification is being used. Authors use personification to allow readers to understand many experiences in human terms that would otherwise be more abstract.

Read the following example of personification in which an author writes of a habit as if it could perform a willful action.

> The many nights I stayed up late while on vacation finally <u>caught up with</u> me when I had to return to work.

In this sentence, the habit of staying up late at night is mentioned as having "caught up with" the author, as if it were an actual pursuer chasing after him. The author suggests that he is experiencing the consequences of suddenly having to change schedules from what he would prefer to what his job required.

Now, notice the following use of personification by an author who is herself an autistic woman as she describes an incident from her childhood.

> Carol's mother got a washcloth and washed my face and hands and legs. There I was. All brand-new. She placed a drink in front of me. I looked at it, waiting to be told what to do. "You can drink it," said the voice. It was a sentence of words, a statement. I looked at the glass and at the mother and at the girl. The girl, sitting across the table, lifted her glass and drank. I was her mirror. I copied her.
> "Where does she live?" said the voice.
> "I don't know. I found her in the park," said another voice.
> "I think you had better take her back there," said the mother.

<u>Fear came and took me away</u>. I stopped being there.

Carol took me by the hand. She led me back to the park. My eyes, like a camera, captured the moment. She lived in another world within that house of hers. I wanted so much to be a part of it. I glared at her—betrayed. <u>The world was throwing me out</u>.

Donna Williams, Nobody Nowhere.

By stating that "Fear came and took me away," the author is personifying the emotion of fear as a way to suggest her lack of control. At the end of the passage, she states that she felt "The world was throwing me out," meaning that she felt alienated and rejected, not just by the people she had just met, but by life itself. Here the author personifies the world, writing of it as if it were actually able to deliberately cast her out.

Next, notice two examples of personification by an author who is discussing the changes in behavior brought about by fear of the AIDS virus.

Fear of sexuality is the new, disease-sponsored register of the universe of fear in which everyone now lives. Cancerphobia <u>taught us</u> the fear of a polluting environment; now we have the fear of polluting people that AIDS anxiety inevitably communicates. Fear of the Communion cup, fear of surgery: fear of contaminated blood, whether Christ's blood or your neighbor's. Life—blood, sexual fluids—is itself <u>the bearer</u> of contamination."

Susan Sontag, AIDS and Its Metaphors.

The author first mentions cancerphobia (the fear of cancer) as if cancer itself has "taught us" to be afraid of the environment. What she actually means is that we have become afraid of cancer-causing agents in the environment. She then ends by describing life as "the bearer of contamination," as if life itself willfully transmits contaminants to us through bodily fluids. Here the author is pointing out the irony that life-giving bodily fluids can contain the AIDS virus.

6h   Symbolism

Another common use of figurative language involves symbolism, which involves one thing being used to represent something else. Symbolism usually involves the use of recognizable images that are understood to stand for something else. Often a symbol will represent another thing that is related to it or that is a part of it.

Like Rodriguez's "restaurant," sometimes a symbol may be similar to a metaphor in that one thing is spoken of as if it were another thing in order to clarify the first through an imaginative comparison. The difference is that in metaphor, the two things compared are dissimilar except for some common characteristic; whereas in symbolism the relationship between the two things is that one thing in some way epitomizes, encapsulates, or represents the other. In this sense, Rodriguez felt that a roadside restaurant symbolizes America in its informality, its temporariness, and its opportunity. Symbolism thus involves the use of one thing to represent or stand for something else.

There are many ways writers use symbolism, all of which involve one thing being used to represent or symbolize another. Read the following sentence in which a common example of symbolism is used.

> There seems to be a general opinion among voters that <u>Washington</u> is out of touch with the real needs of real people.

Here the author uses "Washington" symbolically to represent not the city itself but the federal government that is located there. In this case, a place—Washington—is used to represent an institution—the federal government.

Next, notice how an author uses several examples of figurative language, including symbolism, in a passage about two football quarterbacks.

> The <u>lord of the rings</u>, Joe Montana, is a four-time champion because his 49ers gave him champion colleagues. Sure, Joe is <u>Canton quality</u> even without <u>rings</u>. But given his <u>supporting cast</u>, he was <u>passenger</u> as much as <u>pilot</u> on that Super streak.
>
> Meanwhile, the lord of the records has mostly toiled amid mediocrity in Miami, making contenders of also-rans through sheer, singular will. Marino is <u>Laurence Olivier in a community-theater production</u>.
>
> Greg Cote, "Dan's No. 1."

By referring to "rings" in the first paragraph, the author is using the victory rings received by the Super Bowl champions to represent Montana's Super Bowl victories. By referring to Montana as "Canton quality," the author is using the city of Canton, Ohio to represent the football Hall of Fame that is located in that city. Then the author uses several metaphors. The words "passenger" and "pilot" are used to suggest that the success of Montana's teams was as much a result of his great teammates as his own ability. In the second paragraph, the author indicates that he feels Dan Marino is the better of the two quarterbacks by metaphorically comparing him (as a world-class player on a second-class team) to the great British actor Sir Laurence Olivier performing in an amateur production.

Now read an example of an author using a number of symbolic expressions, as well as similes and metaphors, in an attempt to communicate his view of the Spanish conquest of the Americas.

> Spain cannot be blamed for the crassness of the discoverers. They moved out across the seas stirred by instincts, ancient beyond thought as <u>the depths</u> they were crossing, which they obeyed <u>under the names</u> of King or Christ or whatever it might be, while they watched the recreative New unfolding itself miraculously before them, <u>deafened and blinded</u>. Steering beyond familiar <u>horizons</u> they were driven to seek perhaps self-justification for victorious wars against Arab and Moor; but these things are the <u>surface</u> only. At <u>the back</u>, as it remains, it was the evil of the whole world; it was the perennial disappointment which follows, <u>like smoke</u>, the <u>bursting</u> of ideas. It was the spirit of malice which underlies men's lives and against which nothing offers resistance. And bitter as the thought may be that Tenochtitlan, the barbaric city, its people, its genius wherever found should have been <u>crushed out</u> because of <u>the awkward names</u> men give their emptiness, yet it was no man's fault. It was the force of the pack <u>whom the dead drive</u>. Cortez was neither malicious, stupid nor blind, but a conqueror like other conquerors. Courageous almost beyond precedent, tactful, resourceful in misfortune, he was a man of genius superbly suited to his task. <u>What his hand touched went down</u> in spite of him. He was one among the rest.
>
> William Carlos Williams *In the American Grain.*

This passage is filled with figurative language, including several examples of symbolism. The author begins by using a reference to an attribute of the Atlantic Ocean, "the depths," to represent the ocean itself that the explorers crossed. He then says that the explorers traveled "under the names" of "King or Christ" to mean that they felt or actually had the approval of these authorities. By describing the voyagers as "deafened and blinded," the author does not mean that they were literally deaf and blind but is using metaphors to suggest their ignorance. Then the word "horizons" is used to represent the limits of understanding and knowledge that the explorers felt "driven" or compelled to go beyond.

The author then suggests that behind this "surface" or apparent motivation lies a more fundamental driving force "at the back"—"the evil of the whole world" or a human potential for destruction. Words such as "surface" or "back" are quite commonly used to refer to a superficial level and an underlying cause, but they are metaphors here in the sense that their meanings derive from common understandings of what they mean in a physical sense—an object's surface and rear. The author then uses a simile—"like smoke"—to suggest the disappointing results that he feels inevitably follow "the bursting of ideas," referring metaphorically to the new ideas about the world that were being introduced at that time, in the same way that smoke inevitably follows fire.

Williams then describes how he feels the Aztec capital of Tenochtitlan was destroyed, "crushed out" by Cortez and his band who were driven by "the awkward names men give their emptiness," or by the way they justified the restless drive to conquer that they felt but did not really understand. "Crushed" is used here metaphorically to mean destroyed, not literally smashed; and "awkward names" symbolizes an explanation or rationalization, in the same way that a name represents a person. However, the author does not blame the conquistadors, whom he feels were merely acting out ambitions inherited from their ancestors and that the people of their time also felt, which the author refers to metaphorically as "the pack whom the dead drive." The author ends by referring to Cortez's conquest of the Aztecs as "What his hand touched"—his "hand" symbolizing his conquering army—"went down" or was defeated as an inevitable result of historical forces.

6i Irony

In Chapter 5 we discussed ironic tone, which authors sometimes use to show that what has occurred is the opposite of what one would hope for or expect. Irony also refers to the use of words whose literal meanings are opposite to what is really meant. Authors often use irony in order to emphasize a point through mild-sounding words that indirectly reflect strong feeling.

When the author's intention is to criticize or mock through ironic humor, it is a type of irony called *sarcasm*. Read the following example of an author using irony in a sarcastic way.

One of the rock group Pink Floyd's many contributions to the lowering of American culture to sewer level was a "<u>song</u>" called "Another Brick in the Wall." One of the song's lines was, "We don't need no education." <u>It should be the national anthem of modern American public education</u>, and a reminder of what that education has produced.

Cal Thomas, The Things That Matter Most.

This author is not too happy with the state of American education. He expresses this opinion by sarcastically suggesting that "Another Brick in the Wall," Pink Floyd's antischool song, "should be the national anthem of modern American public education." He is certainly not suggesting that this song should actually be adopted by school systems across the country. What he really means is that because of the poor quality of "what that education has produced," American education deserves no more respect than this song shows. Also, by using quotation marks around the word "song," the author suggests that this is a song only technically and not in any aesthetic sense. This also is a use of irony.

Now, read the next passage, in which an author uses irony to express how he feels about constructing buildings near airports.

The new trend in commercial real estate is to construct tall buildings as close to airports as possible. Washington's National Airport is <u>a perfect example of this imaginative way</u> of using what were once <u>vast wastelands of air space</u>.

Just across the Potomac River, in the small town of Rosslyn, is a silver tower reaching up to the sky; <u>a beacon of welcome</u> to all pilots attempting to land and take off from one of the busiest terminals in the country. A twin building is now going up next to it so that soon there will be two towers instead of one <u>to greet</u> passengers arriving in Washington.

Art Buchwald, "You <u>Can</u> Fool All of the People All the Time."

In this passage, the author uses the example of a building erected near the National Airport to illustrate a recent real estate trend. Though he refers to the building near the airport as "a perfect example of this imaginative way" to use the "vast wastelands of air space" presently lying vacant near the airport, he wants us to know that he really feels that it is quite foolish and even dangerous. In the second paragraph, he calls this building "a beacon of welcome" to pilots and the plan to build another as a way "to greet" passengers to Washington, but he is really suggesting that tall buildings pose a danger to incoming planes and should not be built so near to airports. His use of irony is clearly a sarcastic attempt to show his disapproval.

Finally, read the following passage in which an author comments on what he seems to feel is a prevailing American attitude toward the wilderness.

> In the basin above the cirque I passed shallow lakes, emerald green when viewed from the trail, turquoise blue when seen from above. Cascades tumbled through gorges in the rock, disappearing beneath the casual wreckage of the mountains to emerge as flashing brooks at the head of the lakes. Almost everything in sight was stone or water or vapor, as in the beginning, except for the miniature pastures of grass and turf—<u>like putting greens</u>—where the pikas make their living. The mountain glittered under the sun with that harsh perfection characteristic of God's early work. Almost too perfect; <u>I should have brought a few beer cans to throw around, give the place a natural look.</u>
>
> Edward Abbey, *The Journey Home.*

The author of this passage begins with a description of a basin on a mountain. However, the comparison of the pastures to "putting greens" seems inconsistent with the natural images created in the first part of the paragraph. Then at the end, the statement that he "should have brought a few beer cans to throw around, give the place a natural look" seems out of character with the person who had written the pervious sentences. However, the author has a point he wants to make about Americans, himself apparently included, and what they seem to leave in their wake—"a few beer cans." If that is a "natural look," it is only natural for people with no awareness of their surroundings. Perhaps this is the author's point, made through the use of irony.

Chapter Review

Being able to recognize the emotional or suggestive meanings of certain words—their connotations—is important in understanding an author's meaning, especially when such words have been carefully chosen for their effects. In addition, readers must be familiar with commonly used figurative expressions, or idioms, that are used in a language to communicate specific ideas in vivid ways. Authors also often create original figurative language to express points, clarify ideas, or enhances meanings through concrete, vivid images. Understanding these imaginative and creative uses of language makes reading much more enjoyable and meaningful.

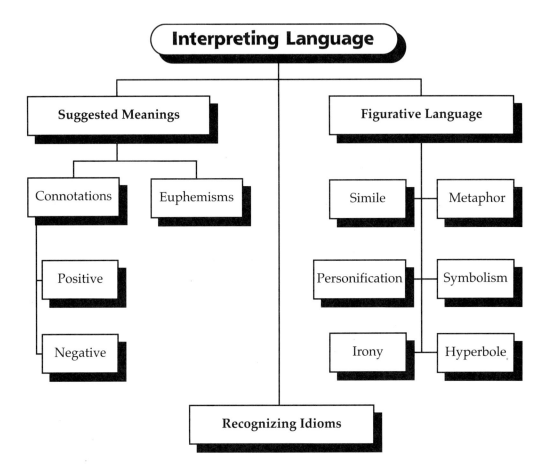

Reading Literature

The word "literature" is perhaps as vague a term as you will encounter in this book, not only because it has several meanings, but also because it means different things to different people. In its broadest use, literature includes virtually everything that has ever been written, from William Shakespeare's plays to Tank Girl comic books. In a narrower sense, literature refers to the written works in a specific subject area, such as psychology or biology, or from a certain culture or nationality, such as French or Chinese literature. In its narrowest sense, and in the sense that the word is probably used in your English classes, literature refers to what in French means "beautiful writing." In this way, literature is distinguished from textbooks, journalism, scholarly writing, and technical writing.

Literature or *literary* writing may thus be defined as that written expression dealing with human experience in finely crafted works with artistic quality. Most of the literature discussed in this chapter includes examples of *prose*—language used in continuous sentences and paragraphs. In addition, *poetry* will also be discussed as a unique form of literary expression involving more condensed language with words chosen for their sound and suggestive power. This chapter will first identify what are generally considered the four main types of writing, and will then discuss some of the most common types of literature, including literary nonfiction, fiction, and poetry.

Recognizing the Modes of Expression

As you read in Chapter 5, authors write for many reasons. Authors may try to describe a situation or an event, explain a topic or situation, or convince readers to accept a certain opinion or perspective. These purposes are closely related to what are commonly called the four modes of expression, the modes of discourse, or the rhetorical modes: narration, description, exposition, and persuasion.

These four modes, or forms of writing, are usually applied to nonfiction. However, narrative and description are also important characteristics of fiction, as you will see later in this chapter. You will often read written pieces that combine some or all of these four modes, and you will also frequently see writing with one of them as its dominant characteristic.

7a   Exposition

Exposition is writing intended to inform, explain, or instruct. *Expository* writing includes everything from a course syllabus to a textbook, and is thus the most common type of writing you will encounter in college courses. Nearly all of the examples you have read in the first six chapters of this book represent examples of exposition. Also, the descriptions of the different author's purposes in Chapter 5 are all examples of the different kinds of expository writing. For this reason, no more will be said about exposition here.

7b   Persuasion and Argumentation

In Chapter 5, *persuasive writing* was defined as all the attempts writers make to influence readers' beliefs or actions concerning some idea or issue. Traditionally, the art of persuasion has been known as rhetoric, described by the Greek philosopher Aristotle as discourse involving logical, ethical, and emotional appeals made by public speakers to their audiences. This classical rhetoric involved highly structured arguments with very specific methods of organization and presentation designed to convince an audience that a certain conclusion or point of view was logical and acceptable. More recent educators and others have adapted this rhetoric to the needs of modern written composition, adding to it and simplifying it into what is now known as *argumentation.* Since Chapters 8–10 will consider both persuasion and argumentation in detail, this chapter will merely mention them as representing one of the four modes of expression.

7c   Description

Description is commonly used in both fiction and nonfiction and involves an author showing what something or someone looks like or what a situation or experience feels like. The purpose of description is to create a sensory image or a mental picture with words. An author using description relies on a lot of details that appeal to the reader's senses—how things look, sound, taste, smell, or feel. Description attempts to portray places, people, and situations in enough vivid detail so readers can visualize or picture in their minds what is being described.

Whereas both expository and persuasive writing always have a main idea or thesis that the author wants the reader to understand or accept, description often has no such focus. However, a descriptive passage is usually meant to make a definite impression on the reader, and in that sense may sometimes have an implied point. In addition, description may either involve an *objective* discussion of how something or someone *appears,* or it may be more *subjective* and show how the author *feels* about what he or she is describing. For example, read the following passage in which a woman describes the walks home she used to take as a little girl with her grandfather. Consider as you read the effect that this description has on you by the mood or feeling expressed in the detail.

> I take Abuelito's hand, fat and dimpled in the center like a valentine, and we walk past the basilica, where each Sunday the Abuela lights the candles for the soul of Abuelito. Past the very same spot where long ago Juan Diego brought down the *cerro* the miracle that has drawn everyone, except my Abuelito, on their knees, down the avenue one block past the bright lights of the *santeria* of Señor Guzman who is still at work at his sewing machine, past the candy store where I buy my milk-and-raisin gelatins, past La Providencia *tortilleria* where every afternoon Luz Maria and I are sent for the basket of lunchtime tortillas, past the house of the widow Marquez whose husband died last winter of a tumor the size of her little white fist, past La Muneca's mother watering her famous dahlias with a pink rubber hose and a skinny string of water, to the house on La Fortuna, number 12, that has always been our house. Green iron gates that arabesque and scroll like the initials of my name, familiar whine and clang, familiar lacework of ivy growing over and between except for one small clean square for the hand of the postman whose face I have never seen, up the twenty-two steps we count out loud together . . . .
>
> Sandra Cisneros, "Tepeyac."

In this description, the author is remembering a past that seems to hold fond memories for her. In describing the various sensations on this walk home, the author is remembering the things that left a lasting impression on her: the feel of her grandfather's hand, the places they pass that she remembers for some meaningful reason, the woman watering her flowers, the iron gates to their house with the scrollwork that reminds her of her own name and that makes a "familiar whine and clang" sound as it is opened with the spot worn through the ivy where that mailman grasped it day after day, and finally the twenty-two steps that they counted together as they climbed.

7d   Narration

In Chapter 4, you read about a chronological pattern of organization. Narration is similar to this in that it also involves describing a series of events. However, a *narrative* more specifically refers to the relating of events in the form of a story, which could be either taken from real life (nonfiction) or from an author's imagination (fiction). Also, a narrative often has some purpose other than to merely tell a tale. It often implies some larger point or theme that the particular story is meant to illustrate or portray.

Similar to the way life is experienced as a series of events in time, a written narrative tells a story. However, because of the impossibility of depicting every single detail of life in writing, a narrative is selective and only includes what the author feels are the most significant events and details. This is how an author makes a point in a narrative, by selecting the events for a story that illustrate a certain point or that lead to a specific outcome. For example, read the following passage from a novel by Toni Morrison that describes an encounter between a man and a woman.

> She opened the heavy door and saw him standing on the other side of the screen door with two quarts of milk tucked into his arms like marble statues. He smiled and said, "I been lookin' all over for you."
>
> "Why?" she asked.
>
> "To give you these," and he nodded toward one of the quarts of milk.
>
> "I don't like milk," she said.
>
> "But you like bottles don't you?" He held one up. "Ain't that pretty?"
>
> And indeed it was. Hanging from his fingers, framed by a silk blue sky, it looked precious and clean and permanent. She had the distinct impression that he had done something dangerous to get them.
>
> Sula ran her fingernails over the screen thoughtfully for a second and then, laughing, she opened the screen door.
>
> Ajax came in and headed straight for the kitchen. Sula followed slowly. By the time she got to the door he had undone the complicated wire cap and was letting the cold milk run into his mouth.
>
> Sula watched him—or rather the rhythm in his throat—with growing interest. When he had had enough, he poured the rest into the sink, rinsed the bottle out and presented it to her. She took the bottle with one hand and his wrist with the other and pulled him into the pantry.
>
> Toni Morrison, *Sula.*

In one sense, this is simply a narrative description of an experience between a man and a woman. However, Sula's acceptance of Ajax's gift of the empty bottle that she suspects he may have acquired by doing "something dangerous" could have symbolic significance. This detail could represent a tendency for Sula to settle for relationships devoid of love but with potentially tragic consequences. So this narrative not only tells a story, but also suggests what it could mean.

Reading Literary Nonfiction

Nonfiction is writing that portrays actual events, persons, or issues. Most nonfiction is perhaps not what one would usually describe as literary, or writing characterized by imaginative or creative style. Nevertheless, you will encounter imaginative or literary nonfiction in books and magazines, as well as in anthologies for English composition courses. Sometimes historical or biographical works are considered literary if the quality of the writing and the influence they have seem to merit it. Also, published diaries or personal journals are sometimes considered literary. Two types of literary nonfiction that will be discussed here include the essay and autobiography. While not all writing of these types is considered literary, these are perhaps the most common forms of literary nonfiction.

7e   The Essay

An essay is a composition that discusses a specific topic. While some essays are book-length, most are relatively short, consisting of anywhere from a few paragraphs to a few pages. An essay usually revolves around a thesis statement—a main point or controlling idea—and may be either expository or persuasive in purpose or may be primarily descriptive or narrative. As opposed to other types of nonfiction writing, a *literary essay* is one that focuses more on human values, ideas, or experiences, rather than on the communication of information. In a literary essay, an author often interprets his or her experiences in an attempt to express cultural, ethical, philosophical, or spiritual meaning and is likely to rely on narration and description as the main modes of expression.

One type of essay that is often considered literary is known as *criticism*, which is the interpretation or evaluation of a work of writing, film, theater, music, or art. Examples frequently appear in newspapers, magazines, and journals and include reviews of books, movies, concerts, albums, and gallery or museum exhibits. There are also many examples of book-length criticisms of the work of authors or other artists. In a critical essay, the author wants to discuss an artistic subject, usually including both positive and negative comments.

When reading a literary essay, try to identify the main point the author is making about the subject under discussion. Also, pay close attention to the author's choice of words, which may reflect a certain feeling that the author wants to communicate. The writer is probably trying to make a certain impression on you through all the details, descriptions, or reflections. So while reading, you want to ask the questions, "What is the author trying to say?" and "What feeling am I expected to have?" With these questions in mind, read the following excerpt from an essay by Richard Rodriguez about American culture based on his observations during his travels around the country.

> We are without a sense of ourselves entire. In the classrooms of America, I heard no term more often in recent weeks than multiculturalism. All over America, in identical hotels, there are weekend conferences for business executives on multiculturalism. The same experts fly from one city to the next to say the same thing: We live in a multicultural America.
>
> What any immigrant kid could tell you for free, on the other hand, is that America exists. There is a culture. There is a shared accent, a shared defiance of authority, a shared skepticism about community. There is a stance, a common impatience at the fast-food counter. Moreover, though the executives at that multicultural seminar do not want to hear it, the deepest separation between us derives not from race or ethnicity but from class. To put matters bluntly, the black executive at Pac Bell or ARCO has more in common culturally with her white colleague than she does with the gang kids in South-Central.
>
> White kids in Santa Barbara know this. They are infatuated with lower-class black style. Ghetto talk, gesture, dress. The suburban kids see in the lower-class black their opposite. As Americans, the suburban kids are infatuated with the defiance of black toughs, with their swagger. Today's rapper is the new Huck Finn. Of course, the white kids want to imitate these outsiders and challenge authority—it is a most American thing to do.
>
> Richard Rodriguez, "Slouching Toward Los Angeles."

In this passage, the author is suggesting that despite what the advocates of multiculturalism may say, theirs is an identifiable American culture characterized by "a shared accent, a shared defiance of authority, a shared skepticism about community" and "a stance, a common impatience." Rodriguez wants you to agree and to feel that there is hope. He wants you to recognize that despite the many differences often thought to divide Americans, there is much uniting us in ways that may be more obvious to "any immigrant kid" than to those of us who are often preoccupied with the differences. This is an essay in which a writer is expressing his view of America.

7f   Autobiography

One important type of literary nonfiction is autobiography. In autobiography, an author recounts events from his or her life as a way to give meaning to personal experience and to communicate to readers how a life has fit into the culture of the time. Autobiographies are thus usually written in narrative form, with authors selecting events and details that they feel are most essential and can create an image of themselves and of the events in which they have participated. Detailed descriptions often play an important part in autobiographies so readers can more easily visualize the places, people, and events related, and perhaps see reflections of their own lives in the experiences portrayed by the author.

When reading autobiographical writing, try to be aware of the meaning behind the events described by asking, "What point is the author trying to make?" Sometimes an author will alternate the portrayal of events with commentaries about these events. These commentaries, or explanations, can provide important clues as to the meaning the author gives to his or her experiences. For this reason, pay careful attention to explanatory comments. Read the following example of autobiographical writing in which an author remembers an incident from her childhood when she snuck out of her house early one morning and went to school to escape the painfully chaotic and confusing situation at home.

"Hey there, young lady. Did you forget to go home last night?" It was Mr. Grunderson, our janitor, whom we all loved. He was nice and he was funny and he was old with white hair, thick glasses and an unbelievable number of keys. I could hear them jingling as he walked across the playfield. I felt incredibly happy to see him.

He let me push his wheeled garbage can between the different portables as he unlocked each room. He let me turn on the lights and raise the window shades and I saw my school come slowly to life. I saw Mrs. Dolman, our school secretary, walk into the office without her orange lipstick on yet. She waved.

I saw the fifth-grade teacher, Mr. Cunningham, walking under the breezeway eating a hard roll. He waved.

And I saw my teacher, Mrs. Claire LeSane, walking toward us in a red coat and calling my name in a very happy and surprised way, and suddenly my throat got tight and my eyes stung and I ran toward her crying. It was something that surprised both of us.

It's only thinking about it now, 28 years later, that I realize I was crying from relief. I was with my teacher, and in a while I was going to sit at my desk, with my crayons and pencils and books and classmates all around me, and for the next six hours I was going to enjoy a thoroughly secure, warm and stable world. It was a world I relied on. Without it, I don't know where I would have gone that morning.

Lynda Barry, "The Sanctuary of School."

In this excerpt from an autobiographical essay, the author shows the significance that school had for her. She first narrates what happened when she went to school early one morning and then explains in the last paragraph how school was such a comforting place for her, an important contrast to what it was like at home. In this essay, the author also makes the broader point that school is a vitally important place, representing for many children the only place where they can experience "a thoroughly secure, warm and stable world."

Reading Fiction

Stories that come from an author's imagination rather than from facts or actual people or events are called fiction. Fiction takes many forms, including the novel, short story, fable, film, and drama. There are also many types of fictional stories, including science fiction, historical fiction, horror stories, comedies, mysteries, and tragedies.

Regardless of the form or type, fiction usually relies on narrative, description, and dialogue. While a film or play is very similar in its structure to a novel or short story, the written script for a play or a film is composed primarily of dialogue—the exact words to be spoken by the characters—with short descriptions inserted concerning the details of the action. On the other hand, because a novel or a short story is meant to be read rather than viewed, it typically incorporates much more description and narrative story-telling, along with the dialogue between characters.

Since most of the fiction you are likely to read will be either novels or short stories, this discussion will focus on these two forms. A *novel* is a book-length fictional narrative, and a *short story* is a shorter fictional narrative, usually just a few pages long.

7g The Elements of Fiction

Both short stories and novels share certain basic elements or features. When reading fiction, the *plot*, or the story itself, is the most important element, but it is also important to recognize other features in order to fully understand and appreciate what an author has created. Read the following descriptions of the different features of fictional narratives. Then read the short story that follows these descriptions, trying as you do to identify the different elements of the story.

Setting   The setting for a story includes the time, place, and circumstances in which it happens. The importance of the setting varies from story to story and may depend on the extent to which the environment affects the characters or events or whether it represents some symbolic idea. Description is thus very important in informing readers of the setting, which may include detailed descriptions of the time period, the physical or geographical location, or the cultural, economic, or social situation in which the characters live.

Characters   The characters are the people, or in some cases animals, depicted in the story. Authors may sometimes provide detailed descriptions of characters, or may allow readers to infer a character's personality from what he or she does and says in the story. Some characters are more important to a story than others. Minor characters may receive little description and may seem one-dimensional and superficial. Other more important characters may seem more complex and may even change and grow during the course of a story. The main character in a story is called the *protagonist,* and an opponent or character causing the conflict is known as an *antagonist.*

Plot   The plot is the main story line, or the events that take place, and the meaning that these events have. It is a sequence of events that occurs within a story and always involves the resolution of some conflict, opposition, struggle, or mystery. A plot is thus more than a chronological sequence of events but also includes the purpose and meaning behind these events. The plot is both what happens and why.

The conflict in a story may take one of many forms. It may involve a main character against some other character, such as a wife trying to escape a violent husband; it may involve a main character versus a group, such as a detective trying to investigate a crime; it may involve a character in conflict with himself, such as a man struggling to overcome self-doubt; or a plot may involve a main character against some external force, such as a foreign student adjusting to American culture.

A plot usually follows a fairly typical sequence: The story begins by introducing the scene or situation and the characters; some problem or complication then arises; suspense builds as the problem or conflict unfolds (as the "plot thickens"); near the end of the story, a peak or climax is reached when the conflict is resolved, the problem solved, or when some turning point is reached; and finally a concluding event or scene ends the story, often with a final realization or understanding. Of course, not all stories follow this sequence. Indeed, some stories seem more a series of descriptive scenes than an actual narrative. However, a plot is usually the central element in a story.

Point of View   The point of view of a story is the perspective from which it is told. The *narrator*, the person supposed to be telling the story, often plays a very important role. The narrator may be what is called *omniscient*, or all-knowing, and tell the story from the perspective of a witness to the action. The following is an excerpt from a short story that has an omniscient narrator, one who is observing but not participating in the story. Notice all the references to the character are in the third person, "he," as if the narrator were observing a scene that in reality could be seen by no one but the character.

> When he passed the barn the horses whimpered softly to him in the cold. The snow creaked under his boots and his breath smoked in the bluish light. An hour later he was crouched in the snow in the dry creekbed where he knew the wolves had been using by their tracks in the sand of the washes, by their tracks in the snow.
>
> Cormac McCarthy, *The Crossing.*

Sometimes, the narrator is a character in the story and refers to "I" or "we" throughout. When this is the case, the narrator may tell the story from a very biased or limited perspective and may sometimes actually seem to have less of an understanding of the significance of events than the reader has. Thus, the narrator of a story may not be the same as the author, but may in fact be as much of a creation as the other characters and the plot. Consider the following example from a novel in which the narrator is a character in the story. Notice how the first person "I" is used and how the narrator tells us what she believes no one else knows about her.

> No one ever understood my wild and secret ways. They used to say Lulu Lamartine was like a cat, loving no one, only purring to get what she wanted. But that's not true. I was in love with the whole world and all that lived in its rainy arms. Sometimes I'd look out on my yard and the green leaves would be glowing. I'd see the oil slick on the wing of a grackle. I'd hear the wind rushing, rolling, like the far-off sound of waterfalls. Then I'd open my mouth wide, my ears wide, my heart, and I'd let everything inside.
>
> Louise Erdrich, *Love Medicine.*

Theme The theme is the central meaning or the main point of the story. Sometimes referred to as the "moral of the story," the theme is similar to the main idea or thesis of expository or persuasive writing. In fiction, the theme is the message that is illustrated through the plot and characters in the story. In some stories, the theme is very important while in others it may be less so, especially if the story is meant primarily as entertainment.

Effect Very similar to an author's tone, as discussed in Chapter 5, the effect of a fictional work is the impression or impact it has on readers or the feeling or *mood* that the story evokes. All the elements in the story—the plot, the characters, the setting, the point of view, and the theme—contribute to the overall effect. Also, the writer's choice of words and use of figurative language contribute to the effect that a story has. An author may intend his or her story to affect readers by evoking moods such as horror, mystery, suspense, romance, amusement, beauty, sympathy, or compassion. Everything in the story thus contributes to its overall effect.

7h A Short Story

Now read the following short story by the English writer Saki (the pen name for H. H. Munro). This story takes place in a house in England around the turn of the twentieth century. As you read this story, keep in mind the meanings of a few terms that may be used in ways you are unfamiliar with. The reference to "a large French window that opened onto a lawn" refers to a pair of doors covered with panes of glass that open outward, and the word "romance" used in the final sentence means a fictitious, imaginative story. Also, the "moor" refers to open land covered with bogs or wet, swampy areas. As you read, try to identify the elements of fiction that have been described above: the setting, the characters, the plot, the point of view, the theme, and the effect.

The Open Window
by Saki

"My aunt will be down presently, Mr. Nuttel," said a very self-possessed young lady of fifteen; "in the meantime you must try and put up with me."

Framton Nuttel endeavored to say the correct something which should duly flatter the niece of the moment without unduly discounting the aunt that was to come. Privately he doubted more than ever whether these formal visits on a succession of total strangers would do much towards helping the nerve cure which he was supposed to be undergoing.

"I know how it will be," his sister had said when he was preparing to migrate to this rural retreat; "you will bury yourself down there and not speak to a living soul, and your nerves will be worse than ever from moping. I shall just give you letters of introduction to all the people I know there. Some of them, as far as I can remember, were quite nice." Framton wondered whether Mrs. Sappleton, the lady to whom he was presenting one of the letters of introduction, came into the nice division.

"Do you know many of the people round here?" asked the niece, when she judged that they had had sufficient silent communion.

"Hardly a soul," said Framton. "My sister was staying here, at the rectory, you know, some four years ago, and she gave me letters of introduction to some of the people here."

He made the last statement in a tone of distinct regret.

"Then you know practically nothing about my aunt?" pursued the self-possessed young lady.

"Only her name and address," admitted the caller. He was wondering whether Mrs. Sappleton was in the married or widowed state. An undefinable something about the room seemed to suggest masculine habitation.

"Her great tragedy happened just three years ago," said the child; "that would be since your sister's time."

"Her tragedy?" asked Framton; somehow in this restful country spot tragedies seemed out of place.

"You may wonder why we keep that window wide open on an October afternoon," said the niece, indicating a large French window that opened onto a lawn.

"It is quite warm for the time of the year," said Framton; "but has that window got anything to do with the tragedy?"

"Out through that window, three years ago to a day, her husband and her two young brothers went off for their day's shooting. They never came back. In crossing the moor to their favorite snipe-shooting ground they were all three engulfed in a treacherous piece of bog. It had been that dreadful wet summer, you know, and places that were safe in other years gave way suddenly without warning. Their bodies were never recovered. That was the dreadful part of it." Here the child's voice lost its self-possessed note and became falteringly human. "Poor aunt always thinks that they will come back some day, they and the little brown spaniel that was lost with them, and walk in at that window just as they used to do. That is why the window is kept open every evening till it is quite dusk. Poor dear aunt, she has often told me how they went out, her husband with his white waterproof coat over his arm, and Ronnie, her youngest brother, singing, 'Bertie, why do you bound?' as he always did to tease her, because she said it got on her nerves. Do you know, sometimes on still, quiet evenings like this, I almost get a creepy feeling that they will all walk in through that window—"

She broke off with a little shudder. It was a relief to Framton when the aunt bustled into the room with a whirl of apologies for being late in making her appearance.

"I hope Vera has been amusing you?" she said.

"She has been very interesting," said Framton.

"I hope you don't mind the open window," said Mrs. Sappleton briskly; "my husband and brothers will be home directly from shooting, and they always come in this way. They've been out for snipe in the marshes today, so they'll make a fine mess over my poor carpets. So like you menfolk, isn't it?" She rattled on cheerfully about the shooting and the scarcity of birds, and the prospects for duck in the winter. To Framton it was all purely horrible. He made a desperate effort to turn the talk onto a less ghastly topic; he was conscious that his hostess was giving him only a fragment of her attention, and her eyes were constantly straying past him to the open window and the lawn beyond. It was certainly an unfortunate coincidence that he should have paid his visit on this tragic anniversary.

"The doctors agree in ordering me complete rest, an absence of mental excitement, and avoidance of any violent physical exercise," announced Framton, who labored under the tolerably widespread delusion that total strangers and chance acquaintances are hungry for the least detail of one's ailments and infirmities. "On the matter of diet they are not so much in agreement," he continued.

"No?" said Mrs. Sappleton, in a voice which only replaced a yawn at the last moment. Then she suddenly brightened into alert attention—but not to what Framton was saying.

"Here they are at last!" she cried. "Just in time for tea, and don't they look as if they were muddy up to the eyes!"

Framton shivered slightly and turned towards the niece with a look intended to convey sympathetic comprehension. The child was staring out through the open window with dazed horror in her eyes. In a chill shock of nameless fear Framton swung round in his seat and looked in the same direction.

In the deepening twilight three figures were walking across the lawn towards the window; they all carried guns under their arms, and one of them was additionally burdened with a white coat hung over his shoulders. A tired brown spaniel kept close at their heels. Noiselessly they neared the house, and then a hoarse young voice chanted out of the dusk: "I said, Bertie, why do you bound?"

Framton grabbed wildly at his stick and hat; the hall door, the gravel drive, and the front gate were dimly noted stages in his headlong retreat. A cyclist coming along the road had to run into the hedge to avoid imminent collision.

"Here we are, my dear," said the bearer of the white mackintosh, coming in through the window; "fairly muddy, but most of it's dry. Who was that who bolted out as we came up?"

"A most extraordinary man, a Mr. Nuttel," said Mrs. Sappleton; "could only talk about his illnesses, and dashed off without a word of good-by or apology when you arrived. One would think he had seen a ghost."

"I expect it was the spaniel," said the niece calmly; "he told me he had a horror of dogs. He was once hunted into a cemetery somewhere on the banks of the Ganges by a pack of pariah dogs, and had to spend the night in a newly dug grave with the creatures snarling and grinning and foaming just above him. Enough to make anyone lose their nerve."

Romance at short notice was her specialty.

In this story, the protagonist is a man who has come to a house in the English countryside to recover from what seems to be emotional stress. He is engaged in conversation by a very imaginative young girl, who turns out to be the antagonist. The setting for this story is in an English house around the turn of the century. The main characters include Vera, a fifteen-year-old girl with a wickedly vivid imagination; Mr. Nuttel, whose name seems appropriate for his mental condition; Mrs. Sappleton, Vera's aunt who it turns out is not as deluded as Vera suggests; and Mr. Sappleton, who appears at the end quite alive. The plot begins with the polite conversation between Mr. Nuttel and Vera, then moves into Vera's imaginative story, building to the climax when Mrs. Sappleton's husband and brothers come home with the dog, and Mr. Nuttel runs off thinking he has seen ghosts; the conclusion of the story unfortunately contains no resolution for poor Mr. Nuttel, but ends with Vera showing again her talent for "romance," for making up fanciful tales apparently for her own pleasure. The conflict has been provided in the form of Mr. Nuttel's increasing anxiety owing to his antagonist's suggestion that his hostess, Mrs. Sappleton, is not all there.

The story is told in the third person from the perspective of an omniscient narrator. The theme of the story seems to be that one tall tale requires another, for Vera had to make up a story to explain to Mrs. and Mr. Sappleton why Mr. Nuttel ran off, in order to cover herself for having scared him with her tale about the hunting party disappearing in the moor three years previously. The author probably intended this to be an entertaining story with no more serious effect than to bring amusement to readers. If it did this for you, then the author has succeeded.

Reading Poetry

Poetry may share some of the same elements as fiction, even including plot and characters. However, poetry is unique as a form of written expression in that ideas are usually written as short lines called *verses* arranged in groups called *stanzas*. Poets also use language in very expressive and suggestive ways in order to compress ideas into powerfully compact forms. In a poem, each word is chosen very carefully for its meaning and its effect, and often for the way it sounds in relation to other words around it. Writers of prose—

language used in continuous sentences and paragraphs (all the writing that has been considered in this book so far)—often use language in similar ways, especially in descriptive passages. However, poets use evocative language and figurative expressions as their main form of communication. Also, whereas prose writing is similar in structure and wording to ordinary speech, poetry often includes words and arrangements of words that are very different from the way a person usually talks or writes. Because this use of figurative language and unusual word arrangement is so important in poetry, you may often have to read a poem more than once to fully grasp its meaning and to appreciate the poet's creation.

7i   Arrangement

One of the unique features of poetry is its form, or the arrangement of words. The form a poem takes is very different from that of prose. In poetry, ideas are presented in verses and stanzas rather than in sentences and paragraphs. Also, poets often use various patterns of rhythm and rhyme in their choice and arrangement of words.

Rhythm and Rhyme   Rhythm and rhyme are the two most common sound elements that poets use to create structure in poems. Similar to the way a regular drum beat keeps the rhythm in music, rhythm in poetry refers to the regular flow produced by the sound of carefully chosen words. This rhythm in poetry is called *meter,* which is based on the number of syllables or the number of stressed or accented syllables in a line or stanza. There are many different traditional rhythmic patterns or meters in poetry. Another common element in poetic arrangement is rhyme. Rhyme is the most commonly used method of using sound for effect in poetry. A poem rhymes if the ends of two or more lines have the same or a very similar sound. Notice both the rhythm and rhyme patterns in the following stanza from a poem about love.

> Oh, give us pleasure in the flowers today;
> And give us not to think so far away
> As the uncertain harvest; keep us here
> And simply in the spring of the year.

> Robert Frost, "A Prayer in Spring."

This is the first stanza of a poem in which Robert Frost expresses the realization that love exists in the present moment rather than in

thoughts of the future. Notice how the last words rhyme in each pair of lines. Also, notice the similar rhythm in the sound of the words in each line.

Free Verse   Though both rhythm and rhyme are certainly elements that distinguish poetry from prose and are perhaps thought of by most people as what defines poetry, not all poems follow such regular patterns. Free verse poetry is based on irregular rhythms and may or may not use rhyme at all. Now read the following three stanzas from another poem about love, this one arranged in free verse.

> By now whatever
> I see is lovely
> seems a reflection of you
>
> Before day I lie watching
> your face asleep
> on the same pillow
>
> Our breath has mingled
> for so many years
> it moves as one

W. S. Merwin, "Long Love."

This poem uses neither rhythm nor rhyme in its arrangement. Each stanza reads more like a sentence of lyrical prose than it does a poem composed of rhythm and rhyme. This is a poem nonetheless, a poem written in free verse.

7j   Content

In addition to the arrangement of words in poetry, the ideas are also expressed in unique ways. While the subject matter of poetry is often the same as with fiction or other forms of prose, poems express ideas in extremely imaginative and evocative ways. Indeed, the unique characteristics of poetry include the expression of ideas through emotions and imaginative language with powerful effects. Read the following descriptions of the elements of poetry, and then look for these things in the complete poem that follows in section 7k.

Emotion   One of the ways in which poetry is unique is in its reliance on emotional expression. Poets may describe persons, places,

and events, but above all they express the feelings that accompany personal experience.

Imagery   Poems do not use the literal language of scientists or journalists. Poets use imaginative images created by figurative uses of language to suggest human emotions, understanding, and experience. For example, rather than describing the qualities of something such as a lake, a poet might describe the effect that seeing a "rippling blue mirror" has on the imagination.

Significance   Poems tend to be about significant topics and try to interpret human experiences in ways that broaden understanding. Poets often attempt to describe experiences for which words are really inadequate. This is why poets must resort to figurative language as they attempt to express their insights.

Effect   Another important characteristic of poetry is the power that poetic expression can have. The effect of a poem may be to evoke in readers an experience of beauty, shame, pain, joy, inspiration, or peace. The condensing of experience into imaginatively constructed language frequently results in a very powerful reading experience, which is illustrated in the poem in section 7k.

7k   A Poem

The following is a complete poem written by e. e. cummings entitled "who sharpens every dull." As you read this poem, notice the patterns of rhythm and rhyme. Also notice how the author expresses an emotional reality more than a physical reality in the world he creates through the images and figurative language used in the poem. Try to understand what these figurative images mean, and allow yourself to feel the effect that these images have.

> who <u>sharpens every dull</u>
> here comes the only man
> reminding with his bell
> to disappear a sun
>
> and out of houses pour
> maids mothers widows wives
> <u>bringing</u> this visitor
> <u>their very oldest lives</u>

one pays him with a smile
another with a tear
some cannot pay at all
he never seems to care

he <u>sharpens is to am</u>
he <u>sharpens say to sing</u>
you'd almost cut your thumb
<u>so right he sharpens wrong</u>

and when <u>their lives are keen</u>
he throws the world a kiss
and slings his wheel upon
his back and off he goes

but we can hear him still
if now our sun is gone
reminding with his bell
<u>to reappear a moon</u>

e. e. cummings

Notice that the last word in every other line either rhymes or has a very similar sound. Also, the poem has a definite rhythm in that every line contains exactly six syllables or vowel sounds. Indeed, the poem almost seems like a nursery rhyme in its simplicity. However, this is more than the simple story of a man who comes to town to sharpen knives.

In what seems more an expression of emotion than of actual events, the imaginative imagery in this poem creates a dreamlike feeling of security and peace. The poem describes a man who is able to cause the sun to set and the moon to rise with the ringing of his bell and who has the ability to "sharpen" the experience of those who come to him, not leaving until "their lives are keen." This man seems to be a magical or mystical figure who has a profound effect on those who come to him. In saying that "he sharpens is to am," "he sharpens say to sing" and that "right he sharpens wrong," the poet seems to suggest that the man directs people inward from the active "is" to the introspective "am," from the literal "say" to the expressive "sing," and from what was "wrong" to what now is made "right." Indeed, this poem seems to represent a transformative meeting—if not literally with an actual person, then figuratively with one's inner self—between our "very oldest lives" and the best of what we all hope to become, the reappearance of "a moon."

Chapter Review

Literature has been defined in this chapter as writing that deals with human experience in works of finely-crafted and artistic prose, or poetry. The problem with this definition is that to consider a book, an article, a story, or a poem as finely-crafted or artistic is of course a matter of opinion. And surely not everyone, not even every English professor, agrees on what qualifies as literature. Nevertheless, this chapter has attempted to discuss literature in a general way in the hopes of clarifying what it includes.

Of the four modes of discourse, exposition and persuasion are most often used in nonfiction, but authors frequently also include narration and description for effect, especially in more literary works and in biographical writing. Fictional writing usually relies on narrative and description to tell a story involving characters in some compelling situation in which a plot develops around a central theme. Poetry may also include both a plot and characters but expresses ideas and feelings in a much more compact way, primarily through evocative language and figurative expressions. In whatever form it takes, literature represents authors' attempts to express the experience of life in all its tragedy, comedy, and profundity through the medium of language.

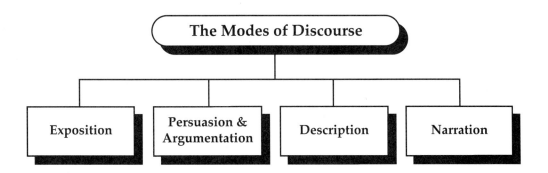

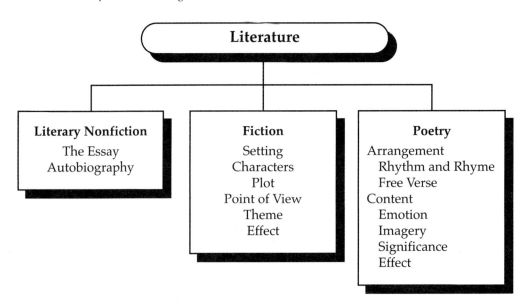

CHAPTER
8

Recognizing
Persuasive Writing

Previous chapters have considered different types of reading material, including both expository and imaginative writing, primarily in terms of understanding the ways authors organize and express their ideas. This and the following chapters will now focus more specifically on persuasive writing and look at how authors structure their attempts to convince readers to accept opinions on various topics.

In Chapter 7, persuasive writing was considered as a broad category containing two types of writing: argumentation and persuasion. Chapters 9 and 10 will focus on argumentation, the type of persuasive writing that relies on reasoned support. This chapter will deal with several things you should be aware of when reading persuasive writing in general. The chapter focuses specifically on persuasion, the type of writing that relies on emotional rather than logical appeals to convince and makes little or no real attempt to present reasonable support.

Persuasion is ever-present in a modern democratic society such as the United States, with a market economy and a social system that recognizes individual rights, freedom of the press, and opportunities for advancement based on merit and personal achievement. In an open country such as this, you are surrounded by advertising, political speeches, the news media, and a variety of printed material ranging from newsletters to textbooks, all of which compete for your attention, your loyalty, or your money.

In this context, persuasion involves attempts to convince you to buy something, to vote for someone, or to believe in something in ways that appeal to your emotions rather than to your logic. For example, when an ad for a new Mazda tells you that you should buy it because "It just feels right," it's not giving you any technical information about the performance, economy, or safety of the car. You are merely being told that owning one will make you feel good. When a certain candidate for the Senate tells you that you should vote for her because she "represents the views of the decent hard-working people of America," you are not being told specifically what she means by this or what she intends to do for those people she claims to represent. She is trying to appeal to the values of enough people to elect her to office. When a newspaper runs a front-page headline about a local sports hero who has been arrested on a drug charge, but it begins an investigative article about the Social Security system on page three, the editors may be highlighting what they think their readers will feel is most interesting and will buy the paper to read about, regardless of the relative importance of the information.

Sometimes people are not at all troubled by such purely emotional appeals, especially when the view presented is one that they already agree with or when the appeal involves something that they desire. Nevertheless, critical readers are willing to make the effort to both analyze and evaluate what they read and are able to judge the effectiveness of a persuasive attempt based on rational rather than prejudiced criteria. Toward this end, you will now examine some things that are important to recognize when reading persuasive attempts: distinguishing between facts and opinions, recognizing persuasive language and author's bias, and identifying different types of fallacies.

Distinguishing between Facts and Opinions

It is important when reading persuasive writing to be able to tell the difference between facts and opinions. As you will see in Chapter 9, the main point of an argument is, by its very nature, an author's opinion. However, the support provided to make it convincing is strengthened when facts are presented as evidence rather than opinions alone. Thus, being able to distinguish between a fact and an opinion is especially important when you are considering the evidence presented in support of a point. Indeed, you will sometimes see examples of writers deliberately attempting to mislead by misrepresenting opinions as factual statements, especially when facts are lacking to support their point.

When considering facts and opinions as types of support, think of a *fact* as something that can be objectively verified or proven in some way. In order for a statement to be considered a fact, you should be able to imagine some practical way to check it out to see if it is true; this verification must be through some form of *objective* evidence, which could include personal observation, research, historical records, or scientific documents. Think of an *opinion* then as something that is *subjective* and makes some value statement or expresses a view toward something that cannot be verified or proven in any way.

Sometimes the line between an objective factual statement and a subjective opinion is a thin one. This is often the case when considering *informed judgments*. For example, if a doctor diagnoses a patient's condition, this may be an opinion, but it is certainly based on an informed, and hopefully extremely knowledgeable, judgment. Similarly, most people would probably agree that a car runs better after a tune-up. This may also be an opinion, but it is one based on experience, and it is one that few people who have ever maintained a car would disagree with. Nevertheless, there are certain ways to help determine whether a statement is a fact or an opinion.

8a   Value Words

Opinions usually involve some expression of value or worth. A value statement is one that uses *value words,* words that express a positive or negative view of something. For example, consider the following two sentences.

> The United States was founded in the late eighteenth century on democratic principles.

> The founding of the United States was the <u>most significant</u> event of the modern era.

The first sentence above is a factual statement because there is an abundance of historical information to verify both when and upon what principles the United States was founded. However, you should consider the second statement to be an opinion because there is no way to prove what is "most significant." The word "significant" is a value word expressing subjective opinion that cannot be proven. Even though many people may agree with the statement, it is still an opinion.

The following is a list of some common value words. Remember that whenever you see any of these words, or other similar words that express value or worth, always consider them to be an expression of personal opinion.

Value Words

absurd	favorable	should
bad	good	significant
beautiful	great	tasteful
best	insignificant	terrible
better	lovely	undesirable
desirable	meaningful	unsatisfactory
disagreeable	meaningless	wonderful
disgusting	preferable	worse
distasteful	satisfactory	worst

It is important to notice the word "should" in the list above and to remember that it always indicates an opinion. Whenever an author is expressing the view that something "should" be done, he or she is expressing an opinion. For example, consider the following two statements.

President Clinton supported efforts to balance the federal budget.

The federal government should end its practice of deficit spending.

In the first sentence, you could perhaps point to things that President Clinton had said that would verify this statement and suggest what he had or had not supported. However, the second sentence is expressing an opinion, for there is no way to verify what the government "should" do. Again, even though many people might agree with the second statement, it is still an opinion.

8b   Predictions as Opinions

Whenever an author makes a prediction about the future, he or she is necessarily expressing an opinion. Although the future may show whether the prediction is accurate, at the time the statement is made there is absolutely no way of knowing if it is true. This is why anytime you read a prediction, you are reading an opinion. Consider the following example.

Now and for many years into the future the opportunity to give the greatest service to one's fellow citizens will be as a member of a police force—the one truly indispensable agency of a free and civil government.

Adam Walinsky, "The Crisis of Public Order."

In this statement, the author is saying that at the present time and "into the future" the "greatest" and most "indispensable" way a person can serve in society is as a police officer. The words "greatest" and "indispensable" are clearly value words expressing opinions about police work. Also, by predicting what will be most valuable "into the future," the author is expressing another opinion.

8c   Facts and Opinions Together

So far we have considered only sentences that contain either factual statements or opinions. However, sometimes a statement can contain both facts and opinions, as in the following example.

> The beautiful statue of the Cuban patriot Jose Marti stands nobly in Miami's Bayfront Park, a monument as much to a people in exile as to a man who died for a cause.

The statements that the statue is of the Cuban patriot Jose Marti and that it is in Bayfront Park are both factual because these can be easily verified by observing both the inscription on the statue and its location. Even to call him a "patriot" merely refers to the historical fact that he worked and fought for Cuban independence from Spain. However, to describe the statue as "beautiful" and to state that it stands "nobly" are subjective opinions that not everyone would necessarily agree with. Also, the last part of the sentence is an opinion concerning the meaning of the statue. By saying that it is "a monument as much to a people in exile as to a man who died for a cause," the author is suggesting that the statue is significant because it represents the influence of Cuban exiles in Miami who must have wanted the statue. Statements of this sort that contain both facts and opinions are quite common and require you to be able to pick out which parts are which in order to fully understand them.

8d   Opinions Masked as Facts

It may seem easy to distinguish between facts and opinions, but it is not always so easy, especially when a writer is trying to mislead you into thinking that an opinion is actually a fact. Consider the following example as such an attempt.

> The fact is that there has been a virtual worldwide contraceptive revolution, as attested to by Francis FitzGerald in the Sept. 12 *New Yorker*. Fifty-five percent of couples in developing countries now use contraception to control their fertility. Many of these countries have majority

Roman Catholic or Muslim populations. The majority of Catholic couples in the United States, of course, employ artificial contraception as a way of reducing the intervals between pregnancies as well as the number of pregnancies in their families.

Leo Sandon, "Emerging Consensus Bypassing Vatican."

The "fact" this author is referring to in the first sentence is the idea that there is a "virtual worldwide contraceptive revolution" going on now. The author says that this is suggested by facts from an article by Francis FitzGerald, some of which are indeed mentioned in the remaining sentences in the quoted passage. However, despite the facts provided, and despite how the reader may personally feel about birth control, to say that the information provided suggests a "revolution"—a complete and fundamental change—is probably not an interpretation that every reader would agree with. Thus, although the author says that his interpretation is a fact, and although facts are used to support it, it is an opinion nonetheless.

Recognizing Persuasive Language

As you read in Chapter 6, a writer's careful choice of words can easily arouse specific emotions or certain responses in readers. An author's consideration for the connotations of the words he or she chooses is thus often very important in successfully persuading readers. However, sometimes if the language is too extreme or too obvious in an attempt to play on readers' emotions, the strategy may backfire, especially if the reader is attentive to such things. It is important for you to be able to spot these somewhat sneaky uses of language. The following paragraphs discuss a few ways that writers sometimes use words in misleading ways for the deliberate purpose of misrepresenting an idea or situation or of persuading readers to accept a certain point.

8e Slanting

Slanting is a way of misrepresenting something by creating either a positive or negative impression as if there were no other way of looking at the issue. Sometimes there may indeed be only one alternative that seems appropriate in a discussion. However, as a critical reader you want to see evidence of this rather than merely accepting an author's assumption that only one view is possible. Slanting is sometimes attempted through a careful selection of facts so that evidence suggesting a different conclusion from the authors' is not mentioned. However, it is often possible to detect slanting in the same way that an author's tone is recognized—by the author's choice of words. Consider the following passage for the way that the choice of words creates a very one-sided impression.

> Unlike other controversial government agencies that merely <u>squander</u> taxpayers' money, the Central Intelligence Agency is a <u>sinister</u> enterprise with a long <u>criminal</u> record. Its sole rationale—engaging in <u>shadowy</u> combat with its equally <u>nefarious</u> communist counterparts—crumbling at about the same time the Berlin Wall did. Without a Cold War to wage, the CIA has become a <u>dinosaur</u> desperate to avoid extinction.
>
> Kevin J. Kelly, "R.I.P. for the CIA?"

This is an excerpt from the beginning of an article advocating the elimination of the CIA. The author makes that point very clear by saying that the CIA does more than "squander" or waste tax money, but that it as a "sinister," "criminal," "shadowy," and "nefarious" organization. These are words that suggest evil intent. Then by calling it a "dinosaur desperate to avoid extinction" the author makes it clear that he feels the CIA has no justification for existence. It seems clear that this author has no intention of giving a balanced treatment of the CIA in any objective way. Even readers who agree that the CIA has outlived its usefulness would likely be put off by this author's extreme language that suggests no possibility of anything positive about the agency. Clearly this slanted language shows a strong bias against the CIA and probably against espionage generally. The point of noting the extreme nature of this author's language is not to suggest that you should disagree with the author or disregard what the author says but rather to recognize that it is not in this article that you will find a balanced, objective discussion of the role of the CIA in a post–Cold War world.

8f   Weasel Words

Words chosen for their emotional effect to persuade readers that something is true or definite without really being proven are often called *weasel words.* These words take their name from their similarity to the practice of weasels who are said to be able to suck the contents out of an egg without breaking the shell. For example, if you read in an advertisement that a certain toothpaste "helps prevent tooth decay," you might think that using this product will keep you cavity-free. However, the word "helps" really means no more than it aids or assists, without making any more promises than could be made for brushing with water alone, which would also "help" prevent decay.

Other words, such as "virtually," "acts on," "works on," and "fights" are commonly used in advertising to state something in a way that makes it sound like more than the words actually mean. Consider these examples.

> Whitepoint appliances are <u>virtually</u> trouble free.
>
> Adams' Cough Syrup <u>acts on</u> your cough control center.
>
> Flake-Off shampoo <u>fights</u> dandruff right in the shower.

While each of these statements certainly sounds good, what these weasel words actually do is make each claim appear to say more than it actually does. While the word "virtually" is meant to create the impression that the appliances are almost completely trouble free, the word actually means "almost but not quite." In other words, no guarantee. Similarly, the words "acts on" and "fights" also sound good but really only mean that the products help but cannot promise a cure.

In a similar way, certain words can be used to *qualify* a statement—to moderate it or make it less definite—while still leaving the misleading impression that something more direct has been said. When writers use qualifying words such as "might," "may," or "could," they are sometimes using them as weasel words to sneak out of a definitive statement while seeming to make one. For example, consider the following excerpt from the opening paragraph of an article about social changes that have taken place in the twentieth century.

> No century in recorded history has experienced so many social transformations and such radical ones as the twentieth century. They, I submit, <u>may</u> turn out to be the most significant events of this, our century, and its lasting legacy. In the developed free-market countries—which contain less than a fifth of the earth's population but are a model for the rest—work and work force, society and polity, are all, in the last decade of this century, qualitatively and quantitatively different not only from what they were in the first years of this century but also from what has existed at any other time in history: in their configurations, in their processes, in their problems, and in their structures.

> Peter F. Drucker, "The Age of Social Transformation."

In this paragraph, the author begins by stating what he feels "may" turn out to be the most significant events of the twentieth century. In the rest of the article, he then goes on to describe in detail what these changes have been. This he does very authoritatively and convincingly. However, by using the word "may" rather than more direct and forceful wording, such as "will" or "will in all probability" or "are likely to," the author is qualifying his thesis and making a much less certain statement. Admittedly, the author is predicting how the changes he describes will be seen in the future, something that he of course cannot know with certainty now. However, the choice of the word "may" seems to lessen the author's commitment to his prediction in a way that should be apparent to an attentive reader.

Recognizing Author Bias

In any attempt to persuade, whether it is a logical argument or an emotional appeal, the author is obviously going to have a view that he or she is trying to express. However, behind the author's stated opinion—and in persuasive writing the main point is always going to be the author's opinion—usually lie stated or unstated opinions, preferences, or positions that necessarily influence the ideas that are expressed, the way that ideas are expressed, and the language used to express them. This is what is referred to as an author's bias— an author's attitude or prejudice that influences his or her opinion on a subject.

For example, if you are reading an article on the opinion-editorial (op-ed) page of a newspaper written by the local chief of police about federal funding for law enforcement, you would expect this person's comments to be biased. You would not be surprised if, because of his job, this person were to favor federal efforts to support the police. His bias would certainly be in favor of support for the police in general and probably in favor of federal support in particular. However, an article on the same topic written by a Republican senator who generally favors less federal involvement in state and local issues would probably express a very different opinion—a preference for local funding for police—undoubtedly reflecting a very different bias—less federal involvement in local issues.

While being able to recognize an author's bias is definitely important in identifying attempts to persuade you of something and in deciding how seriously to take those efforts, remember that an author's bias can be either for or against something and is not necessarily a negative thing. Consider, for example, the following passage in terms of the author's bias concerning the issue of prayer in public schools.

> As a Christian, I quite agree that prayer is not harmful; indeed, my wife and I consider it essential, and want our children to grow up surrounded by it, and partly for that reason they attend a private religious school. But what the Supreme Court has recognized, and school-prayer advocates sometimes miss, is that the ideal of religious freedom means that the state should not express a view on how anyone should pray.
>
> Steven L. Carter, "Let Us Pray."

In this passage from an article about prayer in public schools, the author clearly expresses the Christian belief in the value of prayer. However, on the issue of public school prayer, the author just as clearly expresses opposition, apparently on constitutional grounds. Thus, the author seems biased in favor of private religious expression without interference of any kind from the government, and this bias is in itself neither a positive nor a negative thing; it is merely a preference.

Closely related to the question of author's bias is the concept of tone, which we discussed in Chapter 5. An author's tone may in some cases reflect his or her bias. For example, you may recall from Chapter 5, Peggy Noonan's critical statements about talk shows. Her comments suggest a bias against the types of programs that encourage people to "confuse chatter with communication."

> There's a whole lot of sharing going on out there, and just one of the interesting things about it is it doesn't seem authentic—i.e., the secrets people are sharing don't seem like real secrets but like narrative constructed to give us a claim on the national microphone. One wonders also, Who's listening? Who is learning, being heartened, instructed, shocked? Hemingway once said: Do not confuse movement with action. We are becoming a people who confuse chatter with communication.
>
> Peggy Noonan, "How Have We Changed?"

We also discussed in Chapter 5 objective tone, which refers to writing that shows no emotion, opinion, preference, or bias. When an author writes objectively, he or she is not making any bias apparent. This, however, does not mean that the author has no bias; it simply means that the author is not showing it. In fact, sometimes it may be possible to get hints of an author's bias when such things are considered as the author's background, if we are given any biographical information, or the place the piece is published, if we know something about the philosophy of the publication's editors. For example, consider the following excerpt from the conclusion of an article published in the *Native American Rights Fund Legal Review* by an author who is described in an introduction to the article as an attorney representing the Catawba Tribe.

> It is generally agreed that underlying all parties' reluctance to support a fair settlement was the suspicion that the Tribe had no real leverage; that is, it could not win its case in court. But for the Catawba Tribe there appeared to be few options. More than two centuries of relying on the good will and promises of the State and Federal Governments had resulted only in the loss of their ancestral lands and severe poverty among tribal members. It now appears that a just settlement is possible. And while the proposed settlement can never fully compensate the Tribe for the loss of its lands and economic self-sufficiency, it is hoped that the settlement will, as Chief Blue stated, provide the Tribe and its members with the tools to work with toward a brighter future.
>
> Don B. Miller, "Catawba Tribe v. South Carolina: A History of Perseverance."

The author of this article describes the efforts of the Catawbas to gain the rights to land that they claimed was originally theirs. Despite his relatively objective language, since the author is a lawyer for the tribe and since the article appeared in a publication put out by an organization working for Native American rights, it seems clear that the author is not only in favor of the settlement, but that he is also writing with an underlying bias in favor of the Catawba Tribe.

Identifying Fallacies

As you will see in detail in Chapter 9, successful arguments rely on acceptable support. For this reason, any persuasive attempt should be carefully considered according to the sufficiency and relevance of the support. In other words, evaluating arguments and persuasive writing generally involves deciding how logical a point is or how believable the thesis is after carefully considering the support. With this in mind, we will now look at specific ways that support can be used inappropriately and how writers will sometimes present support that appears to prove their points but that really does not.

When the support for an argument is either incomplete or irrelevant and does not really support what it is supposed to, it can be said to be illogical, and the specific way that it is illogical is called a *logical fallacy*. A logical fallacy is, therefore, the use of inappropriate, illogical, or incomplete support in an attempt to prove a thesis or conclusion. Other fallacies involve ethical and emotional issues that appeal to readers' respect for authority and to readers' values and emotions. These *ethical* and *emotional fallacies* are more commonly found as the main support in persuasive attempts to convince through emotional rather than logical appeals.

These fallacies may sometimes suggest no more than careless writing. However, when they are used deliberately to mislead readers into accepting a point of view or opinion, they are called *propaganda techniques,* and are often found in political campaigns and in advertising, both of which too often resort to emotional rather than logical appeal. In either case, as a critical reader you want to be able to tell when you are reading these types of persuasion. This chapter will list some common logical fallacies (examples of incomplete or irrelevant support), ethical fallacies (examples of misleading appeals to authority), and emotional fallacies (examples of misleading emotional appeals) that you may sometimes find when reading persuasive writing.

8g   Logical Fallacies with Insufficient Support

Sometimes an author attempts to support a point but fails to provide enough support to justify the thesis or conclusion. These are essentially cases where an inference or a generalization is made without enough evidence to justify it. The following paragraphs list, define, and exemplify logical fallacies with insufficient support.

Hasty Generalization   A hasty generalization draws a conclusion from insufficient evidence. Stereotyping is a hasty generalization.

> I have had many conversations with a good friend who considers herself to be a conservative. These discussions have clarified for me the distinguishing characteristic of all conservatives: they refuse to face reality and fail to admit the consequences of their actions.

The conclusion drawn by this author that conservatives "refuse to face reality and fail to admit the consequences of their actions" can be considered a hasty generalization because it seems that it is based on his conversations with only one person. In reality, there are millions of Americans who consider themselves conservatives and who might very well give the author a very different impression—were he to talk to more of them.

False Cause   A false cause suggests that one thing is the cause of another, often simply because it follows the other.

> The present <u>welfare</u> system <u>is responsible for</u> pulling its recipients into <u>a life of dependence</u> that discourages an active search for employment opportunities. Even when jobs open up, welfare recipients don't want to take them because it is easier to <u>sit back and receive welfare checks.</u>

This may be a frequently heard argument against welfare. However, the suggestion that welfare causes laziness—"it is easier to sit back and receive welfare checks"—fails to consider information such as statistics that would show trends toward more low-paying service-sector jobs and fewer higher-paying jobs for unskilled individuals. In other words, there may be more reasons than just the welfare system itself, such as economic trends generally, that discourage welfare recipients from looking for work. Therefore, it is not completely logical to suggest that welfare alone is the cause of a life of dependence.

False Comparison   A false comparison is a false analogy. It compares one thing to another with insufficient evidence to support the comparison.

> Conservative attacks on the National Endowment for the Arts is reminiscent of the Nazi crackdown on what they also considered to be "degenerate art."

This writer apparently considers proposals by some conservative Americans to cut funding for the NEA to resemble censorship of the arts in Nazi Germany. While it may be safe to say that in both cases art that confronts social conventions has been seen as threatening, the kind of repressive measures taken by the Nazis were much more extreme than the mere elimination of government grants to artists, which is all the conservatives are really proposing. The comparison of American conservatives to Nazis on this issue is thus not a fair one.

False Dilemma   A false dilemma claims that there are only two possible courses of action or solutions when, in fact, logic suggests that there must be more possibilities. False dilemma is also known as either-or fallacy.

The goal of education should continue to be <u>the transmission of culture and tradition,</u> rather than <u>the replacement of culture by technology and information.</u> Only people can teach kids to love ideas and learning; all computers can do is teach kids to love computers and to manipulate words and images.

The author here seems to assume that there are only two possibilities for education—"the transmission of culture and tradition" or "the replacement of culture by technology and information"—and that this represents a choice between teachers and computers. However, no evidence is presented to support the idea that the use of computers in education will necessarily make traditional education impossible. Indeed, it is quite possible to conceive of using computers not to replace a traditional curriculum but to supplement it. In other words, logic suggests that there are more than these two possibilities for the future of education.

Appeal to Ignorance   An appeal to ignorance suggests that a point is untrue simply because there is no evidence to support it.

> The belief in a God that answers prayers and who is aware of our actions and thoughts is no more than wishful thinking. The evidence that believers point to from their personal experience cannot be definitively attributed to a personal God. These phenomena could just as easily be explained as qualities of the human brain, in the same way that dreams convincingly recreate experiences in the world.

This author suggests that belief in a personal God is unjustified because there cannot be any factual evidence to prove it. However, even though believers may not be able to present factual evidence that proves the existence of a personal God, the author does not present any facts that disprove it either. The lack of factual evidence does not necessarily disprove something and is certainly not enough to make a convincing argument.

Begging the Question   Begging the question occurs when an assumption is presented without any evidence to support it.

> The recent frequency of prenatal genetic counseling raises the fear that fetuses will be selected for abortion merely on the chance that they may not grow up to meet preconceived ideals of appearance, intelligence, or sexuality.

Even though the fear that the author expresses may indeed represent a horrifying thought, no evidence is presented that prenatal genetic counseling will result in such arbitrary abortion decisions. After reading this statement, we are left wondering why the author fears such a horrible outcome and what evidence points toward this. Because we are not told why or given any evidence at all, this argument fails to convince in any logical way.

Circular Reasoning   Circular reasoning restates a conclusion or main point as if it were itself the support for the conclusion or point.

> One of the most serious problems facing us now is an overabundance of information without any moral guidance to make it meaningful. We lack commonly held values that could help us make the glut of information we are surrounded by intelligible and coherent. Sources of information such as the mass media provide us with more than we can possibly make sense of without some overriding understanding or belief system that can allow us to fit it all into a meaningful context.

This author's point is clear. In fact, it is repeated in different words in all three of the sentences that make up this passage. However, the author never gets around to providing any supporting information to back up the main point. This is an example of restating the main point as if it were its own support, while actually providing no support at all.

Stacked Evidence   Stacked evidence presents only evidence that supports a claim, while failing to present other important information that would contradict or cast doubt on the point being made. Stacked evidence is also known as *card stacking* or *special pleading.*

> Recent research is confirming that on average <u>males tend be more intelligent than females.</u> A recent study conducted at the University of Chicago showed that men account for a higher proportion of geniuses than women, with men representing seven out of every eight people scoring in the top 1 percent on IQ tests. Also, the same study concluded that boys outnumbered girls three to one in the top 1 percent and seven to one in the top 10 percent of math and science test scores. These findings are consistent with <u>the long recognized fact that the average male brain is larger than that of the female.</u>

This author's point is that "males tend be more intelligent than females," and he offers support for this thesis from a research study and a "long recognized fact." While the evidence he provides is indeed accurate, it is by no means complete and actually misrepresents both the University of Chicago study and recent findings about male and female brain size. In fact, the University of Chicago research that the author is referring to also found that men make up the largest proportion of the lowest scorers on IQ tests and that girls outnumber boys in the top five percent on tests of reading comprehension and writing skills, with boys outnumbering girls two to one at the bottom of the scale. As for brain size, recent studies have shown that while male brains do tend to be larger than those of females, female brains contain more brain cells and have a larger tissue connecting the two halves of the brain than do male brains, suggesting that women's brains may work more efficiently than men's brains. Clearly, the author's choice of facts to support his argument is one-sided and misleading.

8h   Logical Fallacies with Irrelevant Support

Sometimes the problem with support may not be that there is an insufficient amount to justify a conclusion, but that what is provided does not directly relate to the thesis. In these cases, the support is misleading and does not actually support the claim at all. The following are examples of logical fallacies that have irrelevant support.

Non Sequitur   Non sequitur is a Latin term meaning "it does not follow." A non sequitur, then, draws a conclusion from unrelated evidence.

> Affirmative action programs have been established to provide access to educational and professional opportunities that have been denied to certain groups in the past. Since white non-Hispanic males have often been at a disadvantage during the last twenty years or so, I feel that I, as a member of this group, deserve special consideration under affirmative action guidelines.

This author's point is that affirmative action guidelines apply to him because he is a white non-Hispanic male, a group whose members have often been passed over for opportunities given to members of minority groups. While the second part of his point may in fact be the case, the definition of affirmative action that the author provides shows that it is meant to aid members of minority groups and women, not people such as himself who have had historical advantages previous to affirmative action programs. His support is thus not relevant to his point.

Two Wrongs Make a Right   Two wrongs make a right fallacy is the justification of a wrong act because a similar act was committed by an opponent or adversary.

> Those Democrats who criticize efforts to open normal trade relations with China because of China's human rights violations commit the hypocritical error of forgetting that it has been they who have also advocated opening relations with Cuba's Fidel Castro, the epitome of a human rights violator. These Democrats have no right to oppose relations with China while supporting loosened restrictions for Cuba.

The author's point about the contradictory nature of some Democrats who support relations with one nation that has a record of human rights violations while opposing relations with another may indeed be accurate. However, this is no justification for suggesting that relations with any human rights violator should be established. Support for relations with one country that violates human rights does not logically justify support for another.

Red Herring   A red herring avoids addressing the real issue by introducing irrelevant or misleading support that is easily criticized.

> Federal funding for the National Endowment for the Arts should be discontinued. Taxpayers don't want and shouldn't be expected to pay for so-called "art" such as Mapplethorpe's sexual perversions and Serrano's sacrilegious trash. It is inexcusable that such things have been supported by tax money through the NEA, which because of such irresponsible decisions should itself be eliminated.

While it is indeed true that some controversial work has been funded by NEA grants, projects of this type have been few and are not representative of what the endowment normally funds. Most of the NEA grant money goes to support projects more suitable to mainstream tastes, including many local dance companies, musical performances, and school art programs. By associating the NEA with highly controversial art that has made up just a small fraction of what it has funded, this critic is attacking something that most taxpayers would probably agree should not be federally supported, but that is not really representative of what the NEA typically funds. In this way the author misrepresents the NEA and effectively avoids the broader issue concerning the role of government in encouraging and supporting cultural life.

8i   Ethical Fallacies

The fallacies listed above represent attempts to support a point with insufficient or irrelevant evidence. Other fallacies attempt to persuade by the use of misleading attacks on an opponent or by an inappropriate reliance on authority. These ethical fallacies are attempts by authors to either inappropriately criticize an opponent's character or to use someone's character as the main support in place of more substantial evidence to support a point.

Argument to the Person   Argument to the person criticizes an opponent's character in a misleading way in an attempt to avoid addressing the person's views or the issue at hand. Emotionally charged names or comments may be used to discredit an opponent by creating a feeling of fear or mistrust in readers. Argument to the person is also known as *ad hominem,* name calling, personal attack, character attack, or guilt by association.

> Senator Izquierda has argued that we should bring the federal budget deficit under control by cutting military spending and by reducing what she refers to as special interest "waste spending." However, it is common knowledge that not long before her election, the Senator had been on the board of directors of a corporation that was forced to declare bankruptcy. Is this the kind of experience that is appropriate for proposing a budget plan for the entire nation? I think not.

This author is suggesting that Senator Izquierda's proposal to control the federal deficit by cutting military spending and what she feels are other examples of "waste spending" should not be taken seriously because of her previous involvement with a bankrupt corporation. The problem with this criticism is that it completely ignores the issues of military spending and the influence of special interest groups on expenditures that the Senator apparently considers inappropriate, and it only addresses an incident from the Senator's past that is not shown to be relevant. It seems that the author is trying to convince his audience by disputing the Senator's qualifications to make a budget proposal rather than through a reasoned discussion of the issues that she is trying to raise.

Straw Man   The straw man fallacy attacks an opponent for holding an unpopular opinion or weak claim that he or she does not really believe. This fallacy misrepresents or distorts an opponent's position in such a way that makes it unacceptable to anyone, even though the opponent does not actually hold that view.

> <u>Mayor Shmoke</u> favors drug legalization, but this is a view held by very few Americans. Indeed, no responsible citizen <u>wants to encourage drug addiction or the crime associated with the use of illicit drugs.</u>

The author is suggesting here that by advocating the legalization of drugs, Mayor Shmoke "wants to encourage drug addiction" and would allow "the crime associated with the use of illicit drugs." These are things that no law-abiding person would support, and are views not actually held by the Mayor. In fact most responsible public figures who support drug legalization hope that these very things will be reduced by reallocating funds and energy into prevention and treatment rather than into the enforcement of laws that many feel are unenforceable. These important issues are avoided here by presenting a misleading attack on views not actually held by the subject.

False Use of Authority   This fallacy uses someone's character or authority to convince readers rather than using actual evidence to support a point.

> Congressman Derecha's <u>proposal to reduce the federal deficit by reducing social spending</u> is both sensible and practical and reflects his expertise in economic matters and his many years of experience with budgetary issues in the House. As a former professor of economics and as a present member of the House Budget Committee, <u>the Congressman is uniquely qualified</u> to formulate a workable plan for our government's fiscal woes.

To suggest that the Congressman is "uniquely qualified" to propose a way to reduce the federal deficit and to address his specific proposal to "reduce social spending" are two very different things. Indeed, this author seems to be avoiding the latter while using the former to convince his audience that the Congressman's plan is "sensible and practical" and "workable." While the Congressman's authority and expertise may be beyond dispute, his specific plan may not be. This author conveniently neglects to discuss the plan itself, relying solely on an attempt to impress the audience with the Congressman's qualifications.

8j Emotional Fallacies

Emotional fallacies rely on misleading information. Emotional fallacies, often used as *propaganda techniques,* play on readers' emotions and appeal to their prejudice, pity, compassion, or fear, rather than addressing actual issues or presenting substantial supporting evidence to back up a point. Slanted, emotionally charged language is often used in these fallacies in attempts to distract or mislead readers.

Appeal to the People   Appeal to the people is a general appeal to readers' emotions—such as fear, prejudice, or patriotism—rather than a reasoned discussion. This type of fallacy is also known as an *ad populum* appeal.

> The American flag is a symbol of everything we hold dear in this country. How many thousands of men and women have died on the battlefields defending our nation, defending our flag? We cannot let these heroic men and women down by allowing the flag to continue to be desecrated in the name of free speech. The Stars and Stripes is as sacred to a patriotic American as the cross is to a God-fearing Christian. We need a constitutional amendment banning any desecration of Old Glory, so that our sacred symbol can remain forever inviolate.

This author clearly wants a constitutional amendment banning any desecration of the American flag, but he fails to provide any more than emotional reasons for doing so. The author is appealing to readers' feelings of patriotism as a way to convince them that an amendment is needed. In order for this argument to be valid, evidence must be provided that shows either the benefits that such an amendment would bring or the harm that could come without one, neither of which this author provides.

Appeal to Pity   An appeal to pity appeals to readers' sympathy. It attempts to convince readers by trying to make them feel sorry for the subject, but without addressing more relevant information.

> Though Mr. James has admitted that he used depositors' money to finance personal expenditures, he was under tremendous pressure and stress to act in a way that anyone can understand. With his wife in and out of hospitals with cancer and three young children at home, Mr. James was faced with responsibilities beyond what he could reasonably

be expected to handle on his salary as a bank teller. He used the money, which he fully intended to repay, to pay for his wife's medical care and to hire a housekeeper to look after the needs of his children while he took care of his professional and personal duties. Because his motives were selfless, Mr. James does not deserve harsh judgment, but deserves compassion and understanding.

Clearly this is an appeal to readers' sympathy. Readers are asked to overlook the fact that Mr. James has embezzled money from the bank where he works, on the grounds that he did it for selfless reasons. His motives may indeed have been selfless, and there may be nothing untrue in the statements made here about him, but the argument is presented in a way that is designed to make readers feel sorry for Mr. James, and thus ignore the fact that he has broken a law.

Bandwagon Appeal   A bandwagon appeal suggests that something should be believed or done because many other people believe or do it. This type of fallacy appeals to people's desire to conform or to be like other people.

> Join the millions of Americans who voted Republican in the last election. Clearly there is a rising tide of voter dissatisfaction with decades of Democratic liberalism and an increasing embrace of conservative values. Add your support to the new majority and join the Republican Party.

This author neglects whatever rational appeals could be made to join the more conservative Republican Party in favor of the emotional appeal to a public who, the writer hopes, wants to be in the majority. This is an appeal to peoples' desire to be like other people and to do what other people do, regardless of its rational merits.

False Needs   False needs appeal to what people value or think they need by creating needs where none exist or by exaggerating real needs.

> Something <u>all of us value</u> is <u>our health and the health of our loved ones.</u> And for this reason we want to be secure in the knowledge that the ones we love will be taken care of in those inevitable times of illness or accident. <u>The only way that security can be provided is</u> through adequate insurance, and such protection is what we at <u>QualityCare</u> offer our clients. Don't gamble with the health of the ones you love the most—trust QualityCare to provide the security you need.

In what appears to be an advertisement for an insurance company, this author appeals to the very real desires for "our health and the health of our loved ones." Even though this need is indeed valid, the association of it with a specific insurance company is less so. While the author does not actually say that QualityCare represents the "only way that security can be provided," he is hoping that this is exactly what readers will believe. Thus, the author is trying to associate the real need for health care with the questionable need for QualityCare insurance.

Glittering Generalities   Glittering generalities make important-sounding general claims with no explanation or evidence that the claims have any basis in reality. This fallacy attempts to make something seem extremely attractive without describing any details.

> Overlooking the sea, the <u>exclusive</u> residential community of Ocean View Estates represents <u>the American dream come true,</u> and it is a place you will be <u>proud to call home.</u>

In an obvious advertisement for a residential development, this passage only tells us one factual thing about Ocean View Estates: It is near the sea. By using such words as "exclusive," "the American dream come true," and "a place you will be proud to call home," the author is trying to make this place seem as attractive as possible without having to really say anything substantial at all. These are examples of "weasel words," discussed earlier in this chapter (section 8f). The emotional effect of these words is meant to convince readers that something is true that has in no way been proven.

Slippery Slope   Slippery slope is an appeal to fear. It claims that a course of action should be avoided because it will lead to undesirable consequences, even though there is no evidence that this will actually happen.

> The end of the Cold War in no way decreases the need for a well-maintained military. In fact, the proliferation of local nationalistic wars, the diffusion of nuclear technology, the increasing danger of terrorist attacks, and the increasing political and economic instability in many parts of the world suggest just the opposite. The United States cannot take the chance of cutting back on military expenditures in a time of such international uncertainty.

This author is arguing for the continuance of military spending at the same level as it was during the Cold War, when the United States was trying to oppose Soviet attempts to spread communism, in order to protect against possible present threats from abroad. He does list some compelling reasons why we should be concerned about the situation in the world today, which he is also suggesting are reasons why the military budget should not be cut. However, the author does not show how these situations directly affect or threaten the United States or how a highly funded American military is necessary to help solve these problems. The author is thus appealing to readers' fears by suggesting that military budget cuts will have dire consequences, without providing any evidence to show that this will actually happen.

Chapter Review

As a member of an open society, you are surrounded by many forms of persuasion constantly tugging at you for your attention and belief. Some of these attempts to convince you represent appeals to your reason, but many appeal solely to your emotions in the hope that you will not examine their logic too carefully. For this reason, it is very important that you read carefully and critically so you can distinguish between facts and opinions, recognize persuasive language, recognize an author's bias, and identify different types of fallacies.

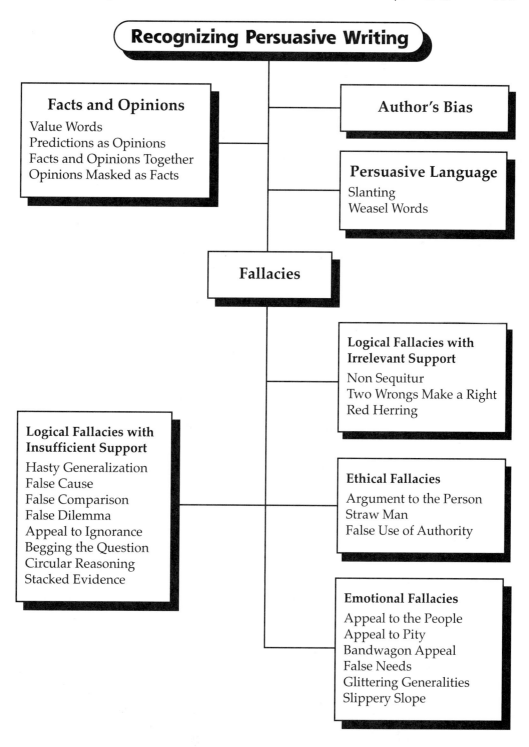

Recognizing Persuasive Writing

Facts and Opinions

Value Words
Predictions as Opinions
Facts and Opinions Together
Opinions Masked as Facts

Author's Bias

Persuasive Language

Slanting
Weasel Words

Fallacies

Logical Fallacies with Irrelevant Support

Non Sequitur
Two Wrongs Make a Right
Red Herring

Logical Fallacies with Insufficient Support

Hasty Generalization
False Cause
False Comparison
False Dilemma
Appeal to Ignorance
Begging the Question
Circular Reasoning
Stacked Evidence

Ethical Fallacies

Argument to the Person
Straw Man
False Use of Authority

Emotional Fallacies

Appeal to the People
Appeal to Pity
Bandwagon Appeal
False Needs
Glittering Generalities
Slippery Slope

CHAPTER
9

Analyzing Arguments

Because you are surrounded by so many attempts to convince you of one idea or another or to buy one product or another, you need to be a discriminating reader and carefully evaluate attempts to influence your thinking. This is especially important in a democracy where elected officials depend upon convincing voters that they are acting in their best interests, and in a consumer society where success often depends on convincing buyers that they need a certain product. Often the success or failure of a campaign or strategy depends on how convincing one is able to be, and examples can be found of such attempts every day in newspapers, magazines, flyers, brochures, and memorandums.

Argumentation is a type of persuasion involving attempts to convince primarily through the use of reasoning and objective evidence. You will find written arguments every day in the editorial pages of newspapers and in opinionated essays in popular magazines, as well as in literary, political, cultural, and academic journals.

This chapter will consider how authors structure written arguments. In Chapter 3, you looked at how authors present main ideas and supporting details. Similarly, this chapter will discuss the *analysis* of arguments—the study of their parts—by looking at how authors present the point or thesis they want readers to accept, try to prove it with supporting evidence, and make assumptions that underlie their choice of certain supporting evidence in their attempt to make a case. Excerpts from argumentative essays will be provided to illustrate each of the parts of an argument.

Identifying the Thesis

An argument is an attempt by an author to convince readers of a certain opinion on a controversial topic by using logically presented and organized support. An argument can be thought of as usually consisting of three parts or elements, two that are stated directly and a third that often goes unstated: the *thesis,* the *support,* and the *assumptions.*

As you saw in Chapter 3, a thesis is the main idea of a multiparagraph essay. Similarly, in an argument the thesis is either a direct statement of the author's main idea or the author's implied main point. Furthermore, because argumentative writing has the specific purpose of convincing readers of some point, the thesis in an argument is the author's opinion that he or she wants readers to accept. Often called a claim, proposition, central argument, or conclusion, the thesis of an argument is what the author is trying to prove. It is the point that the author tries to convince you to accept. Read the following example from the introduction to an op-ed piece about prayer in public schools, in which the author's thesis is implied.

> As a kid I prayed in school. Fast. I can say three "Our Fathers" in the amount of time it takes to eat a Twinkie. The way you do it is, you run "onearthasitisinheaven" and "leadusnotintotemptation" all together. It's as rich in meanings as the multiplication tables.

I'm not making light of prayer here, but of so-called school prayer, which bears as much resemblance to real spiritual experience as that freeze-dried astronaut food bears to a nice standing rib roast.

From what I remember of praying in school, it was almost an insult to God, a rote exercise in moving your mouth while daydreaming or checking out the cutest boy in the seventh grade. It was a far, far cry from soul-searching.

Anna Quindlen, "Lead Us Not."

Though she does not come right out and say so, this author's point is clear. She feels that school prayer is not serious prayer and should not be required of school children. In the article that follows this opening, she counters many of the arguments made by proponents of school prayer, then ends by restating her opinion that "A state of grace owes much, much more to the early years and the everyday acts than to 90 seconds before class." Like this example, you will often find that authors of editorials and op-ed columns leave their theses implied. However, since these are among the most common types of argumentation, you need to become accustomed to analyzing them by using inference to identify the main point.

In argumentation, an author's thesis usually involves one of two types of claims: *factual claims* or *value claims*. In both types of claims, the author's thesis is in the form of an opinion, and in both cases the writer is attempting to convince readers to accept that opinion. However, a factual claim tries to show that something is true, whereas a value claim attempts to pass judgment.

9a Factual Claims

A thesis that makes some factual claim will express a view concerning the existence of something, offer a definition of something, or claim something as a cause. In any case, the writer is attempting to convince readers that something is true by providing supporting evidence in the form of verifiable facts, statistics, or real-life examples. Analogies or quotations from reliable authorities may also be brought in as part of the author's case, but the main evidence in a factual claim will be factual evidence. Consider the following three examples of introductions to articles that contain thesis statements as factual claims.

Example 1

Many aspects of <u>our personalities,</u> it now seems clear, <u>are inborn</u> and resistant to change—a fact, ironically, <u>that makes the</u> role of <u>environment</u> in our lives <u>all the more important.</u>

Winifred Gallaher, "How We Become What We Are."

This statement from a long article states the author's thesis very clearly: "it now seems clear" that human personality is significantly determined by genetics, but the environment is still believed to play an important role. In the rest of the article, the author refers for her main support to the work of several psychiatrists, psychologists, and scientists working in the fields of mental health, psychology, and genetics.

Example 2

What group do you belong to? The UCLA admissions office wants to know. Are you in Group I—"American Indian, African-American or Mexican American/Chicano/Chicana"? In Group II, other "Latino/Latina American"? Group III, "Philipino/Philipina American"? Or Group IV, "All Others," which includes whites and non-Filipino Asians.

   <u>If you're a high school student applying to UCLA, your group number can be critical because race is one of the most important factors in determining admission.</u> Here's how it works, according to a UCLA internal document.

Alexander Volokh and Shechao Charles Feng,
"How Race Adds Up for UCLA Entry."

These two authors begin their article with a clear statement of their thesis in the second paragraph. They go on in the article to show how UCLA's enrollment process works. Throughout the article, they refer to "a UCLA internal document" to support their point that "race is one of the most important factors in determining admission."

Example 3

Life is a mystery, ineffable, unfathomable, the last thing on earth that might seem susceptible to exact description. Yet now, for the first time, a free-living organism has been precisely defined by the chemical identification of its complete genetic blueprint.

The creature is just a humble bacterium known as Hemophilus influenzae, but it nonetheless possesses all the tools and tricks required for independent existence. <u>For the first time, biologists can begin to see the entire parts list, as it were, of what a living cell needs to grow, survive and reproduce itself.</u>

Nicholas Wade, "First Sequencing of Cell's DNA Defines Basis of Life."

This author begins his article by stating his thesis that "For the first time, biologists can begin to see the entire parts list, as it were, of what a living cell needs to grow, survive and reproduce itself." He then goes on in the article to explain the findings of several scientists working in different locations that support this claim.

9b   Value Claims

A thesis that passes judgment or expresses approval or disapproval is called a value claim. A value claim might also make a recommendation for future action or propose a solution to a problem, but what it is essentially doing is expressing a view concerning the quality of something. Here, the supporting evidence may, as in factual claims, take the form of facts, statistics, examples, or expert opinions. However, a value claim is more likely to also include judgments or suggest standards and criteria by which something is judged. Value claims tend to involve more emotional support than factual claims do, and they often appeal to readers' desires for certain outcomes. Now look at some examples of value claims that have been taken from the introductions to articles in which authors try to show that something has positive or negative value.

Example 1

For years Americans have complained about government programs for the disadvantaged that do not work. Now, however, we are on the verge of dismantling <u>affirmative action, the one policy that, for all its imperfections, has helped us achieve the constitutional commitment to the ideal of equity and fairness.</u>

In utilitarian terms, it is hard to find a program that has brought so much gain to so many at so little cost. It has been the single most important factor in the rise of a significant, if still economically fragile, black middle class.

Orlando Patterson, "Affirmative Action, on the Merit System."

This author's point is clear: Though he admits that affirmative action is not perfect, the author feels that it "has helped us achieve the constitutional commitment to the ideal of equity and fairness." The author goes on in this article to try to show that affirmative action has benefited members of minority groups but has not harmed members of the majority. His support includes some statistics and examples but appeals mainly to readers' sense of fairness and equity.

Example 2

> The 5.5 billion inhabitants of this globe are adding 95 million more people to this total every year. We add almost one billion people each decade. The World Health Organization and the United Nations Population Fund estimate that, by the year 2025, nearly nine billion people will live on the Earth, and between 10–14 billion by 2050. <u>The implications of this basic trend—for consumption, production, markets, education, services, the environment, investment, for war and peace—are fundamental.</u>
>
> Paul Kennedy, "Overpopulation Tilts the Planet."

Though this author uses many facts for support throughout the article, as he does in this introductory paragraph, his point is more to show just that the earth's population is increasing. His thesis is that there are significant implications of "this basic trend—for consumption, production, markets, education, services, the environment, investment, for war and peace." The author is expressing concern that the population increase will have negative effects.

Example 3

> Like Pearl Jam's "Jeremy," which tells the story of an alienated kid who blows his head off in school, Nirvana's "Teen Spirit," and indeed all of grunge culture, is rooted in the feeling of damage. Coming out of the get-ahead '80's, it is easy to understand the appeal. Being damaged is a hedge against the illusory promises of consumer culture. For grunges' primary audience, white male teens, damage offers a defense against the claims of gansta rappers and punk feminists. It's a great equalizer at a time when multiculturalism seems to have devolved into competing schools of victimization. <u>Grunge appeals to white kids because it tells them that they're not responsible for the evils of racism and injustices, that they are victims too.</u>
>
> <u>The empowerment you get from listening to these songs lies in unearthing that essential nugget of shame.</u> . . .
>
> Sarah Ferguson, "The Comfort of Being Sad."

In these paragraphs, the author states her main point in an article attempting to explain why white teenagers are attracted to grunge music. She states that grunge expresses "the feeling of damage," "is a hedge against the illusory promises of consumer culture," and "offers a defense against the claims of gansta rappers and punk feminists." Ferguson then states her thesis that grunge makes kids feel that "they're not responsible for the evils of racism and injustices, that they are victims too" and that the music exposes an "essential nugget of shame." While the author admits that she finds it "is easy to understand the appeal," she is also suggesting that white kids who are attracted to grunge are merely trying to escape social realities and expectations. She is thus suggesting that grunge is a negative response by some young people who are basically feeling sorry for themselves.

Identifying the Support

Often referred to as the proof, evidence, reasons, or premises, the support offered for an argument is the information presented in an attempt to prove to readers that the thesis should be accepted. The support may take the form of *logical, ethical,* or *emotional* appeals by trying to increase the readers' understanding, gain the readers' trust, or appeal to the readers' feelings. The following discussion includes explanations of each of these types of support with examples taken from the same articles as were the sample thesis statements listed above.

9c   Logical Appeal

A logical appeal provides factual or objective evidence. Evidence is considered factual or objective if there is a direct relationship between the support and some facts that are objectively verifiable in some way. This type of support is called *logical* because it appeals to the readers' intellect, reasoning, or logic rather than to their emotions.

Logical support for a thesis includes verifiable facts, statistics, observations, examples, or logical analogies. *Facts* are statements about things that can be attested to by others and that can be proven objectively by physical proof or by the testimony of witnesses. *Statistics* are numerical facts, such as information expressed as percentages or amounts. *Observations* involve eye-witness accounts of an event either by the author or by other witnesses. *Examples* are specific instances or cases that illustrate more general patterns or ideas. *Analogies* are logical comparisons that attempt to show how a less familiar situation is similar to another that is better known and can be considered logical if the comparison is one that is commonly observable or is based upon historical evidence. Now read the following examples of these five types of logical support.

Fact   A fact is an objectively verifiable type of evidence.

> Even the simplest organisms possess a daunting length of DNA. <u>Only recently have machines been developed that automate the task of identifying</u> the sequence of A's, T's G's and C's, short for adenine, thymine, guanine and cytosine, the chemical groups that make up <u>the four-letter alphabet of the genetic code</u>. The machines can handle fragments of DNA that are a few thousand letters in length, but it is no simple matter to reassemble the fragments in the correct order as they exist in the organism's genome.
>
> > Nicholas Wade, "First Sequencing of Cell's DNA Defines Basis of Life."

As you recall, this author's thesis had been that "For the first time, biologists can begin to see the entire parts list, as it were, of what a living cell needs to grow, survive and reproduce itself." The factual support here shows that it has not been until recently that a machine was available that could help researchers with the task of analyzing a cell's incredibly complex DNA code.

Statistic   A statistic is a fact in the form of a number.

> A University of California study recently looked at what would happen to UCLA if the admissions office stopped considering race and focused only on academics and socioeconomic disadvantages.
>
> The numbers were striking: <u>Asians today are 42% of the UCLA freshman class. If their race wasn't considered</u> (but socioeconomic disadvantage still was), <u>they'd be at 47% to 48%. Whites are at 28%. If race wasn't taken into account, they'd be at 32% to 35%</u>. Do a bit of subtraction, and you see that <u>10% of the students</u> who'd otherwise be in the entering class—<u>about 350 students every year—are rejected because of the race-conscious admissions program</u>.
>
> > Alexander Volokh and Shechao Charles Feng,
> > "How Race Adds Up for UCLA Entry."

These authors' thesis had been that "race is one of the most important factors in determining admission" into UCLA. The statistics included in this support—the *percentages* of admissions of Asians and whites and the *number* of students affected each year—are meant to show the significant role played by racial considerations in admissions decisions and how many students are affected by this policy.

Observation   An observation provides evidence based on personal experience.

> I came face to face with the essence of grunge culture last summer, when I was out in Seattle interviewing street punks. I was hanging out with a runaway vegan anarchist named Jackie and his street friend Anthony when we decided to go party with their friends from the band Suffocated. We took a shortcut to their house on the outskirts of the U district, tramping through the woods and under the bridge where the "trolls" (street kids) slept when they didn't have a squat to crash, then circling around the back of Safeway to scavenge for moldy sandwiches in the dumpster.
>
> Suffocated's lead guitarist received us nonchalantly, nodding at the 40-ouncers we'd picked up with Jackie and Anthony's panhandling change. Anthony said he wanted to try out his new piercing needle and disappeared into the bathroom upstairs. . . .
>
> Sarah Ferguson, "The Comfort of Being Sad."

These two paragraphs begin the introduction to an article in which the author uses her experience with some street kids in Seattle to show what grunge culture is like. Ferguson offers this description of what she observed to give readers a "face to face" look at the adopted lifestyle of some young people as support for her thesis that "Grunge appeals to white kids because it tells them that they're not responsible for the evils of racism and injustices, that they are victims too." She tries to show that these kids seem to have adopted poverty and an unhealthy lifestyle as ways to express the "essential nugget of shame" that she claims they feel.

Example   An example is a specific case used to illustrate a general idea.

> Slick Willy is the second bull terrier fortunate enough to belong to David Lykken, a psychologist interested in temperament. Temperament, which is reflected in a creature's manner of behavior, is personality's

biological, enduring, and heritable aspect. It greatly contributes to but does not entirely explain personality, much as innate intelligence contributes to but cannot entirely explain ability. <u>Willy's temperament originated when the English bulldog was deliberately crossed with the white English terrier, almost 200 years ago</u>. The nature of the resulting fearless, tenacious fighting machine requires a different sort of nurture than that of dogs bred for complaisance. When Willy can't resist chomping through a plastic jug with his powerful jaws or taking a few extra laps before responding to a summons, Lykken mostly just grumbles, reserving sterner measures for more serious infractions. Harsh treatment would render the feisty animal vicious; permissiveness or neglect would produce an uncontrollable bully. Willy's good behavior depends on an appreciation of his innate disposition and a judicious balance of carrot and stick.

Winifred Gallaher, "How We Become What We Are."

This example of a bull terrier is meant to illustrate the author's thesis that "Many aspects of our personalities, it now seems clear, are inborn and resistant to change—a fact, ironically, that makes the role of environment in our lives all the more important." She is trying to show that because Slick Willy, a bull terrier, has a fierce temperament resulting from almost two hundred years of breeding, he needs a certain care by his owner—"an appreciation of his innate disposition and a judicious balance of carrot and stick"—a treatment that is neither too harsh nor too permissive. This shows that certain inborn temperaments require specific environments in which to thrive and illustrates the author's point that both heredity and environment are important.

Analogy   An analogy is a comparison that is meant to clarify or explain.

Prayer in the schools represents a return to those good old days. They were days in which 12-year-olds didn't carry guns, in which children didn't mouth off to their elders, in which divorce was rare and marriages stuck for life, in which condoms stayed in wallets and out of schools.

They were also days in which black men were strung up from tall trees, women poured caustic cleansers inside themselves rather than face pregnancy, and nobody talked about daddy's drinking.

Queers were sick, women were irrational, and real men taught their sons to use their fists and never mind about their feelings, what are you, a sissy, boy?

Nobody ever seems to remember that part.

<u>The surface of that America gleamed as bright as a breakfront freshly rubbed with paste wax, with no notice taken of what sort of mess might be inside</u>. Some of it truly shone: Main Street, church suppers, the industry, the neighborliness, the embrace of extended family.

But it was also the America in which parents ruled their children but did not know them, nor the children their parents, in which what was handed down from generation to generation was distance and silence.

Anna Quindlen, "Lead Us Not."

Here the author is supporting her thesis that school prayer should not be required of school children. She compares "those good old days" in the past to a "breakfront freshly rubbed with paste wax, with no notice taken of what sort of mess might be inside." She apparently feels that what is now thought of as a better past was really a time when a pleasant appearance hid uglier social realities, similar to a nicely polished breakfront (a cabinet or bookcase with a central part that projects out) that is a mess inside.

9d Ethical Appeal

An ethical appeal is support that makes the author seem trustworthy. Sometimes, authors present information about themselves in order to show readers how reliable and qualified they are to express the views that they hold. More often, authors present the opinions or conclusions of authorities who agree with them or who have arrived at similar conclusions. This type of support may often be in the form of opinions or interpretations that cannot be objectively verified but that can add support to an argument because of the trust readers place in the authority being quoted. These opinions can strengthen an argument if the credibility of the authority is established by the author or is generally well known. These *expert opinions* are presented to make the author's view seem more credible or believable. By either demonstrating his or her own qualifications or by presenting expert opinions, an author is attempting to gain the readers' confidence so they will be more inclined to accept the author's argument.

Author's Qualification A statement of an author's qualification(s) attempts to increase readers' confidence in the author. The following is from a brief biographical sketch of Paul Kennedy, the author of the article "Overpopulation Tilts the Planet." The editors of a newspaper in which this article was reprinted included this information at the end of the first column in order to establish the author's qualifications to address the topic of overpopulation:

> Paul Kennedy, historian and author of *The Rise and Fall of the Great Powers* and *Preparing for the 21st Century,* is co-director of the Independent Working Group on the Future of the United Nations. Appointed by U.N. Secretary-General Boutros-Boutros Ghali, the body is chaired by outgoing German President Richard von Weizsacker and Moreen Quereshi, former prime minister of Pakistan. He wrote this piece for *New Perspectives Quarterly.*
>
> "The Perils of Overpopulation," *The Miami Herald.*

Knowing that Paul Kennedy is the author of two books with impressive-sounding titles, and that he is a co-director of what seems to be an important United Nations group, readers will be likely to take what he says more seriously than if they did not know this information about him.

Expert Opinion   An expert opinion attempts to make readers more likely to trust the author's conclusions by showing that they are supported by other respected authorities.

> In sum, there is today a vast demographic-technological fault line appearing across our planet. On one side of this line are the fast-growing, adolescent, under-resourced, undercatipalized, undereducated societies; on the other side are the rich, technologically inventive yet demographically moribund aging populations.
>
> Perhaps the most glaring cleavage today lies along the Mediterranean, between southern Europe and North Africa. But there are also others—along the Rio Grande in North America, between the Slavic and non-Slavic people of Asia, between Australia and Indonesia.
>
> The greatest challenge global society faces today is preventing this fault line from erupting into a world-shaking crisis. <u>I agree with the Nobel scientist from MIT, Dr. Henry Kendall, who argues that "If we do not stabilize population with justice, with humanity and mercy, then it will be done for us by nature, and it will be done brutally and without pity</u>."
>
> Paul Kennedy, "Overpopulation Tilts the Planet."

The author quotes Dr. Kendall of MIT who agrees with him that it is crucial to deal humanely with the growing disparities between the developed and the underdeveloped areas of the world. The quotation adds significance to the author's argument by including a statement from a highly respected winner of the Nobel prize, making it clear that the author is not alone in his alarm over the population situation.

9e Emotional Appeal

An emotional appeal uses support that appeals to readers' needs or values.

Sometimes an argument will include support that is neither based on factual evidence nor dependent upon the confirmation of authorities. Sometimes an author will try to convince readers by presenting reasons that appeal to their values. This support is subjective or personal because it appeals to readers' beliefs, values, or motivations rather than to their knowledge, understanding, or logic.

This type of support is essentially an appeal to readers' emotions involving an appeal either to their needs or their values. When an author appeals to readers' needs, he or she first tries to identify something that motivates readers, such as the desire for sustenance, security, comfort, or belonging. An appeal to readers' values involves an appeal to what readers think is important, such as responsibility, loyalty, honesty, or courage. By appealing to readers' needs or values, an author is attempting to convince them that the argument is consistent with what they want or think is important. Authors may include this type of support in order to engage readers by trying to get them to identify with the subject or with the author's view.

Appeal to Needs   An appeal to needs attempts to identify the argument with readers' desires or with needs such as security, freedom, love, success, physical well-being, or the fulfillment of one's potential.

> That is why, in the end, change will only come if the average person recognizes, as most now do with respect to environmental issues, that only a global trans-national response to the growing demographic divide from rich and poor societies alike will give the planet Earth a chance to survive. Otherwise the coming deluge of people is certain to swamp all other concerns in the 21st century. Then, hope will be hard to come by.
>
> Paul Kennedy, "Overpopulation Tilts the Planet."

This is the concluding paragraph in Kennedy's article about overpopulation. In his final supporting point, he tries to relate the population issue to readers' personal desires for security and survival and their need to have hope for the future. He appeals to readers' fears by stating that unless "the average person recognizes" the need for international action, there could be a "coming deluge of people" that he suggests would "swamp all other concerns in the 21st century." These are urgent words meant to make readers concerned for their own future and to persuade them—to persuade you—to accept his argument.

Appeal to Values   An appeal to values attempts to identify the argument with what readers think is important.

> Blackness also connotes something positive: the subcultural heritage of African-Americans that in spite of centuries of discrimination has vastly enriched American civilization out of all proportion to the numbers, and treatment of the group creating it. The University of California, like other great institutions of learning, rightly has seen <u>the exposure of all its students to this important minority culture as part of its educational mission</u>.
>
>   This is a noble goal, but it is fraught with dangers. What brought me around to support affirmative action after some strong initial reservations was not only its effectiveness as a strategy for reducing inequity, but <u>also its possibilities for cross-pollinating our multi-ethnic communities</u>. In the process, it could <u>promote that precious, overarching national culture</u>—which I call ecumenical America.
>
> Orlando Patterson, "Affirmative Action, on the Merit System."

This author is suggesting that affirmative action has the positive potential to expose students to African-American culture and to promote "cross-pollinating our multi-ethnic communities" toward what he calls an "ecumenical America"—a nation with unity among its different cultural groups. These points are meant to support his thesis that affirmative action "has helped us achieve the constitutional commitment to the ideal of equity and fairness" by appealing to something that most readers would be likely to value—a united America living in racial and cultural equality.

Recognizing Assumptions

Sometimes referred to as the warrants, the *assumptions* are the generally accepted truths or commonly held beliefs that underlie an author's argument. The assumptions are the ideas that authors assume readers will share with them and that make the support acceptable. Assumptions are almost always unstated and thus need to be inferred. In this sense, the assumptions are not really an identifiable part of an argument in the way that the thesis and support are directly stated or obviously implied. Assumptions are, however, the implied reasons that an author chooses certain types of support that readers would be likely to find convincing and believable.

For example, if an author's thesis is that a vegetarian diet is healthier than a diet that includes meat, and the main supporting point is a reference to a research study conducted by a team of doctors at a well-known university clinic, then the assumption is that the doctors are reliable sources of information and that readers will feel confident in the judgment of these authorities. The author is not likely to state this assumption directly but is more likely to provide enough information about the research and the doctors so that readers will agree with the author's assumption that this is reliable support. The author also assumes that most readers have enough confidence in the findings of clinical research conducted at a university that they are likely to accept this as logical support. An author may decide to explain an assumption, however, if he or she feels that the readers may for some reason be hostile toward the findings or skeptical of the support.

Just as there are different types of theses and support, there are different types of assumptions: *factual assumptions*, based on what most people commonly believe is true or factual; *authoritative assumptions*, based on what most people believe concerning the reliability of certain sources of information; and *value assumptions*, based on what most people believe is most important. Thus, assumptions are highly dependent upon the culture that the author and the readers belong to, for the beliefs concerning truth and importance can vary significantly from culture to culture.

Nonetheless, even though assumptions are perhaps the most difficult aspect of an argument to detect, they are often the most important in deciding whether or not to accept the argument. When attempting to infer an unstated assumption, a useful strategy is to formulate a counterargument representing the opposite of the author's thesis. Try this strategy with the following example of a thesis and supporting point.

<u>Affirmative action in college admissions does more harm than good</u>. When the pace is moving so fast that [affirmative action students] can't

catch up, they end up failing. When you see that black students who don't have the skills are dropping out, then that just reinforces the stereotypes that we [African Americans] are not intelligent and can't achieve, and that is not true.

James Steibel, "UC Affirmative Action: What Does it Mean to Those It Affects?"

This is an argument made against affirmative action by a student who graduated from a community college and plans to transfer to a university. The author's supporting point is that affirmative action students "who don't have the skills" do poorly, which "just reinforces the stereotypes that we [African Americans] are not intelligent and can't achieve." The counterargument to this would be something like the following: "Affirmative action does more good than harm because it allows underprepared African American students the chance to succeed." In this way, it becomes apparent that the author's assumption is that minority students admitted under affirmative action programs are less skilled and are less likely to succeed than other students.

Now consider the following examples of each of the three types of assumptions: factual assumptions, based on common beliefs about what is true; authoritative assumptions, based on the believed reliability of sources; and value assumptions, based on common beliefs about what is important.

9f Factual Assumption

A factual assumption is based on what most people commonly believe is true.

In the introduction from Orlando Patterson's argument quoted earlier in this chapter, he states his thesis that affirmative action "has helped us achieve the constitutional commitment to the ideal of equity and fairness." The following is the first point he uses to support this thesis.

So it is hard to understand why it has become the most contentious issue in the nation. <u>One would have thought that a policy that so many politicians denounced would have adversely touched the lives of at least a substantial proportion of those opposing it.</u>

<u>The facts show just the opposite.</u> A National Opinion Research Center survey in 1990, still applicable today, found that while more than 70 percent of white Americans asserted that whites were being hurt by affirmative action for blacks, <u>only 7 percent claimed to have experienced any form of reverse discrimination</u>. Only 16 percent knew of someone

close who had. Fewer than one in four could even claim that it was something they had witnessed or heard about at their workplace.

Orlando Patterson, "Affirmative Action, on the Merit System."

Patterson's point here is that according to a survey, only a small percentage of white Americans have experienced reverse discrimination as a result of affirmative action programs. Turning his thesis and this support around, a counterargument could state that "Affirmative action is harmful because a survey has shown that it has adversely affected 7 percent of whites." Thus, it becomes clear that this argument hinges on the percentage of whites who said they had experienced reverse discrimination. The author apparently believes this to be effective support on the assumption that most readers will agree that 7 percent is a low figure.

9g   Authoritative Assumption

An authoritative assumption is based on beliefs concerning the trustworthiness of a source.

Later in Patterson's argument, he admits that one of the problems with affirmative action is that it has often been blamed for the "persuasiveness of ethnic separatism" among minority groups on university campuses. However, he then refers to a research study to show that this separatism is not an inevitable result of affirmative action programs.

> Ethnic separatism has also had deleterious academic consequences. In an experiment conducted at the University of Michigan by two psychologists, Claude Steele and Richard Nisbett, a group of disadvantaged minority students who were encouraged to be part of the campus mainstream and made to understand that the highest standards were expected of them, consistently performed above the average for white students and the student body as a whole. Members of a control group who took the familiar route of ethnic solidarity and consciousness-raising performed well below the average.

Orlando Patterson, "Affirmative Action, on the Merit System."

Here Patterson refers to a study conducted by two University of Michigan researchers to show that affirmative action programs that encourage assimilation into the mainstream of student life work better than those that do not. He is relying on readers' respect for a university study by named psychologists that will make their findings persuasive. Turning Patterson's argument around would result in a counterargument stating that "Affirmative action has *not* been effective because it often results in ethnic separation and poor student performance." Thus, Steele's and Nisbett's findings that students who were encouraged to be part of mainstream campus life "consistently performed above the average for white students and the student body as a whole" are crucial, and the effectiveness of this as support depends on readers' acceptance of them as authorities.

9h   Value Assumption

A value assumption is based on what most people believe is important, is more important than something else, or is most important of all.

Next in Orlando Patterson's argument, he goes on to discuss a few problems that affirmative action programs have had and to comment on what he feels should be done as a result. Read the following excerpt in which Patterson makes an assumption about cultural diversity.

> These are all correctable errors. Universities and businesses should return to <u>the principle of integration</u>, to the notion that diversity is not something to be celebrated and promoted in its own right, <u>but an opportunity for mutual understanding</u> and the <u>furtherance of an ecumenical culture</u>.
>
> Orlando Patterson, "Affirmative Action, on the Merit System."

Here, Patterson suggests that the problems with affirmative action can be corrected if institutions "return to the principle of integration" and promote "mutual understanding" rather than the celebration of diversity. A counterargument would be that "The problems of affirmative action cannot be corrected because ethnic separatism is inherent in these programs, and nothing can be done about it." Thus, Patterson's assumption here is that readers will agree with him in the belief that racial and cultural unity is more important than division and separation. He then hopes that agreement on this point will lead readers to also agree with him that affirmative action programs can work if this unity becomes their purpose.

Chapter Review

An argument is composed of three parts: the thesis, the support, and the assumptions. When analyzing an argument, be sure that you first know the issue being discussed. Then read the argument, looking for its three parts.

1.   First, identify the **thesis,** or the main point that the author is trying to prove, and decide what type of claim is being made. A likely place to look for the thesis is in an introduction at the beginning or in a conclusion at the end.

2.   Next, identify the main **support** that the author is providing in an attempt to convince you to accept the thesis.

3.   Finally, as you identify each support, try to infer the **assumption**—the generally accepted truths or beliefs underlying the support—that is meant to make the support believable.

Thesis: The main point of the argument.	
Factual Claims	**Value Claims**
The attempt to convince readers that something is true by providing supporting evidence in the form of verifiable facts, statistics, or real-life examples.	An argument that passes judgment or expresses approval or disapproval.

Support: Evidence presented to support the thesis.		
Logical Appeal	**Ethical Appeal**	**Emotional Appeal**
Support that provides factual evidence, including facts, statistics, examples, or analogies.	Support that makes the author seem trustworthy by presenting information about his or her own credentials or by presenting the opinions or conclusions of authorities.	Support that appeals to readers' needs or values.

Assumptions: The generally accepted truths or beliefs underlying the support.		
Factual Assumption	**Authoritative Assumption**	**Value Assumption**
Based on what most people commonly believe is true.	Based on the trustworthiness of a source.	Based on what most people believe is most important.

CHAPTER 10

Evaluating Arguments

In Chapter 9, we considered the analysis of arguments—identifying the thesis, the main support, and the assumptions underlying an argument—in order to understand how an author organizes material to convince you of something. This chapter will take this discussion a step further and consider the evaluation of arguments—the process of determining their quality. While analysis involves determining *how* an argument is constructed, evaluation involves judging *how well* the author accomplishes this.

When evaluating an argument, you want to consider its *soundness*, or the effectiveness with which an author supports his or her thesis. In determining whether to accept an argument, you should look for support that relies on more than authoritative or emotional appeals. Critical readers should expect to see more than ethical or emotional support in an argument but should want substantial logical support, preferably in the form of factual or other objective evidence. Similarly, when evaluating an argument, you should consider the soundness of the underlying assumptions as well as the support. Sometimes the support may seem accurate or sufficient, but the assumptions underlying it may not always be. This chapter will examine these issues, first through a discussion of ways to evaluate the support and the assumptions, followed by two complete argumentative essays accompanied by evaluative comments.

Determining the Soundness of an Argument

When you are evaluating an argument, or determining its soundness, a skeptical attitude is quite helpful. The first thing you should do when you are evaluating an argument is analyze it by identifying the thesis and the support and by determining the assumptions underlying the support. Once these are understood, ask three crucial questions: "Is there enough support?" "Is the support relevant?" "Do the assumptions underlying the support really justify the support?"

10a   Evaluating the Support

Readers too often take for granted that information must be accurate or truthful simply because it appears in print. This is obviously not always the case, but unfortunately you may not always be knowledgeable enough of the subject under discussion to know whether something is accurate. Nor can you, even as a critical reader, be expected to track down the accuracy of every bit of information you read. For these reasons, you probably tend to have a certain amount of trust in the editors of whatever publication you are reading that they will not publish something without first checking the accuracy of the information presented. However, even if you may lack the technical knowledge to judge information you read, there are logical criteria that you can use to evaluate arguments.

You can and should judge written arguments according to how *believable* you find them. You can first consider how well the evidence presented actually supports the thesis. To accomplish this, you want to try to determine whether the support is both *sufficient* and *relevant* by asking two important questions: "Is there *enough* support to justify the claim?" and "Is the support *directly related* to the thesis?"

Consider the following letter to the editor of a newspaper. It is written by a public school student on the topic of extending the school year. The author's thesis is in the first paragraph, followed by three supporting paragraphs. It ends with a concluding paragraph that summarizes the main point of the argument.

> *Extending the school year would be unnecessary if class time actually were used for teaching and learning.*
>
> Enthusiasm became dismay, and dismay became disillusionment as the truth about public secondary school revealed itself to me last year. <u>In class after class, nothing happened from day to day</u>. Some teachers did not even address the students, or look at us, much less assign us class work: We were expected to kill the time talking among ourselves.
>
> Some days a 10-minute quiz was substance for a 60-minute period. My honors English class spent a week working in groups to color a poster. Students watched movies of literary works and, to keep our eyes glued to the screen, were threatened with being made to read a book. A rare essay assignment submitted in October was returned with a grade in January.
>
> Seven periods out of 10 our honors foreign language class kibitzed with the teacher about proms and clubs and soap operas—in English. As the end of the grading period neared, even less occurred as teachers ignored students to prepare grades.
>
> <u>Except for time spent in the class of one good, conscientious teacher, the months that I spent in school (a "good" school in a good neighborhood) represent little learning</u>. Counting the hours that a school system devotes to core academic courses reveals no truth about the learning experience.
>
> *Adding more such days to the school year will not make our country more economically competitive. Nor will it ensure excellence.* Extending such a school year, however, will steal from public school students time that never can be won back, essential time during which they can replenish some of the natural enthusiasm and creativity diminished by the 180-day school year.
>
> Ellen Bogar, "Make Hours Spent in School Really Count."

Considering the author's argument first by the relevancy of the support, you want to think about whether her two main supporting points are directly related to her thesis that "Extending the school year would be unnecessary if class time actually were used for teaching and learning." Her two main supporting points—"In class after class, nothing happened from day to day" and "Except for time spent in the class of one good, conscientious teacher, the months that I spent in school . . . represent little learning"—are certainly about the lack of learning experienced in school.

The next question to ask concerns the sufficiency of the evidence provided to support the thesis. In other words, are these two major supporting points and the minor support the author provides enough to make her thesis convincing? For her first supporting point, she provides examples of her English and foreign language classes to illustrate that few constructive activities go on. However, her second point has less to back it up. She merely states that she has learned very little in her core courses without any evidence to explain this. The type of support she provides consists entirely of logical appeals in the form of personal observations and experiences. This piece indeed represents a compelling statement from one student's perspective that extending the school year alone will not guarantee more learning. However, in and of itself, it is perhaps not a complete argument against extending the school year.

The following discussion about ways to evaluate an author's assumptions will refer you back to this student's argument as an example, which may clarify why this is not a complete argument against extending the school year.

10b   Evaluating the Assumptions

As you may recall from Chapter 9, the assumptions in an argument are the unstated and generally accepted truths or commonly held beliefs that the author thinks readers are likely to share and that underlie his or her argument. When evaluating an argument and considering its believability—how well you feel the evidence supports the thesis—you need to think about the assumptions underlying the support. You may also recall from Chapter 9 that a useful strategy to uncover the author's assumptions is to play the devil's advocate and think up counterarguments—arguments that oppose what the author is saying. This is also a useful strategy to see how well the author's points hold up.

To evaluate an author's assumptions, you must not only consider the sufficiency and relevance of the support, you must also consider to what extent the support is based on some commonly accepted truth (factual assumption), on sources of information that most people consider reliable (authoritative assumption), or on what most people believe is important (value assumption). To evaluate the assumptions in this way, ask the following questions: "Is the support based on some commonly accepted truth?"; "Is the support based on sources of information that are generally considered reliable?"; or "Is the support based on what most people believe is important?"

Look back at the argument written by the public school student about extending the school year, this time in terms of the assumptions she is making with regard to her support. Remember, her argument is basically that extending the school year will not increase learning because very little learning goes on in school. Her first supporting point is that "In class after class, nothing happened from day to day." She then goes on to give examples mainly from her English and foreign language classes to show that this is so.

> Some teachers did not even address the students, or look at us, much less assign us class work: We were expected to kill the time talking among ourselves.
>
> Some days a 10-minute quiz was substance for a 60-minute period. My honors English class spent a week working in groups to color a poster. Students watched movies of literary works and, to keep our eyes glued to the screen, were threatened with being made to read a book. A rare essay assignment submitted in October was returned with a grade in January.
>
> Seven periods out of 10 our honors foreign language class kibitzed with the teacher about proms and clubs and soap operas—in English. As the end of the grading period neared, even less occurred as teachers ignored students to prepare grades.
>
> Ellen Bogar, "Make Hours Spent in School Really Count."

What she is basically trying to show here is that extending the school year would be useless because so few educational activities actually go on in school. However, a counterargument to this could be that "Extending the school year would be beneficial because it would more closely coincide with parents' work schedules." This counterargument makes the author's assumption clear, that the students' needs are the main consideration in extending the school year. However, as the counterargument shows, this may not necessarily be the case.

Her second supporting point—"Except for time spent in the class of one good, conscientious teacher, the months that I spent in school . . . represent little learning"—really makes the same assumption. Again, even though her assumptions logically suggest that her support is relevant and important in a discussion of the issue of extending the school year, her support is probably not enough to make a complete argument on this topic.

Evaluating Arguments

To sum up, when evaluating an argument, you want to consider the three parts—the thesis, the support, and the assumptions—and decide how well the support and assumptions actually lead to and lend support to the thesis. Thus, when evaluating an argument, do the following.

1. First, be sure that you have identified the **main point** the author is making, **the main support** that the author is providing, and the **underlying assumptions** that are meant to make the support believable.

2. Next, evaluate the support by considering it in terms of its **sufficiency** and **relevance**. Do so by asking the following questions.

   "Is there **enough** support to justify the claim?" (sufficiency)

   "Is the support **directly related** to the thesis?" (relevance)

3. Finally, evaluate the **assumptions** by considering the **believability** or **reasonableness** of the support. Do so by thinking up an opposing point to what the author is saying and by asking the following questions.

   "Is the support based on some **commonly accepted truth**?"

   "Is the support based on **sources of information** that are generally **considered reliable**?"

   "Is the support based on **what most people believe is important**?"

Now consider the following article by Barbara Ehrenreich on the controversial topic of drug legalization that originally appeared in *Time* magazine. The article itself appears below in the column on the left, and evaluative comments appear on the right. As you read it, look for the parts of the argument—the thesis, support, and assumptions. Notice that throughout the article, different type formats are used to indicate the thesis and support: the thesis is in *bold italic* type; the main supporting points are in **bold** type; main supporting points in paragraphs are <u>underlined</u>.

Kicking the Big One
by Barbara Ehrenreich

Evaluative Comments

An evil grips America, a life-sapping, drug-related habit. It beclouds reason and corrodes the spirit. It undermines authority and nourishes a low-minded culture of winks and smirks. It's the habit of *drug prohibition,* and *it's quietly siphoning off the resources that might be better used for drug treatment or prevention.* Numerous authorities have tried to warn us, including most recently the Surgeon General, but she got brushed off like a piece of lint. After all, drug prohibition is right up there with heroin and nicotine among the habits that are hell to kick.

Admittedly, <u>legalization wouldn't be problem-free</u> either. <u>Americans have a peculiarly voracious appetite for drugs</u>, and probably no one should weigh in on the debate who hasn't seen a friend or loved one hollowed out by cocaine or reduced to selling used appliances on the street. But if drugs take a ghastly toll, *drug prohibition has proved itself, year after year, to be an even more debilitating social toxin.*

Consider **the moral effects of marijuana prohibition**. After booze and NyQuil, pot is probably America's No. 1 drug of choice—a transient, <u>introspective high</u> that <u>can cure nausea</u> or make the evening sitcoms look

Introduction

The thesis is that drug prohibition has had negative effects and should be replaced with treatment and prevention strategies.

Here she admits that legalization would have its own problems because of Americans' desire to take drugs. She then restates her thesis that prohibition has caused even more problems.

Support

Her first supporting point is that there are moral effects of marijuana prohibition: It is contradictory and hypocritical that a relatively harmless drug used by many Americans is

like devastating wit. <u>An esti-mated 40 million Americans have tried it</u> at some point, from Ivy League law professors to country-and-western singers. Yet <u>in some states, possession of a few grams can get you put away for years</u>. What does it do to one's immortal soul to puff and wink and look away while about 100,000 other Americans remain locked up for doing the exact same thing? <u>Marijuana prohibi-tion establishes a minimum base-line level of cultural dishonesty</u> that we can never rise above: the President "didn't inhale," heh heh. It's O.K. to drink till you puke, but you mustn't ever smoke the vile weed, heh heh. One of the hardest things a parent can ever tell a bright and ques-tioning teen-ager—after all the relevant sermonizing, of course—is, Well, just don't get caught.

But **the prohibition of cocaine and heroin may be more corro-sive still**. Here's where <u>organized crime</u> comes in, the cartels and kingpins and Crips and Bloods. These <u>are the principal beneficia-ries of drug prohibition</u>; without it they'd be reduced to three-card monte and numbers scams. Legitimate entrepreneurs must sigh and shake their heads in envy: if only the government would ban some substance like Wheat Chex, for example, so it could be marketed for hundreds of dollars an ounce.

illegal and can lead to arrest and im-prisonment. The assumption here is that marijuana use is harmless. How-ever, she does not provide any evi-dence to show that this is so.

She assumes her readers will agree with her that marijuana is harmless and therefore should be legalized. She feels that this would eliminate the hypocrisy of adult users or for-mer users having to feel guilty about those who are in jail for the same thing or being in the awkward position of having to tell kids not to use it.

Her second supporting point is that the prohibition of cocaine and heroin has had even more serious conse-quences: It has led to organized criminals who have profited from the sale of these illegal drugs. Her as-sumption here is that organized crime has flourished over the illegal drug trade. Though she provides no proof of this, she assumes that most readers will agree with her, and in this she is probably right.

Yes, <u>legal drugs, even if heavily taxed and extensively regulated, would no doubt be cheaper than illegal ones</u>, which could mean <u>more people sampling them out of curiosity</u>. But this danger has to be weighed <u>against the insidious marketing dynamic of illegal drugs</u>, whose wildly inflated prices <u>compel the low-income user to become a pusher and recruiter of new users</u>.

Drugs can kill, of course. But **drug prohibition kills too**. <u>In Washington, an estimated 80% of homicides are drug related, meaning drug-prohibition related</u>. It's <u>gunshot wounds</u> that fill our urban emergency rooms, not ODs and bad trips. **Then there's the perverse financial logic of prohibition**. The <u>billions we spend a year on drug-related law enforcement represents money not spent on improving schools and rebuilding neighborhoods</u>. Those who can't hope for the lasting highs of achievement and self-respect are all too often condemned to crack.

So why don't we kick the prohibition habit? Is it high-minded puritanism that holds us back, or political cowardice? Or maybe it's time to admit that **we cling to prohibition** for the same reason we cling to so many other self-destructive habits: **because we like the way they make us feel**. Prohibition, for example, tends to make its advocates feel

She goes on, however, with a more controversial point: even though legalization would lead many people to try drugs out of curiosity, it would be beneficial for society by eliminating the incentive that criminal drug pushers now have to recruit new users. She is assuming that legalization is the only way to eliminate the criminal drug trade, which many readers will not agree with, especially without more convincing evidence.

Her next point is that there are other harmful effects of drug prohibition: Many deaths have resulted from prohibition, and it has deflected money away from more useful social and educational purposes. She is making two assumptions here: First, that it is more important to end drug-related shootings and deaths than it is to continue drug prohibitions; and second, that it is more important to spend money on social and educational programs than on costs related to drug prohibition. While many readers would possibly agree with these assumptions, without more information to explain them, it seems that she is essentially implying a false dilemma fallacy—allowing only for two extreme possibilities without providing enough information to support her assessment of the situation.

Next, Ehrenreich makes the point that Americans want drug prohibition because it makes them feel they are doing the right thing.

powerfully righteous, and militant righteousness has effects not unlike some demon mix of liquor and amphetamines: the eyes bulge, the veins distend, the voice begins to bray.

But the most seductive thing about prohibition is that it keeps us from having to confront all the other little addictions that get us through the day. It's the NutraSweet in the coffee we use to wash down the chocolate mousse; a dad's "Just say no" commandments borne on martini-scented breath. "Don't do drugs," a Members Only ad advises. "Do clothes." Well, why "do" anything? Why not live more lightly, without compulsions of any kind? Then there's TV, the addiction whose name we can hardly speak—the poor man's virtual reality, the substance-free citizen's 24-hour-a-day hallucinatory trip. No bleary-eyed tube addict, emerging from weekend-long catatonia, has the right to inveigh against "drugs."

When cornered, the prohibition addict has one last line of defense. We can't surrender in this war, he or she insists, because we'd be sending the "wrong message." **But the message we're sending now is** this: Look, kids, **we know prohibition doesn't work**, that it's cruel and costs so much we don't have anything left over with which to fight the social causes of addiction or

Also, she says that prohibition is an excuse not to have to deal with other types of legal addictive behavior, such as drinking coffee and alcohol, eating sweets, and watching television. She is making two assumptions in these two paragraphs: First, that feeling right is not the same as doing right; and second, that drug use is no worse than the other types of addictive behavior that she lists. While her first assumption is one that most people would probably agree with, the second is one that most probably would not, at least not without a good deal of factual evidence showing the actual effects of these different types of behavior, none of which the author provides.

Conclusion

Her final point is that adults are sending a contradictory message that is not fooling kids: Even though prohibition does not work, it makes adults feel good to pretend that it does. She suggests that kids' response to this message is to ignore adults' advice.

treat the addicts, **but**, hey, **it feels good**, so we're going to keep right on doing it. <u>To which the appropriate response is, of course, heh heh</u>.

We don't have **to quit** cold turkey. **We could start with marijuana, then ease up on cocaine and heroin possession, concentrating law enforcement on the big-time pushers**. Take it slowly, see how it feels. One day at a time.

Finally, Ehrenreich recommends that drugs be gradually legalized, with law enforcement concentrating only on organized crime.

Most of the evaluative comments above are either summaries of the author's thesis and her supporting points or evaluations of her assumptions, some of which seem reasonable and some of which seem less so. Concerning the support itself, the questions remain: "Is there enough support to justify the claim?" and "Is the support directly related to the thesis?" The following outline of the thesis and supporting points may help evaluate the argument.

Thesis: Drug prohibition has had negative effects and should be replaced with treatment and prevention strategies.

- A. Moral effects of marijuana prohibition
    1. A relatively harmless drug
    2. Used by many Americans
    3. Illegal and can lead to arrest and imprisonment
- B. Prohibition of cocaine and heroin, more serious consequences
    1. Organized crime
    2. Drug pushers recruiting new users
- C. Other harmful effects of drug prohibition
    1. Deaths resulting from prohibition
    2. Deflected money away from social and educational purposes
- D. Reasons people want drug prohibition
    1. People feel they are doing the right thing
    2. An excuse not to have to deal with other addictive behavior
- E. Adults sending a contradictory message to kids

      F.   Suggestions
          1.   Gradual legalization
          2.   Law enforcement concentrating only on organized crime

Thus, while the support all directly relates to the thesis, the author seems to rely almost completely on the persuasive logic of her points rather than on any substantive factual evidence. She includes no references to authorities and states nothing that would suggest her expertise on the subject. She makes a lot of assumptions that readers may or may not agree with. Her tone is mocking and sarcastic—"a low-minded culture of winks and smirks"; "What does it do to one's immortal soul to puff and wink and look away"; "the President 'didn't inhale,' heh heh. It's O.K. to drink till you puke, but you mustn't ever smoke the vile weed, heh heh"; "militant righteousness has effects not unlike some demon mix of liquor and amphetamines: the eyes bulge, the veins distend, the voice begins to bray." This almost makes it seem that she is writing for readers who already agree with her, or simply to shove it in the face of those who don't. In any event, regardless of how you feel about the issue of drug legalization, the argument that Ms. Ehrenreich has put together lacks substantive support, and it would probably only be acceptable to those who can accept her assumptions, many of which seem questionable without more evidence. Even those readers who can appreciate her brand of humor would probably have to admit that this article is much better at pointing out hypocrisies than it is at presenting a well-structured, convincing argument.

Now read one more example of an argumentative essay, this one by the columnist Ellen Goodman. This argument is on the same topic as the student's essay that you read earlier in this chapter—extending the school year—but from a different perspective. As you read, notice the different type formats that indicate the thesis and support: *thesis*, **major supporting points**, <u>main support.</u>

Turning Hands on School Clock
by Ellen Goodman

The kids are hanging out. I pass small bands of once-and-future students, on my way to work these mornings. They have become a familiar part of the summer landscape.

These kids are not old enough for jobs. Nor are they rich enough for camp. They are school children without school. The calendar called the school year ran out on them a few weeks ago. Once supervised by teachers and principals, they now appear to be in "self care."

Like others who fall through the cracks of their parents' makeshift plans—a week with relatives, a day at the playground—they hang out. With a key in each pocket.

Passing them is like passing through a time zone. **For much of our history**, after all, **Americans framed the school year around the needs of work and family**. In 19th century cities, schools were open seven or eight hours a day, 11 months a year. In rural America, the year was arranged around the growing season.

Now, only 3 percent of families follow the agricultural model, but nearly all schools are scheduled as if our children went home early to milk the cows and took months off to work the crops. Now, three-quarters of the

Evaluative Comments

Introduction

The thesis of this article is suggested in the title and implied in the first two introductory paragraphs—the school year should be lengthened so that kids are in school more during the year.

Support

Ms. Goodman begins her support with some reasons why she feels that the school year should be extended.

First, she argues that the present school calendar no longer meets the needs of working parents. The assumption she is making in this point is that the school calendar should be based on family work patterns. She backs up this assumption with facts that the agricultural model with long summer time off is no longer relevant for the vast majority of American families and that most mothers now work. She mentions the average work hours for parents, which supports the point that they cannot be home when their school-age children get out of school. Probably few parents would dispute these points.

mothers of school-age children work, but the calendar is written as if they were home waiting for the school bus.

The six-hour day, the 189-day school year is regarded as somehow sacrosanct, a cherished American Tradition. But **when parents work an eight-hour day and a 240-hour year**, it means something different. It means that many kids go home to empty houses. It means that, in the summer, they hang out.

"We have a huge mismatch between the school calendar and the realities of family life," says **Dr. Ernest Boyer**, head of the Carnegie Foundation for the Advancement of Teaching. "Children spend a huge amount of time alone without any interaction with adults."

Dr. Boyer is one of many who believe that a radical revision of the school calendar is inevitable. **"School, whether we like it or not, is custodial and educational.** It always has been."

His is not a popular idea. Schools are routinely burdened with the job of solving all our social problems. Can they be asked now to synchronize our work and family lives?

It may be easier to promote a longer school year on its educational merits, and indeed, **the educational case is compelling**. Despite the complaints and studies about our kids' lack of

She then quotes Dr. Ernest Boyer to reinforce the point that the school calendar does not match parents' work schedules. By quoting this recognized authority in the field of education, she is adding credibility to her opinion.

The second quote from Dr. Boyer also supports the assumption that the school calendar should accommodate family needs: School provides a custodial—a day-care, caretaker, or supervisory role—as well as an educational service. However, she admits that this idea has been controversial.

The second main reason the author gives for lengthening the school calendar is that it would increase learning. Her assumption is that more time

learning, the <u>United States still has a shorter school year than any industrial nation</u>.

In most of Europe, the school year is 220 days. In Japan, it is 240 days. While classroom time alone doesn't produce a well-educated child, <u>learning takes time and more learning takes more time</u>. The long summers of forgetting take a toll, particularly on the have-nots—on those who have no summer sorts of learning.

As Boyer says, "<u>The learning curve does tend to drop in summer</u>. But the pathologies of <u>being adrift in summer with only your peers</u> has graver consequences."

The opposition to a longer school year comes <u>from families</u> that want to and can provide other experiences for their children. It comes from <u>teachers</u>. It comes from tradition. And surely from <u>kids</u>. But <u>the crux</u> of the conflict has been over <u>money</u>. To extend school hours and days just to keep kids at their seats is expensive. To do more than that, costs.

But we can, as **Boyer suggests**, begin to turn the hands of the school clock forward slowly. The first step is to <u>extend an optional after-school program</u> of education and recreation to every district. The second step <u>is a summer program with its own staff</u>, paid for by fees for those who can pay and vouchers for those who can't.

The third step will be the hardest: **a true overhaul of the school**

spent in school equals more learning. She tries to back this up by referring to the longer school years in Europe and Japan, implying that students there learn more. Most readers are probably familiar with test scores that routinely show European and Japanese students outscoring American students, but Goodman does not give any evidence that the reason for this is more time in school, other than to quote Boyer who expresses a similar view. There could be other reasons for the poor showing of American students. Indeed, remember the letter-to-the-editor from the high school student quoted earlier in this chapter?

Goodman then lists those who oppose a longer school calendar, including the main objection—the additional costs. By doing so, she admits that her idea is not necessarily a popular one.

Her final point is to summarize Dr. Boyer's suggestions for phasing in a longer school year, resulting in a completely different schedule that would be more accommodating to parents' working lives.

Here Goodman is assuming that these changes would indeed be

year. Once school was carefully calibrated to arrange children's schedules around the edges of family needs. Now, working parents, especially mothers, even teachers, try and blend their work lives around the edges of the school day.

better for parents, an idea that she has already shown not all would agree with.

So it's back to the future. Today there are too many school doors locked and too many kids hanging out. **It's time to get our calendars updated**.

Conclusion

The author ends with a clear statement of her thesis in the final sentence.

Ellen Goodman's thesis, of course, is that the school calendar should be lengthened: "It's time to get our calendars updated." She supports this opinion with two main points: First, the present school calendar no longer meets the needs of working parents; and second, a longer school year would increase learning. She also is making two assumptions that underlie these points: First, the school calendar should be consistent with family work habits; and second, more school time means more learning. The first of these assumptions is one that most Americans would probably agree with, especially with all the information she brings to support it. The second one, however, seems less certain, especially considering the article by Ellen Bogar quoted earlier in this chapter.

In terms of the relevancy and adequacy of her supporting points, an outline should help make these issues clearer.

Thesis: The school calendar should be lengthened.
  A. Reasons for lengthening the school year
    1. To meet the needs of working parents
      a. originally for farm families
      b. families now work all year
      c. Boyer
        1. mismatch
        2. custodial mission of schools
    2. To increase learning
      a. other nations
      b. long summer vacations
  B. Opposition to the idea
  C. Boyer's recommendations

Clearly Goodman's supporting points are relevant to the topic: They all relate directly to the issue of a longer school calendar. However, the question of adequacy—Is there enough support to make her argument convincing?— is a little more involved. The author makes it very clear that the present school calendar is out of synch with parents' work schedules. She does not, however, make as convincing a point about the educational merits of a longer school year. This seems to be the weakest part of her argument. Even though she mentions several times that the long summer vacations lead to kids "hanging out," the author seems biased in favor of the parents here, focusing much more attention on the needs of parents than of the children. More specifically, she seems most concerned with less well-off parents, those who are not "rich enough for camp" or who can't "provide other experiences for their children." While most parents would probably appreciate this focus, by leaving out the important perspective of the experience of students themselves, Ms. Goodman perhaps lessens the overall persuasive effect of her argument.

Chapter Review

When evaluating an argument, you want to first consider the three parts—the thesis, the support, and the assumptions—and then decide how well the supporting points and the assumptions actually lead to and lend support to the thesis.

1. **Thesis:** First, be sure that you have identified the **thesis** (the main point the author is making), the main support that the author is providing, and the underlying assumptions that are meant to make the support believable.

2. **Support:** Next, to determine how well the **evidence** actually supports the thesis, critically question the support by asking the following questions:

    "Is there enough support to justify the claim?"

    "Is the support directly related to the thesis?"

3. **Assumptions:** Finally, question the **assumptions** by asking the following:

    "Is the support based on some commonly accepted truth?"

"Is the support based on sources of information that are generally considered reliable?"

"Is the support based on what most people believe is important?"

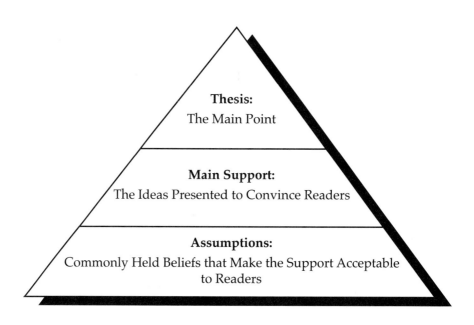

Acknowledgments

Unless otherwise indicated, everything in these chapters has been written by Don Meagher. Some of the example passages had been originally written by the author for Miami-Dade Community College, which has generously granted permission for their use here. The following is a list of sources for previously copyrighted material quoted in the book.

Abbey, Edward. *The Journey Home.* New York: Plume, 1977. (Quote from pp. 220–221.)

The American Heritage Dictionary, Third Edition. New York: Houghton Mifflin Company, 1994. Reproduced by permission from *The American Heritage Dictionary, Third Edition,* Paperback edition. (Quotes from pp. viii and 531.)

Amis, Martin. "Buy My Book, Please." *The New Yorker,* June 6/July 3, 1995, pp. 96–99. (Quote from p. 98.)

Arms, Karen, and Pamela S. Camp. *Biology: A Journey into Life,* Second Edition. Philadelphia: Saunders College Publishing, 1991. Reprinted by permission of the publisher. Photograph, Figure 1-12, reprinted by permission of Photo Researchers. (Excerpt adapted from pages 12–13.)

Barry, Lynda. "The Sanctuary of School." *New York Times,* "Education Life," January 5, 1992, Section 4A, p. 58.

Bogar, Ellen. "Make Hours Spent in School Really Count." *The Miami Herald,* May 9, 1995, p. 12A.

Boorstin, Daniel J. *The Discoverers: A History of Man's Search to Know His World and Himself.* New York: Vintage Books, 1985. (Quote from p. 566.)

Brogan, D. W. *The American Character.* New York: Time Inc., 1956. (Quote from pp. 3–4.)

Browning, Michael. "A Pox upon MTV Bozos for Debasing Our Civility." *The Miami Herald,* 12/30/94, pp. 1F–2F. (Quote from p. 1F.)

Buchwald, Art. *"You Can Fool All of the People All the Time."* New York: Putnam, 1985. (Quote from p. 168.)

Bussey, Jane. "Death, Misery in the Mountains of Mexico." *The Miami Herald,* July 29, 1995, pp. 1A, 25A. (Quote on p. 25A.)

Calvino, Italo. *Marcovaldo.* Translated from the Italian by William Weaver. New York: Harcourt Brace Jovanovich, 1983. (Quote from p. 36.)

Carter, Steven L. "Let Us Pray." *The New Yorker,* Dec. 5, 1994; pp. 60–74. (Quote from p. 62.)

Cisneros, Sandra. "Tepeyac." *Woman Hollering Creek and Other Stories.* New York: Vintage Books, 1991. (Quote from pp. 22–23.)

Cote, Greg. "Dan's No. 1: He Has Never Had Strong Support." *The Miami Herald,* 12/29/94, p. 1D.

Cowan, Jon and Rob Nelson, "Age Discrimination—Against the Young." *Los Angeles Times,* August 7, 1994, p. M5.

cummings, e. e. "who sharpens every dull." *Complete Poems 1904–1962.* New York: Liveright, 1991. (Quote from p. 624.)

Doob, Christopher Bates. *Sociology: An Introduction.* Fort Worth, TX: Harcourt Brace College Publishers, 1995. (Quotes from pages 253 and 344.)

Douglas, Marjory Stoneman. *The Everglades: River of Grass.* St. Simon's Island, GA: Mockingbird Books, 1947. (Quote from p. 33.)

Doyle, Arthur Conan. "The Red-Headed League." In A. Conan Doyle, *The Illustrated Sherlock Holmes Treasury.* New York: Avenel Books, pp. 16–30, 1976. (Quote from p. 17.)

Drucker, Peter F. "The Age of Social Transformation." *The Atlantic Monthly,* November 1994, pp. 53–80. (Quote from p. 53.)

Ehrenreich, Barbara. "Kicking the Big One." *Time,* February 28, 1994, p. 70.

Erdrich, Louise. *Love Medicine.* New York: Bantam Books, 1984. (Quote from p. 216.)

Ferguson, Sarah. "The Comfort of Being Sad." *Utne Reader,* July/August 1994, pp. 60–62. (Quotes from pp. 60 and 60–61.)

Figueroa, Angelo. "Must Fight Back on Affirmative Action." *The Miami Herald,* August 4, 1995, p. 27A.

Frady, Marshall. "The Children of Malcolm." *The New Yorker,* October 12, 1992, pp. 64–81. (Quote from p. 72.)

Frost, Robert. "A Prayer in Spring." *Poems by Robert Frost.* New York: Signet Classic, Penguin Books, 1990. (Quote from p. 40.)

Gabler, Robert, Robert J. Sager, and Daniel L. Wise, *Essentials of Physical Geography.* Fort Worth, TX: Harcourt Brace College Publishers, 1993. (Quotes from pages 181, 374, and 515.)

Gallaher, Winifred. "How We Become What We Are." *The Atlantic Monthly,* September 1994, pp. 38–55. (Quotes from pp. 39 and 39–40.)

Gates, Henry Louis Jr. "Heroes, Inc.: Dr. King, Deified and Digitized." *The New Yorker,* January 16, 1995, pp. 6–7. (Quote from pages 6–7.)

Goodman, Ellen. "Turning Hands on School Clock." *Boston Globe,* July 8, 1990.

Guinier, Lani. "To Heal the Nation, We Must Talk." *The Miami Herald,* 12/30/94 , p. 19A.

Havel, Vaclav. *Summer Meditations.* New York: Vintage Books, 1993. (Quote from p. 6.)

Hillerman, Tony. *The Ghostway.* New York: Avon Books, 1984. (Quote from p. 12.)

Hitt, Jack. "How a Pilgrim Progresses." *New York Times Magazine,* August 14, 1994, pp. 36–39. (Quote from p. 36.)

Joseph, Yonette. "The People Column." *The Miami Herald,* January 4, 1996, p. 2A.

Kelly, Kevin J. "R.I.P. for the CIA?" *Utne Reader,* July–August 1995, pp. 16–20. (Quote from p. 16.)

Kennedy, Paul. "Overpopulation Tilts the Planet." *New Perspective Quarterly,* Fall 1994, pp. 4–6. (Quotes from pp. 6, 4–5.)
   Biographical information from introduction to article by Paul Kennedy, "The Perils of Overpopulation," *The Miami Herald,* July 31, 1994, p. 1M.

Lebowitz, Fran. *Metropolitan Life.* New York: E. P. Dutton, 1978. (Quote from p. 16.)

Liebeman, Shari, and Nancy Bruning. *The Real Vitamin & Mineral Book.* Garden City Park, NY: Avery Publishing Group, 1990. (Quote from p. 3.)

McCarthy, Cormac. *All the Pretty Horses.* New York: Vintage Books, 1992. (Quote from p. 93.)

———, *The Crossing.* New York: Vintage Books, 1994. (Quote from pp. 3–4.)

Merwin, W. S. "Long Love." *Finding the Islands.* San Francisco: North Point Press, 1982. (Quote from p. 53.)

Miller, Don B. "Catawba Tribe v. South Carolina: A History of Perseverance." *Native American Rights Fund Legal Review,* Vol. 18, No.1, Winter/Spring 1993. pp. 3–13. (Quote from p. 13.)

Morrison, Toni. *Sula.* New York: Alfred A. Knopf, 1973. (Quote from pp. 124–125)

Moseley-Braun, Carol. "How Have We Changed?" *American Heritage,* December 1994. (Quote from pp. 77–78.)

Noonan, Peggy. "How Have We Changed?" *American Heritage,* December 1994. (Quote from p. 80.)

Patterson, Orlando. "Affirmative Action, on the Merit System." *New York Times,* August 7, 1995, p. A11.

Provenzo, Eugene F., Jr. *An Introduction to Education in American Society.* Columbus, Ohio: Charles E. Merrill, 1986. (Quote from pp. 127–128.)

Quindlen, Anna. "Lead Us Not." *New York Times,* December 7, 1994, p. A23.

Rathus, Spencer A., and Jeffrey S. Nevid, *Adjustment and Growth: The Challenges of Life.* Fort Worth, TX: Harcourt Brace College Publishers, 1995. (Quotes from pages 193 and 358.)

Rodriguez, Richard. *Days of Obligation: An Argument with My Mexican Father.* New York: Viking, 1992. (Quote from pp. 54–55.)

———. "Slouching Toward Los Angeles." *Los Angeles Times,* April 11, 1993, pp. M1, M6.

Rothchild, John. *Up for Grabs: A Trip through Time and Space in the Sunshine State.* New York: Viking, 1985. (Quote from p. 56.)

Saki (H. H. Munro). "The Open Window." *Short Stories and the Unbearable Bassington.* Oxford: Oxford University Press, 1994, pp. 97–100.

Sandon, Leo. "Emerging Consensus Bypassing Vatican." *The Miami Herald,* September 11, 1994, p. 4M.

Silko, Leslie Marmon. *Ceremony.* New York: Penguin Books, 1977. (Quote from pp. 217–218.)

Sontag, Susan. *AIDS and Its Metaphors.* New York: Farrar, Straus and Giroux, 1988. (Quote from p. 73.)

Steibel, James. "UC Affirmative Action: What Does it Mean to Those It Affects?" *Los Angeles Times,* July 14, 1995, p. B9.

Tannen, Deborah. "And Rarely the Twain Shall Meet." *The Washington Post,* National Weekly Edition, January 9–15, 1995, p. 25.

Thomas, Cal. *The Things That Matter Most.* New York: Harper Collins, 1993. (Quote from p. 178.)

Trillin, Calvin. "Messages From My Father," *The New Yorker,* June 20, 1994, pp. 56–78. (Quote from page 61.)

Tuchman, Barbara. *The First Salute: A View of the American Revolution.* New York: Alfred A. Knopf, 1988. (Quote from p. 5.)

Turner, Frederick. *Beyond Geography: The Western Spirit against the Wilderness.* New Brunswick, NJ: Rutgers University Press, 1983. (Quote from p. 255.)

Volokh, Alexander, and Shechao Charles Feng, "How Race Adds Up for UCLA Entry." *Los Angeles Times,* July 18, 1995, p. B9.

Wade, Nicholas. "First Sequencing of Cell's DNA Defines Basis of Life." *The New York Times,* August 1, 1995, pp. B5, B9. (Quotes from p. B5 and B9.)

Walinsky, Adam. "The Crisis of Public Order." *The Atlantic Monthly,* July, 1995, pp. 39–54. (Quote from p. 54.)

Wiesel, Elie. *Night.* Copyright © 1960 by MacGibbon & Kee. Copyright renewed © 1988 by The Collins Publishing Group. Reprinted by permission of Hill and Wang, a division of Farrar, Straus & Giroux, Inc. (Quote from pp. 105–106.)

Williams, Donna. *Nobody Nowhere.* New York: Times Books, 1992. (Quote from p. 17.)

Williams, William Carlos. *In the American Grain.* New York: New Directions, 1956. (Quote from p. 27.)

Wilson, Edward O. *Naturalist.* Washington, DC: Island Press, 1994. (Quote from p. 351)

Index